CHINESE AMERICA

HISTORY AND PERSPECTIVES

1998

CHINESE HISTORICAL SOCIETY OF AMERICA

The editorial committee would like to express our deepest appreciation to the Lawrence Choy Lowe Memorial Fund for their generous support of our publication.

Publication of *Chinese America: History and Perspectives 1998* is sponsored in part by a grant from Grants for the Arts of the San Francisco Hotel Tax Fund and the Lawrence Choy Lowe Memorial Fund.

Chinese Historical Society of America
Publisher

Asian American Studies
San Francisco State University
Sponsor

Contents

Introduction

Chinese, from their earliest arrival in the Americas, have been persecuted. As the essays in this volume reveal, however, Chinese have endured. Some have even risen to great heights. And although many of the communities established in the nineteenth century were destroyed either through physical violence or by the slow strangulation of Exclusion, a few have not only survived but been revitalized through new waves of immigration.

Him Mark Lai's "Potato King and Film Producer, Flower Growers, Professionals, and Activists" explores the experiences of Chinese from Huangliang Du (in the Pearl River Delta) who settled in Northern California. As indicated by the title, immigrants from this region entered a wide variety of occupations: Chin Lung, the Potato King, was also an astute businessman with investments on both sides of the Pacific; Jun You Jew played a pioneering role in the Chinese film industry in America; members of the Chinese Flower Growers Association in the San Francisco Peninsula helped establish a flower market in the city; political activists worked to better the lives of Chinese on both sides of the Pacific, with some, like Dr. Wong Him, fighting against the segregation of Chinese children in San Francisco's public schools, and others, like American-born George Young, serving in the Chinese Air Force. Using Chinese- and English-language sources, Lai places these—and other—individuals in a textured context that allows us to see the fine nuances necessary for understanding history.

In "The Fake and the True: Researching Chinese Women's Immigration History," Judy Yung, great-granddaughter of Chin Lung, the Potato King, carefully delineates the myriad complications in Chinese immigration arising from sixty-one years of Exclusion, focusing in particular on how women were affected. The stringent, patently unjust Exclusion laws placed the burden of proof on Chinese immigrants to prove their legal right to enter the United States. This burden, in turn, gave rise to clever stratagems by Chinese to circumvent the laws. Some of these strategies, while contributing to the successful immigration of one individual, would later cause difficulties for another person within the same family, as Yung illustrates through the immigration experiences of her

great-grandmother in 1893 and her mother in 1941. Painstakingly piecing together her forebears' affidavits, transcripts of interrogations, coaching book, and oral histories, Yung illuminates the challenges faced by Chinese women immigrants and those who research and write their history.

In "'The Inconveniences Resulting from Race Mixture,'" Larissa N. Schwartz examines the 1911 massacre of Chinese in Torreón, Mexico, that left 303 Chinese and five Japanese dead. Where previous scholarship has attributed the anti-Chinese violence in the northern states of Mexico to the disparity between the Chinese and the indigenous people, lower-middle-class, and middle-class Mexicans, Schwartz suggests that the perceived economic and racial threat of the Chinese was also part of a revolutionary struggle to define a Mexican national identity.

Zeng Ying, sharing her preliminary findings on the "Development of the San Diego Chinese American Community," takes us north of the border. Her essay, based on two months of fieldwork in 1996, reveals the internal workings of the community, including such diverse groups as descendants of nineteenth-century immigrants from the Pearl River Delta and new immigrants from Southeast Asia, as well as the external conflicts between the Chinese community and mainstream society.

Finally, Edmund D. Jung's poignant "He's a Chinaman" provides a timely warning for those who would like to think race prejudice in the workplace is no longer an issue for Chinese Americans. A third-generation American of Chinese descent and an army veteran who served in the South Pacific at the end of World War II, Jung was subjected to subtle and blatant discrimination in his work as a medical doctor at a Veterans Administration hospital by the chief of medicine, an immigrant from Europe. Jung, refusing to accept the role of victim, fought back with the help of Chinese for Affirmative Action and the support of the San Francisco Chinese community. His ultimate victory, however, was Pyrrhic.

As always an attempt was made to be consistent in the Chinese transliterations within each essay, but no attempt was made to make them consistent throughout the publication.

Potato King and Film Producer, Flower Growers, Professionals, and Activists

The Huangliang Du Community in Northern California

by Him Mark Lai

Huangliang Du (Wong Leung Dou) was formerly an administrative region in the southwest corner of the Pearl River Delta.[1] It consisted of the present Doumen County (area: 358.3 sq. mi.; population in mid-1980s: 261,001) plus offshore islands now part of Xiangzhou District in Zhuhai Municipality (area: 144.9 sq. mi.; population in the mid-1980s: 30,535) (see Table 1). This was the political subdivision that existed when immigrants from the region came to America. Doumen is somewhat smaller than San Mateo County (454 sq. mi.) in the San Francisco Bay Area. Huangliang Du, including the offshore islands, is slightly larger; however, the total population is still only about half that of highly urbanized San Mateo.

HISTORICAL GEOGRAPHY

The Pearl River Delta is a relatively recent geological formation. About six thousand years ago, during the late Quaternary Period, the West, North, Pearl, East, and associated rivers of the region were discharging their waters southward into a shallow island-studded bay opening into the South China Sea. At the head of this bay was the port of Guangzhou (Canton). As the river water slowed in the bay, alluvial soil carried from upstream deposited to create dry land. In time islands became mountains and hills separated by river channels and valleys. The largest of these in the Huangliang Du region became Huangyang (box tree) Mountain with an elevation of 1,906 feet.

By the Song dynasty much of the bay had become dry land; it became Xiangshan County in A.D. 1162. This area saw the denouement of the Song empire in 1278, when pursuing Mongol Yuan forces crushed the main forces of the Song resistance at Yaimen in Xinhui, adjoining present-day Doumen to the west. Many the defeated settled in the region, helping to develop the area further. In 1642 the Portuguese occupied Lampacao, an island in what was to be Huangliang Du, as one of their bases to pursue the China trade. By the late 1550s, however, they had moved their operations to the more strategically located Macao, a peninsula off the southeastern tip of Zhuhai.

After the Manchu Qing dynasty succeeded the Ming during the mid-seventeenth century, Sanzao and other offshore islands became some of the bases from which Ming loyalists together with pirates continued to harass the Qing.[2] In order to prevent the loyalists from linking up with Ming sympathizers inland, the Qing court issued decrees in 1662 and 1664 ordering evacuation of the coast for fifty *li* (about seventeen miles). Much of the Pearl River Delta region was directly affected.

The evacuation order was not lifted until two decades later. Some inhabitants returned. New settlers also arrived from nearby Xinhui as well as from land-poor areas in northeast Guangdong such as Huiyang and Lufeng.[3] The Xinhui heritage is still strongly evident in the region in that, unlike the rest of Zhongshan, the local dialect closely resembles the Cantonese spoken in neighboring Xinhui. In 1731 the Qing government designated this region Huangliang Du. During the Republican era that administrative subdivision was abolished, with the portion on the mainland becoming the Eighth District of Xiangshan. Sanzao and other offshore islands became the Seventh District. In 1925 the name of Xiangshan was changed to Zhongshan (Chungshan) in honor of Sun Zhongshan (Sun Yat-sen).

In 1961 the southeastern part of Zhongshan and islands off the Pearl River Delta became Zhuhai County. In 1965 Doumen became a separate county comprising the former Eighth Area of Zhongshan and a small part of neighboring Xinhui (see map). In 1979 Zhuhai County became the Zhuhai Municipality. In 1983 Doumen County was placed under the jurisdiction of the municipality; the territory that used to be Zhuhai County became Xiangzhou District.

EMIGRATION

With easy access to the ocean, this area early became an emigration area. By the last half of the eighteenth century Huangliang Du people were known to be active in Southeast Asia.[4] Huangliang Du people also moved to nearby Macao to engage in businesses or to find work. When Hong Kong developed as an international port and entrepôt after the

TABLE 1

LAND AREA AND POPULATION STATISTICS FOR MODERN
TOWNSHIPS IN THE REGION FORMERLY OCCUPIED BY
HUANGLIANG DU

Locality	Land Area (sq. mi.)	Permanent Population	Mobile Fishing Population
Townships, Doumen County			
TOTAL	358.3	261,001	
Jing'an[1]	49.7	50,593	
Doumen[1]	40.6	36,971	
Shangheng[2]	19.3	22,231	
Liuxiang[3]	24.8	18,050	
Lianxi[1]	16.2	15,685	
Baijiao[1]	48.0	30,183	
Qianwu[1]	24.5	16,530	
Wushan[1]	46.3	23,393	
Pingsha[1]	74.1	36,528	
Hongqi[1]	14.8	10,837	
Townships, Xiangzhou District (offshore islands only)			
TOTAL	144.9	30,535	3,603
Nanshui[1]	35.4	7,123	
Sanzao[1]	30.1	11,078	
Xiaolin[1]	28.9	7,247	
Wanshan[5]	11.6	1,028	1,383
Dan'gan[4]	15.4	758	820
Guishan[4]	5.4	895	1,400
Hengqin[5]	18.1	2,406	

Source: Guangdong sheng Zhuhai shi dimingzhi (Gazetteer of geographical names of Zhuhai City, Guangdong Province) (Guangzhou: Guangdong keji chubanshe, 1989); referenced hereafter as *Gazetteer of Geographical Names of Zhuhai*.

[1] Was part of Huangliang Du.
[2] Was part of Xinhui until 1965.
[3] Was part of Xinhui and Zhongshan.
[4] Was part of Bao'an.
[5] Was not part of Huangliang Du.

Opium War, it also became a magnet, attracting Huangliang Du emigrants seeking better opportunities. Some, particularly those from Sanzao and other offshore islands, found work in the fisheries or served on ships sailing international routes. The proximity of Hong Kong also facilitated its use as a way station for Huangliang Du people to go abroad. However, the majority of Huangliang Du people living away from the home villages settled in Hong Kong and Macao.

The estimated populations from various different townships in Doumen County and the offshore islands living in Hong Kong, Macao, and countries abroad are listed in Table 2. Of the approximately 17,000 from Doumen County, in the United States the largest number are found in California, chiefly in the San Francisco Bay Area. Smaller concentrations dwelled in Los Angeles, Honolulu, and New York City.[5] A high percentage of the immigrants originated from villages in Doumen Township (area: 40.6 sq. mi., slightly smaller than the area of San Francisco) on the western side of Doumen County.[6] The population abroad from this township is between 85 and 90 percent of the population still living in the area.

There are fewer emigrants from the smaller populations of the offshore islands. An estimated 20,000 live outside the borders of China, mostly in Hong Kong and Macao, but small numbers are also found in Western Europe, the United States, Australia, Southeast Asia, and Latin America. Most came from Sanzao Island. In the United States the largest concentration of people from the offshore islands is in New York City, where there are several thousand. In the 1990s there are several hundred to a thousand in the San Francisco Bay Area.[7]

IN THE NEW WORLD

People from Huangliang Du were among the earliest Chinese to settle in North America. The earliest recorded pioneer was Yuan Sheng from Tianxin Village, Sanzao Island. Around 1820 he boarded ship at Macao and voyaged to Europe and America. When the ship berthed in New York City, he decided to stay.[8] Later he traveled to Charleston, South Carolina, to be a merchant. He became a Christian and a naturalized American citizen. He even claimed to have voted the Republican ticket. When the California Gold Rush began, Yuan was among the first wave of Chinese to settle in San Francisco around 1850. Known as Norman Asing (or Assing) to San Franciscans, Yuan became a leader in the young Chinese community. In 1852 he wrote a letter defending the Chinese when Governor Bigler of California urged a ban on Chinese immigration.[9]

At that time there were already numerous Chinese immigrants in California. Yuan urged his compatriots to organize for mutual aid and protection from external threats as well as for social control. In September 1852, Asing together with Cai Libi (Lai Bik Choi) of Shangzha and Liu Zuman (Jou Moon Lau) of Qianshan, both in present-day Xiangzhou District of Zhuhai, founded Yeong Wo Association to aid immigrants from Xiangshan, Dongguan, and Zengcheng.[10] Yuan became the first head of the association, but "an attack of haemorrhages [sic]" soon forced him to yield the position to Tong K. Achik of Tangjia in present-day Xiangzhou District.[11]

When Californians turned from mining gold to developing other sectors of the economy, Chinese immigration

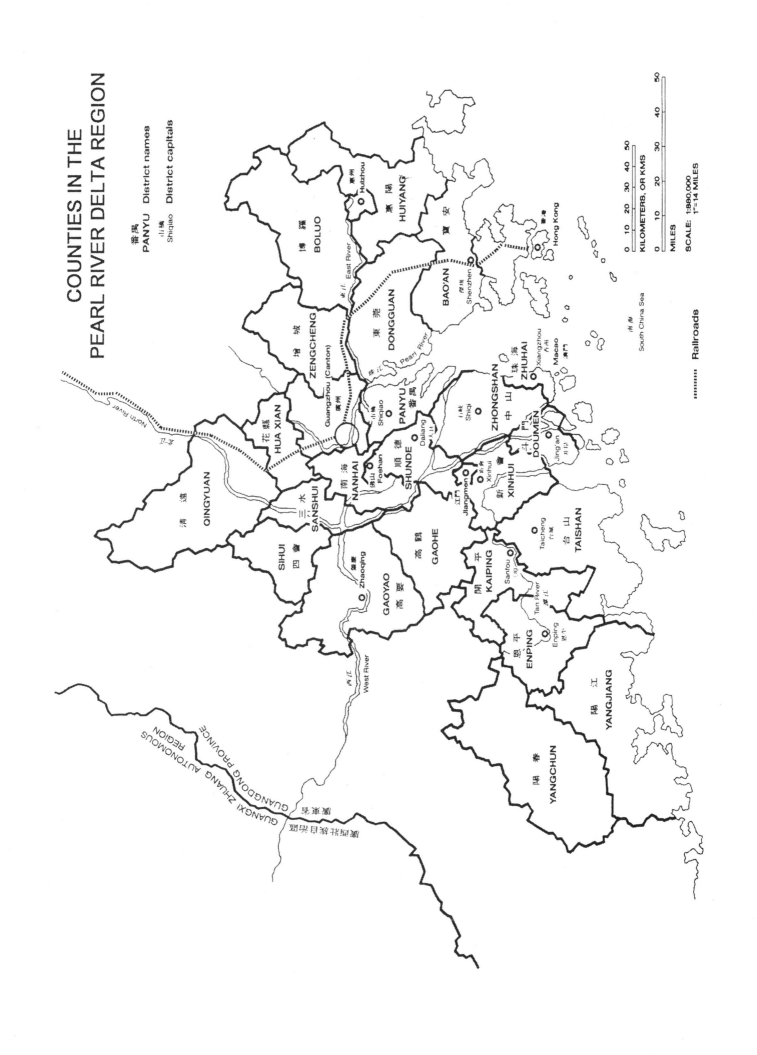

COUNTIES IN THE PEARL RIVER DELTA REGION

PANYU District names
Shiqiao District capitals

North River

OINGYUAN

SIHUI

SANSHUI

HUA XIAN

ZENGCHENG

BOLUO

East River

HUIYANG

Huizhou

DONGGUAN

Pearl River

BAO'AN

Shenzhen

Hong Kong

South China Sea

Guangzhou (Canton)

NANHAI

Foshan

SHUNDE

Daliang

PANYU

Shiqiao

ZHONGSHAN

Shiqi

ZHUHAI

Xiangzhou

Macao

DOUMEN

Jing an

GAOHE

XINHUI

Xinhui

Jiangmen

GAOYAO

Zhaoqing

West River

KAIPING

Santou

TAISHAN

Taicheng

Tan River

ENPING

Enping

YANGCHUN

YANGJIANG

GUANGXI ZHUANG AUTONOMOUS REGION

GUANGDONG PROVINCE

50
40
30
20
10
0
KILOMETERS, OR KMS

30
20
10
0
MILES

SCALE: 1:880,000
1"=14 MILES

••••••• Railroads

TABLE 2

DISTRIBUTION OF CHINESE ORIGINATING FROM
TOWNSHIPS OF DOUMEN AND OFFSHORE ISLANDS

Locality	Population in Hong Kong/ Macao	Population Overseas	Total Population Abroad
	Townships, Doumen County		
TOTAL	102,135	25,122	127,257
Jing'an[1]	12,100	3,450	15,550
Doumen[1]	25,820	6,440	32,260
Shangheng[2]	8,455	920	9,375
Liuxiang[3]	4,500	840	5,340
Lianxi[2]	2,500	765	3,265
Baijiao[1]	14,660	2,106	16,766
Qianwu[1]	15,380	2,885	18,265
Wushan[1]	13,520	4,620	18,140
Pingsha[1]	4,200	2,075	6,275
Hongqi[1]	3,000	1,021	4,021
	Townships, Xiangzhou District (Offshore Islands Only)		
TOTAL			16,250
Nanshui[1]			544
Sanzao[1]			13,200
Xiaolin[1]			305
Wanshan[5]			400
Dan'gan[4]			500
Guishan[4]			501
Hengqin[5]			800

Source: Gazetteer of Geographical Names of Zhuhai.

Note: In an interview on Dec. 14, 1993, the Zhuhai Overseas Chinese Affairs Office gave the following unpublished revised figures for 1992:

Doumen County: Chinese overseas and in Hong Kong, Macao: 151,000; Chinese overseas: 41,000 in thirty-eight countries including the United States, Cuba, Peru, Chile, Canada, Australia, Malaysia; United States (including Hawaii): 17,000. Sanzao: Chinese overseas in more than a dozen countries and in Hong Kong, Macao: 20,000.

[1] Was part of Huangliang Du.
[2] Was part of Xinhui until 1965.
[3] Was part of Xinhui and Zhongshan.
[4] Was part of Bao'an.
[5] Was not part of Huangliang Du.

increased dramatically. The population under the jurisdiction of the Yeong Wo Association increased to more than twenty thousand by the late 1860s.[12] During this period Huangliang Du immigrants also began to immigrate into Hawaii, where California's rapid development stimulated growth of the islands' sugar industry.

Chinese abroad very early on organized *huiguan* and *shantang* for mutual help. Membership was based on area of origin in China. A function of these groups was to ship the dead back to the home village in China for burial. The existence of a *shantang* for Huangliang Du immigrants in California was not evident in early accounts. But from the fact that similar organizations for other Xiangshan areas were documented at an early date, it is reasonable to assume that such an organization also existed to perform this important religious function for Huangliang Du immigrants.[13] However, a formally organized *shantang* for Huangliang Du immigrants in California apparently did not appear until late in the nineteenth century.

The establishment of a new Chinese cemetery at Colma, near San Francisco, by the Chinese Six Companies in 1889 may have spurred the formal establishment of Hee Shen Association for Huangliang Du immigrants in the 1890s.[14] During this period social needs as well as the need for protection against external threats also led to the formation of the fraternal group Yee Ying Association for Huangliang Du immigrants. This group was dominated by the more numerous clans, and about a decade later, smaller Huangliang Du clans formed a second fraternal group, the Hip Sen Association.[15]

Around this period Huangliang Du immigrants in the Hawaiian kingdom also formed Huangliang Du Fushan Tang on Maui, and Huangliang Du Gongsuo and Huangliang Du Jilu (name changed to Jishantang in 1906) in Honolulu.[16] There is no formal organization for Huangliang Du people in New York, but there is a Chung Shan Association, founded in 1920. There is a Sanzao Gongsuo, which existed as Sam Jo Kong Fong for many years. During the 1940s a Sam Jo Kong Fong also existed for a short time in San Francisco.[17]

The Chinese Exclusion laws barred Chinese labor from the United States from 1882 to 1943. However, America still held the promise of a better life for many Chinese, and they devised many stratagems to circumvent the ban and gain entry. Some seamen jumped ship at ports, became stowaways on trans-Pacific vessels, or were smuggled into America from neighboring countries. By far the most common method of entry was to claim exempt status as a merchant, as a merchant's spouse and children, or as citizens and citizens' offspring. Thus many Huangliang Du immigrants paid mercantile establishments to list them as partners. Others bought papers claiming citizenship status as American-born or as native-born, often with surnames different from their original surnames.

FARMERS AND BUSINESSMEN

Many Huangliang Du immigrants to America settled in San Francisco, and the city became the site for most organized activities of concern to the Huangliang Du community in the continental United States. As was typical in practically all overseas Chinese societies, merchants played a leading role in the community. There has been insufficient research to identify Huangliang Du merchants and businesses during the early days of the San Francisco Chinese community, except for Norman Asing, mentioned above. But by the end of the nineteenth century several Huangliang Du merchants had emerged to play prominent roles. A major store at the turn of the century was Sing Kee, rice importer and seller of general merchandise located at 808 (the address changed to 756 after the 1906 earthquake) Sacramento Street.[18] The store's owner was Lung Chin (also known as Hong Dai Chan) from Nanshan Village. Chin arrived in San Francisco around 1882 and began working at Sing Kee soon after. He learned English at the Chinese Baptist Church.[19] During the late nineteenth century he began leasing land in the Sacramento–San Joaquin river delta, growing crops such as asparagus, beans, onions, and potatoes. In 1912 Chin bought 1,100 acres near Stockton and named it the Sing Kee Tract. It was probably the only tract in California named after a Chinese store. After California passed the 1913 Alien Land Act, Chin acquired about 2,000 acres near Klamath Falls, Oregon, to raise potatoes. Thus, during the early twentieth century Chin became known as the Chinese counterpart of George Shima, the Japanese "potato king." Many Huangliang Du immigrants worked on Chin's farm, and a Huangliang Du community sprang up in Stockton's Chinatown, where Chin in 1915 became part owner of Poo Wo Tong, an herbalist and general merchandise store at 137 South Hunter Street.[20]

Chin continued his agricultural enterprises in San Joaquin County until 1924, when additional restrictions imposed by a second Alien Land Act in 1920 and an amendment in 1923 forced Chin to close down his California farming operations. He also gave up farming in Oregon after that state also enacted an Alien Land Law in 1923. However, some families who went north with Lung Chin remained in Oregon. One was Hushan Village's Sam Wong Chin, who with his family eked out a living for many years growing potatoes. During World War II the farm profited by raising and supplying quantities of Chinese cabbage to the Japanese internment camp at nearby Tule Lake.[21]

Lung Chin invested part of his capital in the Shanghai Trunk Company in San Francisco in 1923. This business became a gathering place for Huangliang Du people, especially those from Nanshan, and operated until around 1939.[22] Chin also bought land and made investments in his native China.[23]

Another major entrepreneur was Jun You Jew, also known as Fook Jew, who came from Nanmen Village around 1908. Jew was manager of the Chung Sun Wo store and silent partner in the Shew Hing Lung store. In the 1920s he acquired Mon Ming Hotel and Shanghai Noodles in San Francisco. Around 1923 he founded Hip Sing Chong, a general merchandise store at 12 Ross Alley, to handle remittances to China. In the 1930s, when Huangliang Du people had become established in the flower industry on the San Francisco Peninsula, Jew's nephew James Jew opened Canton Flower Shop around 1934. Using the same storefront as Hip Shing Chong, the shop also became a gathering place for Huangliang Du people.[24] It was not the first Huangliang Du florist, but it was one of the oldest and most successful.

Jun You Jew made major investments in California agricultural enterprises. He had a shaky start, incurring losses in rice farming in Colusa. Undaunted, he leased land near Isleton to raise asparagus. In 1928 Jew formed Kwangtung Corporation. In 1929 the corporation purchased 2,665 acres near Dos Palos in Merced County. It soon moved its operations to 1,660 acres at nearby Firebaugh to the southeast. In 1944 Kwangtung Corporation became Jew Fook Corporation, headed by Jew's grand-nephew Richard. Richard managed the initial parcel together with land purchased by a corporation formed in 1947 by several former Kwangtung Corporation stockholders and another parcel he bought separately. It was the largest Chinese-owned farm in the area.[25] Fook Jew also entered a partnership with Dan Louie to acquire more than two thousand acres in Imperial Valley. Later the partnership was terminated and the holdings divided between the partners, with Jew keeping 1,800 acres. The land was sold in 1958, but the new owner leased the parcel to Jew's nephew Edwin Chew.

Jun You Jew also played a pioneering role in the Chinese film industry in America. In 1926 he became vice-president, deputy manager, and a member of the board of directors of Zhonghua Yizhi Yinghua Gongsi (Chinese educational films company). The company's first film, made in Hollywood, was *Xue Pinggui quan zhuan* (Story of Xue Pinggui), with Anna May Wong playing one of the roles.[26] Jew financed his second son, Joseph Sunn Jue, when the latter organized the New Art Film Company and made his first film, *Yaomo zhi yue* (The demon's cavern) in 1926. In 1933 Joseph Sunn Jue formed Grandview Film Company in San Francisco. The company's first production, *Gelü qingchao* (Blossom Time), was one of the earliest sound motion pictures made in the Cantonese dialect. It premiered in San Francisco and afterward was shown in China, where it was an acclaimed success. Joe Sunn Jue then moved his studio to Hong Kong. After the War of Resistance against Japan broke out in 1937, Jue returned to America in 1939 and made several color feature films using 17 Old Chinatown Lane in San Francisco Chinatown as his studio. He also formed a corporation to build and operate a movie theater in San Francisco. Fook Jew bought a building at 756–58 Jackson Street and turned it over to the corporation at cost. Unlike two other contemporary Chinatown movie theaters that were converted from theaters for Cantonese operatic performances, this theater had to be completely remodeled. Grandview Theater opened in 1940.[27] The theater closed and the building was sold in 1976.[28]

Kwong On & Co. and Chung Sun Wo were major Huangliang Du general merchandise stores in San Francisco. The former was founded around 1894 by members of the Chen (Chan) clan of Nanshan and the Huang (Wong) clan of Dahaochong. After the 1906 San Francisco earthquake, Kee Wong became manager. The business operated until around 1935. After the founding of the Republic Wong founded the *jinshanzhuang* (*gamsaanjong*) Wing Shun Tai in Hong Kong.[29]

Chung Sun Wo was founded by Jim Mock and others at the turn of the century. It ceased operation about 1922. Around 1927 the store reopened as Shew Hing Lung. It lasted until 1942. By then it was managed by Xinhui immigrants, although several of the eighty partners were from Huangliang Du.[30] Another business with partial Huangliang Du ownership was the herb shop Tin Suie Tong. During the 1930s this store provided postal and remittance services for immigrants, particularly those belonging to Doumen's Mok (Mock) clan.[31] On the eve of World War II, in around 1938, Zhao Yanxin (Yin San Jew) of Nanmen founded Comfort Shoes at 754 Grant Avenue. It was one of the few Chinese-owned shoe stores in Chinatown. However, more important than its footwear sales (although this undoubtedly was convenient for many in Chinatown), the store also handled remittances to China after Hip Shing Chong closed down. The business closed in the early 1950s.

PROFESSIONALS AND WORKERS

Similar to other Chinese immigrants to California of the period, most Huangliang Du immigrants were either shopkeepers, restaurant workers, domestics, gardeners, or cooks. One remembered by many was Mo Yiya (Yik Ngah Mok) from Chishuikeng, who held the position of chief cook at the Angel Island Immigration Station for many years before World War II. His kitchen staff, most of whom were also from Huangliang Du, played a crucial role in maintaining communications between Chinese on the outside and Chinese detainees at the immigration station. When a member of the kitchen staff had a day off, he would visit San Francisco and pick up coaching messages from a business such as Shew Hing Lung. This message would then be smuggled into the hands of the detainees at mealtime.[32] This system continued for many years, until the station closed.

A small number of professionals also became respected individuals in the community during the first half of the twentieth century. At the turn of the century one of the best known herbal physicians in San Francisco was Dr. Henry Wong Him from Dahaochong. Wong was a domestic cook who was said to have been encouraged by his employer to become an herbal physician outside Chinatown. He became wealthy treating non-Chinese patients and was a silent partner in a number of Chinese businesses ventures such as Kwong On and Shew Hing Lung. During the late nineteenth century he also bought eighty-five acres (near the present Agnew State Hospital) in Santa Clara County, where he had a Chinese pear orchard, then the largest of its kind in the United States.[33]

Dr. Wong Him did not have a medical license, but his son, also known as Henry Wong Him, obtained an M.D. degree at the Hahnemann School of Homeopathy in San Francisco. Although the younger Wong Him was licensed to practice Western medicine, he preferred to practice herbal medicine with his father. However, he was on the medical staff of Chinese Hospital when it opened in 1925, and he donated $3,000 toward the purchase of an X-ray machine for the hospital.[34]

Another respected herbal physician was Zhao Shunzhi (Sun Jee Jew). Sun Jee Jew played a key role in bringing a halt to a bloody feud between Nanshan and Lishan villages in Doumen. In 1915 a dispute between the two villages had led to violent fighting, causing casualties and serious economic dislocations. Jew and Ging Chan, manager of Stockton's Poo Wo Tong, raised funds from fellow townsmen in America for the relief of refugees fleeing the fighting. When the fighting threatened to escalate in 1916, Jew and Chan stepped in and successfully mediated an end to the fighting and the signing of a peace treaty.[35]

Herbal physician Chen Jingshan (Ging Saan Chan) was principal at the Yeong Wo Chinese School. He also set a precedent as the first president of the Yeong Wo Association, and hence the first member of the board of presidents of the Chinese Consolidated Benevolent Association, to be elected from the local membership of the Hee Shen Association. That move had become necessary when the Chinese government during the 1920s refused to continue issuing diplomatic visas for *huiguan* presidents to come to America to head their respective organizations.[36]

Other men of letters pursued careers as Chinese school teachers and journalists. One was Huang Baohuan (Bou Waan Wong) of Dahaochong Village, who gained notoriety during his sojourn as an editor at the Kuomintang newspaper *Young China* from the late 1920s to the early 1930s. His commentary attacking the Ning Yung Association published in the paper in 1927 ignited a controversy that resulted in a Ning Yung Association boycott of *Young China*. The controversy lasted eight years and required mediation by the governor of Guangdong Province before it subsided.[37] Another jounalist was Shek Ng Mock of Chishuikeng, who immigrated in 1920. Mock taught at the Yeong Wo and Chung Wah Chinese schools during the late 1920s. He then became an editor at the *Chinese Times,* where he was subsequently promoted to chief editor and served until the early 1940s.[38]

As Chinatown gradually became modernized during the first half of the twentieth century, Western-educated professionals also appeared. One pioneer of Huangliang Du ancestry was Man Quong Fong, born in San Francisco in 1883. Fong opened Republic Pharmacy in November 1912. It was said to be the first such Chinese-owned establishment in America. Fong graduated as a pharmaceutical chemist from the University of California in 1914.[39]

Dr. Henry D. Cheu, who came to the United States when he was ten, was one of the first Western-trained physicians of Huangliang Du origin. Cheu worked his way through Stanford University and was the third Chinese to graduate from Stanford Medical School. In 1930 Dr. Cheu joined the Chinese Hospital staff.[40]

Before World War II it was difficult for Chinese American professionals to find work in mainstream America. Many college graduates often had to change their callings or to depart for China to try to build a career. A fortunate few, however, were able to enter the professions in this country. An American-born of Huangliang Du ancestry, Chen Qinxue (Kan Hok Chan), was said to have served as interpreter at the Angel Island Immigration Station during the 1920s.[41] In 1937 John Young, son of San Jose store owner Soong Quong Young, became a petroleum engineer in Southern California, first with the Conservation Committee of California and then with Standard Oil. In both cases he was the only engineer of Chinese descent with the firm.[42]

During this period the pervasive discrimination against Chinese was an obstacle preventing many talented Chinese from even considering careers in the arts and literature. However, in some cases the younger generation was willing to take the risk. It is said that Mo Guangdong (Gwong Dong Mok), grandson of Jim Mock, was saxophonist with a band in the theatrical circuit; however, his career was cut short by an early death.[43] In the realm of fine arts, George Chann of Nanshan Village ancestry received a full scholarship from the Otis Art Institute of Los Angeles, where he majored in painting from 1934 to 1938 and graduated with honors. Chann had exhibitions while at the school and was awarded a special easel. After World War II he taught painting in China and in San Francisco and then opened a small gift shop in Los Angeles.[44]

ON THE SAN FRANCISCO PENINSULA

The writer has not yet been able to determine the year the first Huangliang Du immigrant moved to the San Francisco Peninsula to make a living. But as suburban San Mateo and Santa Clara counties developed following the Gold Rush, the Chinese population in the region also increased; however, by 1900 it had declined due to the Chinese Exclusion Laws (see Table 3). Many were domestics and gardeners working on estates in San Mateo and Santa Clara counties; others were truck gardeners and small farmers, among them immigrants from Huanglian Du. Small Chinatowns also sprang up in the peninsula towns of San Mateo, Menlo Park, Mayfield, and San Jose to serve this Chinese population. Typically each Chinatown had one or more general merchandise stores that

TABLE 3

CHINESE POPULATION IN SAN FRANCISCO PENINSULA, 1860–1900

	San Mateo County	Santa Clara County
1860	6	22
1870	519	1,525
1880	596	2,695
1890	448	2,723
1900	306	1,738

became social centers for fellow villagers and often also fronted for gambling houses catering to the Chinese. Often there were also a restaurant and a laundry or two in the neighborhood and, in the larger Chinatowns, perhaps even a rooming house.

The San Mateo Chinatown was in existence as early as the 1870s with a cluster of businesses around B and Second avenues. By the turn of the century another small Chinatown had developed around the Hop Yick store at First and Claremont. Chinese from Taishan and Huangliang Du owned most of the establishments, among which were interspersed some Japanese businesses. This Chinatown disappeared before World War II. A smaller Chinatown in nearby Menlo Park, however, lasted until the 1950s. Chinese establishments in that cluster were mostly owned by Huangliang Du people. One store, Hip Cheong Jan, later became the clubhouse for the local chapter of Hip Sen Association.[45]

In adjoining Palo Alto, however, Chinese had to fight for the right even to establish businesses in that town close to Stanford University, where many Chinese were working. Plans to open a Chinese laundry in Palo Alto failed in 1893, when citizens pressured the building owner to cancel the lease.[46] In 1905 B. F. Hall acting on behalf of Mock Wo and Ah Fong, who may have been of Huangliang Du origin, applied for a permit to operate the Cardinal Restaurant in town. When the city clerk refused to issue the license, Hall took the matter to court, and the restaurant subsequently opened quietly, establishing a precedent for other Chinese businesses in Palo Alto. Two years later Gee Beng Mock and Kee Leung, both from Huangliang Du, were able to open City Cafe without any disturbances. Leung, who had been a cook at the Phi Delta Theta house on the Stanford campus, later built one of the early apartment houses in Palo Alto, the Palm Court Apartments.[47] However, Palo Alto never did have a Chinatown, and customers of Chinese businesses were primarily drawn from mainstream American society.

A small Chinatown existed in Mayfield (annexed by Palo Alto in 1925), south of Palo Alto, for many years. This Chinatown had mostly Huangliang Du people, although there were some from Sze Yap. Mayfield's citizens were imbued with the same anti-Chinese sentiments as their neighbors, but as lamented by the *Palo Alto Times* in 1903: "Citizens of May-field are meeting with difficulties in their efforts to dislodge the Chinese quarters. It is not easy to find land upon which to place them, and such tracts as can be had the Chinese will not accept." Thus, in spite of continued harassment, the small Chinese enclave managed to survive; however, it disappeared long before World War II.[48]

The largest Chinatown in Santa Clara County was at San Jose. It was first formed at Market and San Fernando streets during the 1860s. By the late 1880s the Chinatown had become a bustling community with more than a thousand inhabitants. At this time the city of San Jose was envisioning construction of a modernized downtown area where China-town was located. When the Chinese showed a reluctance to move from the area, arsonists set fires that destroyed China-town on May 4, 1887. The displaced Chinese then leased land at Fifth and Taylor streets from John Heinlen and built a new Chinatown that became known as Heinlenville.[49] But by the late 1920s the Chinese population had declined as older Chinese died, retired, or returned to China while the younger generation departed to seek better opportunities. In 1931 the Heinlen Company went bankrupt, and the land was turned over to Pacific National Bank of San Francisco, who began razing Chinatown. The last vestige of Chinatown did not disappear, however, until 1949, when the Ng Shing Gung temple was finally demolished.[50]

Most of the inhabitants of Heinlenville were Sze Yap, but branches of the Young Wo and Sam Yap associations also existed. The principal Huangliang Du general merchandise store during the twentieth century was Kwong Wo Jan (Quong Wo Chan). Soong Quong Young, who immigrated from Longtan Village in 1881, was an employee at the store. In 1892 he became a partner and in 1907 sole owner. The store was a gathering place for people from Huangliang Du and other areas of Xiangshan.[51]

TRUCK GARDENS, SEED FARMS, FLOWER NURSERIES

Many Huangliang Du immigrants were small farmers in the agricultural sector of the San Francisco Peninsula, on a modest scale. They were probably among the Chinese that began tending vegetable patches in Santa Clara and San Mateo counties during the 1870s. By the 1880s a number of Chinese were also working on peninsula estates as gardeners. This period saw the beginnings of the cut flower industry on the Peninsula, when Italian farmers began growing violets along-side their vegetables. They were soon joined by Chinese gardeners and farmers who realized that growing flowers for the market was a good means to augment their income. Thus by the turn of the century Chinese were already marketing cut flowers, as described in the following news item depicting the scene at the Southern Pacific station at Third and Townsend streets in San Francisco: "Chinese with great baskets like lidless trunks came ambling from the station, eight or ten of them, each with his offering of fresh flowers where-with to pile high the light burden to be borne up Third Street by the express wagons."[52]

During this period cut flowers were still regarded mainly as a source of supplemental income, and for some years into the twentieth century Chinese farmers on the Peninsula still focused on produce as their principal crops. For example, Huangliang Du people were said to have operated three truck farms on the site of the present Palo Alto city hall. The land was divided into three sections and farmed by three companies, each owned by eight to ten partners. They raised vegetables such as tomatoes, string beans, celery, squash, and cucumbers and sold the produce on consignment to San Francisco merchants.[53]

Information is vague regarding whether nineteenth-century flower vendors and growers were of Huangliang Du origin; however, a support system based on clan solidarity as well as a common region of origin in China soon enabled Huangliang Du people to dominate certain sectors of agriculture on the Peninsula. The same factor also worked to promote their dominance on Chinese seed farms. At first these farms were located near San Jose at the south end of the Peninsula, but around the turn of the century the operations moved to the Hollister–Gilroy–San Juan Bautista area. Many members of the Huang (Wong) clan of Dahaochong ran such farms, and at one time during the first half of the twentieth century there were as many as seven such farms near Hollister.[54]

The Huangliang Du community generally credits the Stanford farm near Palo Alto as being the first to hire Huang-liang Du people as gardeners. With Palo Alto as a center, they spread to other parts of the San Francisco Peninsula. The pioneer was said to be Jim Mock from Chishuikeng. Mock appears to have arrived in California before the 1880s, when he became a supervisor of Chinese workers on the Southern Pacific Railroad. Afterward he became a foreman on the Stanford farm. Taking advantage of his position, Mock assisted many Huangliang Du fellow clansmen and fellow townsmen to find employment on the farm. They in turn helped their relatives and friends. Thus numerous immigrants of Huangliang Du origin came into the area. According to one informant, up to the early 1920s practically all Chinese gardeners on the Stanford estate were from Huang-liang Du, as were many cooks in Stanford University fraternity and sorority houses. Many second-generation Mok (Mock) clan members were born in and around Palo Alto.[55]

Mock apparently left Stanford's employ when the farm became the Stanford University campus. As mentioned previously, he became one of the founders of Chung Sun Wo in San Francisco. Mock also learned flower cultivation from a Japanese gardener and around the early 1900s became the first Huangliang Du villager to grow sweet peas, asters, and chrysanthemums near San Carlos. He taught these horticultural skills to Mo Yuqin (Yee Him Mock), who in 1908 became the second San Carlos grower.[56] Charlie Wong, formerly supervisor of a C. C. Morse seed farm at Hollister, moved to San Carlos with his family in 1918, also to grow sweet peas, asters, and chrysanthemums.[57]

Another pioneering family was known to American society as Yee; however, their Chinese surname was Zhao (Jue, Jew, Chew). The progenitor of the clan worked on the Hopkins estate in San Mateo County as a gardener. As time went on, local people sought him out to buy flowers. Yee then leased a quarter- or half-acre near the estate and worked on it on a part-time basis, growing chrysanthemums, asters, and sweet Williams in an open field. Yee grew flowers commercially during the early 1900s and became known as Ah Sam. His descendants continued growing commercial cut flowers using the same name.[58]

After World War I ended, potato prices declined sharply, and many Huangliang Du farmers in the San Joaquin delta decided that the developing San Francisco Peninsula offered better opportunities than potato farms in the San Joaquin delta. The influx of Huangliang Du people into the Peninsula continued after 1910. Some were members of the Lin (Lum) clan of Dahuan, the Chen (Chan, Chin) clan of Nanshan, and the Tan (Tom, Hom) clan of Paishan. They were joined by villagers belonging to other clans. Thus by the 1920s the Peninsula had a relatively large concentration of Huangliang Du people.[59]

Huangliang Du people were also dispersed widely in rural parts of the Peninsula. Some were gardeners, while others grew produce. Many also raised cut flowers to augment their incomes. But as time elapsed, the cut flowers became an increasingly important part of their annual incomes. Before the 1920s sweet peas, asters, and chrysanthemums were the principal crops. Since each flower blooms at a different time of the year, this combination ensured the grower of a source of income during most of the year.[60] During the early years the Chinese growers carried cut flowers to San Francisco in reed baskets, taking the train or the streetcar line that ran from San Mateo to San Francisco. They would rent a room in Chinatown in the building above the store Chung Sun Wo, where they would keep the flowers and spend the night before going to the flower market early the next morning.[61] The Mee Brothers (the family's Chinese surname was Tan [Tom or Hom]) nursery was said to be first to purchase a Model T Ford to transport flowers to San Francisco.

Chinese growers soon found asters and chrysanthemums to be more profitable than sweet peas and turned to these crops. The need for a central outlet to store and distribute the cut flowers led to the formation of the Chinese Flowers Growers Association around 1924–25. Each member of the group bought hundred-dollar shares to form a flower market in San Francisco. Later, as the number of growers increased, the association members decided to limit membership in the

market to twenty-six, with newer growers being excluded.[62] This market, under the name of Peninsula Flower Gardens Market, became part of the flower terminal complex that opened at Sixth and Townsend streets in 1956. The two other buildings of the complex were those of the larger Japanese American California Flower Market, with 135 members, and the predominantly Italian San Francisco Flower Growers Association.[63]

Around World War I Ah Sam became one of the earliest growers to have cut flowers shipped to other parts of the United States. However, during this early period, Chinese growers did not handle shipment of their products outside the local area. In 1931, during the depths of the Great Depression, San Carlos grower Charlie Wong's son ventured into the flower-shipping business when he opened Wong and Sons in San Francisco Chinatown. The outlet was both a retail florist and a shipper of cut flowers. However, within a few years the business failed. During the late 1930s Wong tried again, teaming up with his brother-in-law, and established the more successful Wong and Chan, wholesale shippers, on the Peninsula.[64] Another early shipper was Lee Brothers, whose owners came from Liwuwei. They had run one of the early Chinese-owned nurseries in the San Carlos area. The Lee Brothers packed "pom-poms, China mums, Heather-violets, Belmont Gardenias, and callas."[65]

Because asters were grown outdoors, they required minimal investment in equipment and were favored by growers with limited capital. During the late 1930s aster growers comprised the majority of flower growers. They numbered between twenty and thirty, located mostly around Redwood City and Menlo Park. Some later also located near East Palo Alto.[66] During this period before World War II there were few families; the growers thus lived bachelors' lives. In their spare hours they would visit San Francisco or San Jose Chinatown, or frequent gambling houses and stores in the smaller Chinatowns of San Mateo, Menlo Park, and Mayfield.

Most aster farms were tended by two- to three-man partnerships. The plots were located on the flatlands with parcels generally three to five acres in area. Aster crops, however, contaminated the soil with a virus that rendered the land unsatisfactory for a succeeding aster crop. Thus growers had to make frequent moves to virgin land.

Chrysanthemum crops, in contrast, did not impose such restrictions, and the growers could invest in long-term capital improvements on their parcels. During the late 1920s about a dozen nurseries were located in the San Mateo area between 25th and 33rd avenues, at the site of the College of San Mateo and around the golf course along Highway 92 beyond Hillsdale. Others were closer to San Francisco, in the San Bruno area, where the Golden Gate National Cemetery is today. They were all on leased hillside land facing east to take full advantage of the sunshine and to provide protection from frost and the ocean fog. Mee Brothers was one of the largest Chinese-owned nurseries during this period.[67]

Although chrysanthemum growers tended to stay longer at a location than aster growers, creeping urbanization and rising land values also motivated them to relocate to cheaper land in less urbanized areas. Chew Chin's nursery is said to be the first to move south to Woodside. By the eve of World War II there were some twenty nurseries of five to ten acres in the area. At the time Chin's nursery was the largest at approximately twenty acres. He had six to seven nephews working for him.[68]

Nursery owners developed techniques to control and improve the yield of chrysanthemums at an early date. During the 1920s the Mee Brothers nursery, which was located in the flatlands rather than on a hillside, was first to use cheese-cloth to cover and protect the plants. In 1931 the nursery introduced the use of black cloth to induce bud initiation. At that time it was also the only grower to use steam heat to sterilize the soil and to heat the greenhouses. Most growers during this period were small and thus lacked the capital to introduce such improvements.[69]

The alien land laws barred many Chinese growers from owning land. Faced with pervasive discrimination against Chinese during the 1920s and 1930s, many also considered themselves sojourners in this country. Most growers therefore leased their parcels and were not greatly motivated to spend much on capital expenditures. Thus, even though the Chinese and the Japanese had entered the flower-growing business at approximately the same time, the Japanese growers soon assumed the leadership role in developing the industry. During the pre–World War II era, Italian and Japanese at one point each made up about 45 percent of the growers in the region, while 10 percent were Chinese.[70]

THE PEAKING AND THE DECLINE OF THE CUT FLOWER INDUSTRY

During World War II many flower growers served in the armed forces, and many growers turned to garden produce. After the war the political and social status of the Chinese in America improved with the relaxation and repeal of many anti-Chinese laws and practices. This change diminished the sense of alienation among Chinese in America, and the attitude that this country was to be a permanent home for themselves and their descendants began to evolve.

After the war the relaxation of immigration laws allowed many families to be reunited in this country. During the period of postwar prosperity many growers improved their economic status. Many bought parcels of land and turned from asters to the more profitable chrysanthemums. Nurseries became family-operated businesses and the number of growers increased.

The increased availability of air cargo services for shipping cut flowers enabled growers to develop a national market. This expanding market for flowers motivated nursery owners to invest in technological innovations to improve and main-

tain their competitive positions. Chrysanthemum nurseries moved from the hillsides to the flatlands. Cheese-cloth houses erected on redwood posts began to be superseded by steel-framed glass greenhouses. Around 1952 Charles Foo Chan was first to use electric lights to control the growth rate of chrysanthemums. The use of steam heating became universal around 1956 to sterilize the soil and to heat greenhouses. Fan cooling with a pan of water to lower the greenhouse temperature in summer was first used around 1958 to improve the quality of the blooms. Techniques were also introduced for direct planting and rooting in sand beds, thus eliminating the need for transfer planting.[71]

With the increased number of Chinese flower growers, some felt that there was a need to organize to strengthen their bargaining power in negotiations with suppliers, shippers, and florists. Since membership in the existing Chinese Flowers Growers Association was limited to twenty-six, a number far smaller than the forty-five to fifty-five growers during the mid-1950s, Charles Foo Chin and Mo Huanwen (Foon Man Mok) led in the founding of the more inclusive Bay Area Chrysanthemum Growers Association around 1956. Membership was limited to Huangliang Du growers. Chinese aster growers also formed the Northern California Aster Growers Association. The Chrysanthemum Growers Association was headquartered in Mountain View, but in 1981 loans from members enabled it to build and move into a new headquarters at Ringwood Avenue, San Jose.[72]

America's prosperity in the 1960s ushered in a golden era for nursery owners. Huangliang Du nurseries increased to around a hundred, providing livelihoods for some five to six hundred Huangliang Du people. The owners were predominantly from Doumen, but a significant minority originated from Sanzao. During the 1960s Fuzhou immigrants also entered the field to become competitors.[73] The number of aster growers declined to a minority, as shown by the eighteen members in the Northern California Aster Growers Association in 1970 as compared to eighty in the Bay Area Chrysanthemum Growers Association. During this period some growers began to try to diversify their crops as a buffer against the caprices of the market. T. S. Chan Nursery, founded by Lung Chin's son in 1948, in 1967 became the first Chinese nursery to grow roses, a crop with high profit margins. By that time T. S. Chan's son, Gordon, was managing the business. Gordon Chan was the only Huangliang Du nursery owner with a formal education relating to the field, having received a degree in ornamental horticulture from California Polytechnic Institute in 1959. In the early 1970s two other Chinese nursery owners went into roses, while four or five grew carnations.[74]

By this time chrysanthemums had become the single biggest crop among agricultural products in Santa Clara County, valued at $9,392,000 in 1968. This figure represented 12.4 percent of the value of all agricultural production. Chrysanthemums were grown on 158.8 acres, for a value per acre of $59,000. Tomatoes, the second cash crop, had a value per acre of only $980. At the time the Chinese produced about half the chrysanthemum crop and nearly all the asters.[75]

The rapid postwar urbanization of the Peninsula, however, exerted constant pressure, forcing the growers to move southward to cheaper land. Flower nurseries had not existed in Belmont, where some early growers started, since the 1940s. They disappeared from Woodside Road near Redwood City after the 1950s. During the early 1940s the first Chinese growers had entered Santa Clara County, settling near Palo Alto. By the 1950s most of the aster growers were on Stanford University land. By the 1960s they had begun moving to the Berryessa District in San Jose. A similar fate befell the chrysanthemum growers. By the early 1950s the last nurseries had left the San Bruno region. By the late 1950s and early 1960s, about the time College of San Mateo built its campus the last Chinese grower left the San Mateo area. In the 1950s many nurseries were located near Mountain View and Sunnyvale, but rapid urbanization of that area during the 1960s accompanying the rise of Silicon Valley forced nursery owners to move again. Most chose to join their aster-growing fellow villagers in the Beryessa District. By the mid-1970s the bulk of the growers had relocated there. There were five to six growers in the Cupertino area from 1959 to 1985. Some moved to Milpitas and Fremont. Others moved south to the area around Gilroy and Morgan Hill, where it was hoped the urban frontier would not arrive soon.[76]

Even during this period of prosperity, uncertainties were already clouding the future of many nurseries. Many growers' offspring, especially those who had acquired professional or technical educations, were reluctant to follow in their parents' footsteps. But up to the mid-1970s the influx of new immigrants into the industry more than offset those dropping out, so that by 1978 the number of nurseries had actually increased to 125, with ten in asters, two in roses, and the rest in chrysanthemums. About 110 were from Doumen, ten Fujianese, and the remainder Cantonese from areas other than Doumen. A typical nursery consisted of about two acres of covered area tended by members of the family and three hired employees (usually Mexicans, in contrast to the 1950s, when they were practically all Chinese). The average annual gross income of the nurseries ran between $50,000 and $100,000.[77]

In 1979 a disagreement within the Bay Area Chrysanthemum Growers Association over construction of a new clubhouse led twenty-eight members to withdraw to form the United Flower Growers Association. Since by this time there were an increasing number of non–Huangliang Du growers, and growers of Huangliang Du ancestry could no longer monopolize the field, both organizations accepted as members all Chinese growers, regardless of area of origin.[78]

During this period a basic change had occurred in the domestic market for chrysanthemums. Around 1971 chrysanthemums began to be imported from countries with lower production costs. Then came the Arab oil embargo of 1973, and domestic nurseries found production costs zooming steeply upward. Less expensive imported pompon chrysanthemums expanded their share of the American market from 5.6 percent in 1971 to 73.5 percent in 1988. Cut flowers in Santa Clara County dropped from a $35 million industry in 1980 to $22 million by 1990. By 1989 cut flowers had yielded their position as the leading agricultural commodity in Santa Clara County and had slipped to third place behind nursery crops and mushrooms. Newcomers from the Indochina Peninsula, including ethnic Chinese, also began entering the field during the late 1970s and early 1980s to compete against existing growers for a shrinking market.[79]

With these adverse developments the number of active growers in the Bay Area Chrysanthemum Growers Association decreased from 140 in the late 1970s. By 1997 the organization had eighty-three growing members and seventy-one retired members. There are no growers left in the Milpitas area, about eight growers around Alviso on Highway 237, and three in San Jose. The rest are located near Morgan Hill, Gilroy, San Martin, and even Watsonville south of San Jose. There are about seventy chrysanthemum growers but only one (in Watsonville) grower of roses.[80] The remaining active growers have turned to raising Chinese vegetables, primarily for the growing Asian market in the Bay Area. A few ship their produce to mainstream supermarkets as far away as Seattle. About half the former members chose to retire. As urbanization of the South Bay Area continued unabated, nursery owners such as Cupertino's Marshall Mok and San Jose's Gordon Chan and William Mok (grandson of Yee Him Mock) either sold their land at premium prices to developers or developed their landholdings themselves as housing and shopping malls.[81]

In the 1990s a decreased number of Huangliang Du people are still active in the flower-growing sector of the Bay Area economy. The number from Sanzao has increased relative to those from Doumen, so that they now are said to number almost half.[82] However, they have entered a field that faces many uncertainties as it is buffeted by changing winds in the domestic and international economies.

CHANGING TIES WITH THE ANCESTRAL LAND

Early Huangliang Du immigrants, similar to most Chinese immigrants, continued to maintain strong ties to their home villages. With the rise of Chinese nationalism after the late nineteenth century, they also expressed interest and concern in developments in the ancestral land more generally. Some participated actively in Chinese political movements advocating a strong and modern China. Many were particularly active in the revolutionary movement led by Sun Yat-sen. During the first decade of the twentieth century, merchant Kee Wong was active raising funds for the movement. The Imperial Qing government was said to have put a price on his head, and Wong had to use the name Huang Rui (Yoey Wong) to avoid arrest. After the founding of the Republic, Wong was active in the Kuomintang-led movement in America opposing President Yuan Shikai's usurpation of power in China. He also served variously as an officer in the General Branch of the Nationalist Party of China (Kuomintang) in the United States through the mid-1920s.[83]

Another activist was San Jose merchant Soong Quong Young, proprietor of the Kwong Wo Jan store, who joined Sun Yat-sen's revolutionary organization Tongmenghui. After the founding of the Republic he continued to be active in the successor organization, the Kuomintang. In 1923 Sun Yat-sen appointed him to head the party's San Jose liaison office.[84]

From Nanshan Village came three notable supporters of Sun Yat-sen. Chen Yaoyuan (You Foon Chan) arrived in Stockton in 1906 to take over operation of his cousin's store Tuck Wo and Company, and soon joined the Tongmenghui. He became head of the local chapter and a close associate of Sun Yat-sen. In 1911 he sold his business to help finance the revolution. After the founding of the Republic, Chan became affiliated with the San Francisco party organ *Young China*. In 1915 he helped to organize the first party convention held in San Francisco. He also participated in establishing a program in America to train aviators for Sun Yat-sen's forces. In 1922 Sun appointed Chan to be general secretary of the Kuomintang general branch in San Francisco that supervised all party branches in the Americas. In 1925 Chan was elected one of the delegates from America to attend the Second Party Congress in China. In 1929 Chan became an alternate member of the Central Committee of the Kuomintang in China.[85] Fellow villager Chen Zesan (Jaak Saam Chan) became a member of the board of directors of the general branch of the Kuomintang in San Francisco in 1921. He served the party organ *Young China* in various capacities as member, officer on the board of directors, as well as editor up to the 1950s.[86] A third activist was Ging Chan (also known as Chen Jiazheng [Gai Jing Chan]), manager of Stockton's Poo Wo Tong herbshop. In 1930 Ging Chan was a stockholder in Chicago's Kuomintang organ, *San Min Morning Paper*. In 1933 he introduced a resolution at a meeting of Kuomintang delegates to ask the Chinese government to take action to resist Japanese aggression in China. In 1937 he was appointed by the *Young China* board of directors to a committee to study methods to improve the paper's operations.[87] The elder Dr. Wong Him and Jun You Jew were also active Kuomintang members.[88]

During the early decades of the Republic, when the Kuomintang was striving to unify China under its rule, the party often appealed to Chinese abroad for support. One of the young Chinese who answered the call was Chen Yousheng (Yau Shing Chan) of Nanshan, who had immigrated to the United States around 1913. Chan learned aviation at the Kuomintang-sponsored aviation school in Redwood City, California, and then returned to Guangzhou in 1921 to join the Kuomintang government's embryonic air force. He served

in various capacities and by 1940 had been promoted to be section head of the administrative section of the Aviation Commission.[89]

Japanese aggression against China during the 1930s aroused nationalistic feelings among Chinese in America. Some Chinese Americans hastened to join in the defense of ancestral land. Most notable were those who fought in China's outnumbered air force. After the Japanese invasion of Manchuria in 1931, Lin Shihan (Shihon Lam) of Niwan Village, then living in Mexico, arranged to go to San Diego to take flying lessons and then enlisted in the Guangdong air force in 1932. During the War of Resistance against Japan, Lam was appointed commanding officer of a military airfield in Guizhou Province.[90] Some young men made the ultimate sacrifice while serving in China. One was American-born George Young, son of Soong Quong Young, who became the first instructor in China to teach parachute jumping techniques. He was killed during the Sino-Japanese War when his plane crashed into a mountainside while flying with poor visibility.[91] Another was Huang Huajie (Wah Git Wong) of Dahaochong, who had immigrated into America in 1913. After graduating from the aviation school sponsored by the Chinese Six Companies in 1939, he enlisted in the Chinese Air Force. He was killed in a mishap at the Kunming Airport in 1941.[92]

Chinese resistance against the ruthless Japanese military machine inspired an outpouring of patriotic fervor in the Chinese community. Chinese Americans generously donated time and money to support the war effort. For example, in 1944 Jun You Jew was one of two people making the second largest donation at $20,000 to a fundraising campaign commemorating the seventh anniversary of the outbreak of the war.[93] He and Jaak Saam Chan served on the executive board of the China War Relief Association of America (CWRAA) and were among the many Huangliang Du people actively involved in war relief activities. Women also played active roles. Huang Zuyi (Jook Yee Wong), Jun You Jew's wife, was director of the women's section of CWRAA. She also became chairwoman of the Chinatown chapter of the Women's New Life Movement Association of China.

Soon after the end of the conflict in 1945 the cold war between the Western powers and the Socialist bloc began. China also lapsed into civil war. The victorious Communists founded the People's Republic of China (PRC) in 1949 and aligned with the Socialist bloc, while the defeated Nationalist government fled to Taiwan. At this critical juncture, the Korean War began, giving the United States a pretext to intervene in the Chinese civil war by extending its protection over Taiwan. The entry of PRC troops into the Korean Peninsula in late 1950 led to hostilities between them and United Nations troops, led by the United States. The presence of two governments, one on the mainland and the other on Taiwan, each claiming to be the legitimate rulers of the Chinese nation, polarized Chinese abroad. It was not until recently, as confrontation between Taiwan and the China mainland has relaxed, that the political atmosphere among the Chinese in America has changed accordingly.

The situation that developed within the Huangliang Du community in America was no different from that among other Chinese in America. Those who were active Kuomintang members actively helped Taiwan to extend and maintain political control over public opinion in the Chinese community. Active in the party organ *Young China* was J. P. Wong of Dahaochong. Wong had immigrated to the United States in 1913 and joined the Kuomintang in 1922, and soon he was serving as an officer in the San Francisco branch of the party. He returned to China in 1929 and did not return to this country until the Nationalist regime on the China mainland collapsed in 1949. In 1951 Wong became proprietor of the Hang Ah Teahouse. He also was elected to the board of directors of *Young China* and became its manager in 1954. In 1974 Wong was appointed consultant to Taiwan's Overseas Chinese Affairs Commission. However, in 1980, after U.S. relations with the PRC had improved, Wong visited his ancestral village in Doumen. The following year, 1981, he and fellow Kuomintang member and artist George Chann accepted invitations from the Guangdong provincial government to attend the seventieth anniversary commemoration of the 1911 Revolution.[94]

Another loyal Kuomintang supporter was flower grower Zhao Shusheng (Shue Shang Jew) of Nanmen, who served as a *Young China* board director and consultant to Taiwan's Overseas Chinese Affairs Commission.[95] In the 1980s one of the most active supporters of the Taiwan regime was flowershop owner Mo Xiangxing (Cheung Hing Mok), who variously served as secretary of the General Branch of the Kuomintang in America and president of the Chinese Anti-Communist League. He was also a member of the board of *Young China*. In the 1980s the Taiwan government appointed him an overseas Chinese affairs commissioner. In 1986 he was elected to serve in Taiwan's Legislative Yuan as a representative of the Chinese in America.[96]

Because of the tense relations between the PRC and the United States, and the anti-Communist atmosphere in this country, there were few overt expressions of support for the PRC by Chinese in America during the 1950s and 1960s. But by the late 1960s, with the rise of a more liberal atmosphere in America brought about by the Civil Rights movement, attitudes in the community began to change. Journalist Maurice Chuck (also known as Huang Yunji [Wan Gei Wong]) of Dahaochong Village, who immigrated in 1948, was one of the first to express this new orientation openly. Chuck was an active member of the pro-PRC Chinese American Youth Club in the 1950s and was harassed by the U.S. government for his political beliefs. When the political situation began to change, he was hired as Chinese editor of the liberal weekly *East/West* in 1967. In 1969 Chuck became a founder of *Chinese Voice*, a newspaper advocating better U.S.–PRC relations.

In 1972 Chuck started *San Francisco Journal*, another paper with a similar editorial policy.[97] Chuck was also active in creative writing in the Chinese language. In 1995 he began publishing *The Literati*, a bimonthly journal devoted to literary works by Chinese in America.

Similar to other emigrants from the Pearl River Delta, Huangliang Du emigrants had long remitted money to their ancestral villages for family support and public projects. However, because the emigrant population was relatively small compared to such areas as Taishan and Kaiping, few schools and hospitals were built in the region through contributions from abroad. In the 1930s Huangliang Du Chinese in America raised funds to expand the Hefeng Middle School in the town of Doumen. However, the outbreak of the Sino-Japanese War forced postponement of the project, and the Hee Shen Association diverted the money to purchase a building. After World War II, Zhao Shunzhi (Sun Jee Jew) and Chen Jingshan (Ging Saan Chan), both former herbal physicians in San Francisco who had retired to Doumen, started a campaign in 1950 to raise money from abroad to expand the school facilities. A two-storied classroom building with a memorial plaque inscribed with the characters *qiao ze shilin* (fellow villagers abroad confer beneficence upon our community of scholars) was dedicated in 1951.[98]

With the opening of the PRC in the 1980s, immigration from Doumen and Sanzao increased dramatically. Many in the Huangliang Du community in America resumed contacts with relatives in the area, while young people visited the ancestral villages in search of their roots. Some Chinese Americans of Huangliang Du ancestry forged commercial links with or invested in business ventures in the PRC. Others became active making educational and cultural contacts with China. An example was restaurant owner Kam Hong Kwong of Xiaohaochong, who in the 1980s proposed establishing a college in Zhongshan to meet the needs of the developing economy. Groundbreaking and recruitment of students for a Sun Wen College (the name was changed to Zhongshan College in 1995) began in 1984. Kwong was an active member in the New China Education Foundation that in 1988 sponsored five Zhongshan middle school students to study in an American high school. In 1993 he initiated another foundation-sponsored activity, a summer study program in Guangdong that included Chinese language lessons and visits to various points in the Pearl River Delta, including the students' ancestral villages.[99]

From 1978 through 1987 Huangliang Du people abroad and in Hong Kong and Macao donated about RMB$1,120,000, benefiting more than twenty middle and primary schools. Additional contributions went toward funding other public facilities for a modern society. Among the most generous donors were the late John Young and his wife Mary. In 1984 the couple donated $10,000 to the First County Middle School, followed by $10,000 in 1986 to the County Third Middle School to set up scholarship funds. In 1987 they donated art objects valued at $10,000 to the County Library to set up an exhibition room dedicated to the memory of Soong Quong Young and $5,000 to help plan a county museum. After John Young passed away in 1987, his family donated HK$1,280,000 and art objects to establish the John Young County Museum. Another generous donor was William Mock, who since 1987 donated a total of HK$1,370,000, including RMB$180,000 to build Jingsheng Primary School at Bajia, $40,000 to purchase an X-ray machine for the County People's Hospital, and more than $10,000 to the First Middle School to establish an electronic classroom and a Shuangsong Library. In 1995 Mary Young and William Mock were among a group of twenty-eight overseas investors and donors honored by being made honorary citizens of Doumen.[100] On October 15, 1996, they were the only two from Doumen among 802 outstanding foreign investors honored by the Guangdong provincial government for their contributions during the seventeen years of China's open door reform policy.[101]

INTO THE AMERICAN MAINSTREAM

Even while many in the Huangliang Du community in the United States were concerned with developments in the ancestral land, others in the community were sinking roots in America and were becoming increasingly involved in events in American society. As early as the turn of the century, Dr. Wong Him, the San Francisco herbal physician, made history when he fought against the segregation of Chinese children in San Francisco public schools. His daughter Katie was excluded from Clement School in San Francisco's Richmond District in 1902 in accordance with Section 1662 of the Political Code of California and was ordered to attend Chinese Primary School in Chinatown. Wong Him then filed a complaint in the United States Circuit Court, alleging that the law violated the Fourteenth Amendment of the U.S. Constitution in that it denied equal protection of the law to citizens of Chinese descent. In the racist clime of the day, however, Dr. Wong Him lost the case.[102] In 1908 the Chinese Consolidated Benevolent Association (CCBA) appointed him to serve on a twenty-one-member planning committee to work with Imperial Commissioner Liang Qinggui to establish a Chinese school in San Francisco. He subsequently donated $300 to the school building fund.[103]

Man Quong Fong, founder of the Republic Pharmacy, was also active in community affairs. After the 1906 earthquake and fire in San Francisco, he helped to manage the Chinese refugee tent city located on the shores of Lake Merritt in Oakland, California. He then served as secretary to the Chinese consulate. He also became a member of the Chinese school planning committee appointed by the CCBA.[104] Fong was secretary for the Chinese Chamber of Commerce in 1913 and English secretary for China Mail Steamship Company, the first Chinese-owned steamship company in America, in 1915. He was also one of the founders of the Soo Yuen Association.

Owing to prejudice against Asians, particularly on the Pacific Coast, Chinese participation in mainstream society was very limited during the first half of the twentieth century. The turning point was World War II. After the Japanese attack on Pearl Harbor catapulted America into the war, many Huangliang Du people entered the war industries. Flower growers became truck farmers for the duration of the conflict. In common with other Chinese Americans, many entered the armed forces. A few served in the China-Burma-India theater, as was the case of Huang Zhaojun (Siu Gwan Wong) from Wankou Village, Qianwu. Wong has the distinction of having served in both the Chinese and U.S. air forces. He learned aviation in America and in 1934 joined the Guangdong air force. Subsequently he quit the Chinese Air Force and returned to the United States. During World War II he joined the U.S. Air Force and was assigned to the Fourteenth Air Force as an aerial spotter for the artillery.[105] A few Huangliang Du people became commissioned officers in the armed forces. One of these was John Young, the younger son of Soong Quong Young. John Young volunteered for duty and was sent to serve in the China-Burma-India war theater. Young started as a second lieutenant, but by the end of the war he was a captain. Young joined the reserves after his discharge, and during the Korean War he was recalled to active duty and was eventually promoted to full colonel. In 1946 he was cited for the Grand Order of the Cloud and Banner, China's highest decoration.[106] Another with a distinguished military record was James Leung, who went to officers' training school during the war and was sent to Germany with U.S. Army Unit 356, Civil Affairs, in 1947. Afterward he stayed in the reserves and was promoted to full colonel in 1960.[107]

In the period immediately preceding U.S. entry into the conflict, as American industries began tooling up to help England defend against German attacks, Chinese Americans with technical education were finding job opportunities where none existed before. Jun You Jew's son Lawrence Jue began as a junior naval architect at Mare Island Navy Yard in 1940, after he received a Master of Science degree in mechanical engineering from the University of California, Berkeley. By 1958 he had become chief naval architect at the San Francisco Naval Shipyards and had made significant contributions to submarine design. He was the principal designer of Sealab II, a manned underwater habitat, and received the Superior Service Award, the Navy's second highest award for civilians. In 1943 Jue was a founding president of the San Francisco chapter of the Chinese Institute of Engineers. This was the first organization promoting the interests of the increasing number of Chinese American engineers in the San Francisco Bay Area.[108]

The war brought about repeal of the Chinese Exclusion acts, and the situation of Chinese in the United States began to improve perceptibly. With this better economic status, more Chinese American venture capital began to be invested in various enterprises. The efforts among flower nursery owners have been described in a previous section. Many others opened businesses. A major departure from the groceries and restaurants traditionally connected with Chinese in America was the U.S. Enterprise Corporation, founded by John Young and his brother-in-law George Hall in San Francisco. The corporation produced Wing Nien brand soy bean sauce and was one of the few Chinese-owned manufacturing firms in America. Some immigrants from Sanzao skilled in Western cookery became mainstays on the staff of Chinatown businesses such as the Ping Yuen Bakery.

Chinese Americans also took advantage of U.S. government veterans' education benefits to enter medicine, engineering, science, education, and other professional and clerical fields to form a new middle class. Members of this new middle class did not limit their activities to the traditional organizations but also became active in various newer organizations such as the Chinese Chamber of Commerce, the Chinese American Citizens' Alliance, and various veterans groups. They also began to establish contacts in mainstream America and even to venture into mainstream politics. Chinese Americans of Huangliang Du ancestry participated actively in these developments.

The decades after 1960 saw even greater middle-class participation in community and civic affairs to elevate the status of the Chinese in America and to improve the quality of life in the Chinese community. Many who participated were of Huangliang Du ancestry. One of the earliest was Alan Wong of Dahaochong ancestry. Wong became interested in social issues during the late 1960s, when he was a member of the San Francisco Council of Churches. He participated in the Economic Development Council established during the War on Poverty program initiated during late 1960s. In 1969 he taught the first collegiate course on the Chinese community at San Francisco State College. Wong entered elective politics in 1965, when he served on the Democratic Party County Central Committee. In 1982 and 1986 he was elected to the San Francisco Community College Board.

Naval architect Lawrence Jue was also a community activist. He headed a Save Our Schools Committee in 1973 that successfully lobbied the San Francisco school board to find funds to retrofit and seismically upgrade three elementary schools serving the Chinatown area rather than closing them.[109] In 1974–78 he and Connie Young Yu, daughter of Col. John Young, were members of a legislature-appointed committee to make recommendations for preservation of the Angel Island Immigration Detention Station. Jue also headed the committee to choose the Chinese inscription on the memorial tablet erected at the site. Connie Young Yu later was active in the South Bay community, participating in the project to restore San Jose's Ng Shing Kung temple, and has published authoritative works on the Chinese in Santa Clara County.

In San Francisco civil engineer William Chin of Xiazhou represented the Chinese Six Companies in 1994 to negotiate with the city government on the implementation of regulations for handicapped access during seismic retrofitting of Chinatown buildings.[110] In 1987 attorney Arnold Chin, another of Lung Chin's grandsons, became one of the few American-born to head the Yeong Wo Association and the Chinese Six Companies. Chin was president of the Chinese Chamber of Commerce in 1994–95.[111] He also serves on the board of the Angel Island Immigration Station Foundation that works to preserve the historic site. From the late 1960s, Dr. Donald Cheu, son of Dr. Henry Cheu, has been appointed to local and state positions in emergency and disaster care and has received numerous commendations and awards.[112]

Judy Yung, of Paishan ancestry, served on the San Francisco Library Commission, in 1976–78 under Mayor Moscone. In 1975 she established the Asian Branch of the Oakland Public Library, the first such public collection in the country. She also headed a research project to develop the first exhibition on Chinese American women's history—which opened in 1983—and has often written on the subject.[113] Yung is currently professor of American Studies at University of California, Santa Cruz. Developer Pius Lee from Bajia, active in the Chinese Chamber of Commerce, headed the California-Taiwan Sister State Committee in 1984–85. He became police commissioner in 1988 under San Francisco Mayor Art Agnos.[114]

In spite of increased political participation, Chinese on the American mainland have yet to match the record of Hawaii's Senator Hiram Fong, who was of Doumen ancestry. Fong was elected to national office and held office until he retired. On the mainland Man Quong Fong's daughter-in-law March Fong ran successfully for the Alameda County school board in the 1960s. Elected to the California State Assembly in 1966 and secretary of state in 1974, she became one of the most successful Chinese American politicians in California. In 1994 she became ambassador to Micronesia. Her son Matthew in turn was elected California's state treasurer in 1994.[115]

In Santa Clara County, Gordon Chan, grandson of Lung Chin, was the first Chinese American member of the County Farm Bureau. From 1985 to 1989 he served on the County Planning Commission. In 1992 he was appointed to the County Fair Board. He also served on the Trails Master Plan Committee of the County Parks and Recreation Commission from 1993 to 1996.[116] College professor Paul Fong, grandson of a Huangliang Du flower grower, was the first from such a South Bay family to be elected to public office. During the mid-1990s he was elected to the Foothill–De Anza College District board.[117] In 1995 Fong's home also became the headquarters for the successful campaign to elect Michael Chang as the first Chinese American to serve on the Cupertino city council.[118] In 1996 Alameda County judge Ming Chin became the first Chinese American to be appointed to the California Supreme Court. Chin was the youngest son of Oregon farmer Sam Wong Chin.[119]

In the cultural field, in 1997 Jessica Yu won the coveted Oscar Award in the Best Documentary Short category. Just as her staunchly Nationalist great-grandfather Soong Quong Young was noted for his role in helping to shape historical destiny in China, her name now occupies a permanent niche in the annals of America for her contribution to the best in the film arts.[120]

CONCLUDING WORDS

A striking phenomena of the Huangliang Du community in northern California is its high incidence of activists in the political arena during the twentieth century. This activism may have to do with the fact that the Pearl River Delta is a region that for centuries was influenced by contacts from abroad. Such contacts led to a psychology favorable toward acceptance of new ideas. During the nineteenth century the Zhongshan-Zhuhai-Doumen region was on the frontline for receiving attacks on traditional China launched by Western aggressors. Thus it was not surprising that, at the turn of the century when Sun Yat-sen from the same region began promoting his ideas for changing and modernizing China, he found many sympathetic ears and attracted many followers among Huangliang Du people. These pioneers through their examples not only spurred the continuation of activism among their descendants, but also served as models, stimulating activism within the Huangliang Du community.

The basic history of the Huangliang Du community in northern California, however, parallels that of other Chinese American communities formed by immigrants from Guangdong's Pearl River Delta and their descendants. Through hard work and perseverance over many decades, many succeeded in upgrading their social and economic status. Because they came from a relatively small area in China and spoke the same dialect, these immigrants formed a close-knit community. Mutual aid based largely on feelings of kinship and regional bonds enabled them and fellow villagers to enter and expand their role in certain sectors of the economy. This phenomenon was most noticeable in their role in the development of the San Francisco Peninsula cut flower industry.

When the community became established in California, it continued to maintain close ties with the home villages in China. This was particularly true before World War II, when many immigrants had come without their families. Many at that time considered themselves sojourners in this country

and returned to China when they retired. In the half-century since the end of World War II, however, most Huangliang Du immigrants' families have been reunified in this country. With that resolution has come a realization that America for all practical purposes has become the permanent home for themselves and their posterity. Although the continued influx of immigrants in recent decades has served to sustain regional bonds both within the community in California and with ancestral villages in China, the changed status of the community in America has greatly weakened feelings of regional solidarity as individuals have increasingly become active participants in the American mainstream.

This tendency is particularly marked among the increasing number of American-born, some reaching even the fourth or fifth generations. Many have entered occupations in the larger society in the professional and technical fields. With their increasing integration into the American mainstream, they have become actively involved in developments in American society, and regional feelings have become even less meaningful as a factor in their personal and business relationships.

NOTES

1. In this essay all transliterated Chinese geographical names, except for widely accepted ones such as Hong Kong and Macao, are given in Mandarin transliterated into Hanyu pinyin. For names of institutions and individuals, the spellings customarily used in America are preferred. If only the Chinese characters were available, the name appears in pinyin with the Cantonese transliteration in parentheses. Personal names customarily used in America and Cantonese transliterations of Chinese names are given with surname last per Western practice. Individuals' names in Mandarin are given with the surname first per Chinese practice.

2. Huang Qichen, *Aumen lishi* (History of Macao) (Macao: Macao Historical Society, 1999), 40–43; *Xiangshan xianzhi, xubian* (Guangzhou: Mobaolou, 1923), vol. 16, folio 1a.

3. Zhao Fuchong, "Mulong sui zhong" (Grave of mulong year), in *Doumen wenshi* (Doumen literature and history), 1st collection (Doumen: Zhengxie Doumen xian weiyuanhui wenshi ziliao gongzuozu, 1985), 59–60; Zhao Guoyong, "Xue jun banban de 'yijie' shijian" (The bloody "moving the boundary" incident), *Doumen wenshi*, 2d collection (Doumen: Doumen xian zhengxie wenshi ziliao weiyuanhui, 1986), 49–51; Zhao Guoyong, "Doumen ge xingzu yuanliu gaikuang" (A survey on the origins and development of various Doumen clans), Part 1, *Doumen wenshi*, 4th collection (Apr. 1987), 48–50; Part 2, *Doumen wenshi*, 5th collection (Oct. 1987), 49–55; Liang Zhenxing, Wen Liping, "Sanzao dao jianshi" (Brief history of Sanzao Island), *Zhuhai wenshi* (Zhuhai literature and history), 5th collection (Zhuhai: Zhongguo renmin zhengzhi xieshang huiyi Zhuhai shi weiyuanhui wenshi ziliao yanjiu weiyuanhui, 1987), 63–73.

4. "Doumen xian qiaowuzhi" (Gazetteer of Doumen overseas Chinese affairs) (draft) (Doumen, 1988), 7. Referenced hereafter as "Gazetteer of Doumen Overseas Chinese Affairs."

5. "Gazetteer of Doumen Overseas Chinese Affairs," 9.

6. *Jiushan chongjian Yanghe guan miao gongjin zhengxinlu* (Record of income and disbursements for reconstruction of the Yeong Wo Association building and temple in San Francisco) (San Francisco: Yeong Wo Association, 1900). Referenced hereafter as *Record of Yeong Wo Association*. The count of Huangliang Du donors listed by village of origin on folios 10b to 13a was used to estimate the number of immigrants from the various villages to California.

7. Interview with Kong Chow, Nov. 3, 1995. Referenced hereafter as interview with Kong Chow.

8. Ou Tianqi, "Zhonghua, Sanyi, Ningyang, Gangzhou, Hehe, Renhe, Zhaoqing, Keshang ba da huiguan lianhe Yanghe xinguan xu" (Joint preface from the Chinese Consolidated Benevolent, Sam Yap, Ning Yeung, Kong Chow, Hop Wo, Yan Wo, Sue Hing, and Haak Sheung associations congratulating Yeong Wo Association on its new building), in *Record of Yeong Wo Association,* no page numbers.

9. Norman Asing, "To His Excellency Gov. Bigler," *Daily Alta California,* May 5, 1852.

10. "Joint preface from the Chinese Consolidated Benevolent, Sam Yap, Ning Yeung, Kong Chow, Hop Wo, Yan Wo, Sue Hing, and Haak Sheung Associations Congratulating Yeong Wo Association on Its New Building"; "Report of the Committee on Mines and Mining Interests"; California State Assembly Document No. 78 (Sacramento), dated Mar. 9, 1953.

11. Carl T. Smith, *Chinese Christians: Elites, Middlemen, and the Church in Hong Kong* (Hong Kong: Oxford University Press, 1985), 47.

12. *Sacramento Daily Union,* Nov. 27, 1869.

13. A news item in *The Oriental,* June 1856, reads as follows:

> On the 28th day of the fourth moon a two-and-a-half mast English ship Shidianchenbolu carried 336 coffins [containing bones] of late fellow townsmen to Guangdong. The cost for renting the ship as well as the expenses to exhume and move the bodies from the mountains, this city and other places and to purchase the coffins was covered by the generous subscriptions from the fellow townsmen of each *du.* There were 138 coffins of late fellow townsmen of Jishan Tang of Shang Gongchang Du, 25 coffins of Mushan Tang of Long Du, 23 coffins of Dunshan Tang of Renzi Du, 12 coffins of Chengshan Tang of Dening Du, 17 coffins of Jishan Tang of Sizi Du, 2 coffins of Guishan Tang of Guzu Du, 94 coffins of Bao'an Tang of Dongguan, 17 coffins of Yi'an Tang of Zengcheng. Besides there were eight coffins of bones of people from other distant locations whose expenses were paid by relatives.

The names of six out of the eight organizations mentioned above are the same as the corresponding organizations today. The names of the modern Long Du and Dening Du organizations are Tongshan Tang and Deshan Tang respectively. The date of this item is much earlier than the founding dates claimed by most of these organizations. It may be that these organizations at this early date were activated only when the need arose to take care of the dead and that they took on other functions and evolved into some degree of permanence only toward the end of the nineteenth century.

14. Li Puzhen (P. C. Lee), "Liushan jiyao" (Summary history of the Chinese cemetery), in *Meiguo Sanfanshi liu huiguan chongxiu Liushan fenchang zhengxinlu* (Record of income and disbursements for the rebuilding of the Chinese cemetery by the six *huiguan* of San Francisco in America) (San Francisco: Chinese Cemetery Association, 1953), 1.

15. Interviews with John Mock, Nov. 2, 1969; Apr. 26, May 17, 1970 (referenced hereafter as interviews with John Mock); Zhou Zhangcai, "Xieshantang lishi leshu" (A short history of Hip Sen Association), *Doumen xiangyin* (The Voice of Doumen), no. 23 (fall 1992), 17.

16. *The Chinese of Hawaii* (Honolulu: Overseas Penman Club, 1929), 97, 100; *The Chinese of Hawaii, Vol. II* (Honolulu: Overseas Penman Club, 1936), 36.

17. *The Chinese Community in New York City* (New York: Chinese Community Research Bureau, 1950), 182; interview with Kong Chow.

18. Interview by Judy Yung with Lung Chin's fourth son, Gway Chin (referenced hereafter as Yung interview with Gway Chin), July 29, 1979; interview of the author with John Chin (referenced hereafter as interview with John Chin), Nov. 13, 1995.

19. Sucheng Chan, *This Bittersweet Soil: The Chinese in California Agriculture, 1860–1910* (Berkeley: University of California Press, 1986), 207–8; Yung interview with Gway Chin; interview of author with Mary Chan, Oct. 23, 1995.

20. Wells Fargo and Co.'s Express, Directory of Chinese Business Houses, San Francisco, Sacramento, Stockton, Marysville, San Jose, Portland, Virginia City, Nev. (San Francisco: Wells Fargo and Co., 1878), 32; same Directory dated 1882, 49; interview with John Chin; notarized partnership lists dated May 13, 1887; Aug. 12, 1891; Aug. 16, 1893; Lung Chin's Statement to U.S. Immigration Service, Nov. 9, 1904; Jan. 11, 1912; Dec. 27, 1917.

Lung Chin's name did not appear on the 1887 partnership list. However, the 1891 and 1893 lists put Lung Chin at the head of the list and were signed by him. The 1893 list also stated that he had been a San Francisco resident for fourteen years and a member of Sing Kee for eleven years.

Sing Kee appears to have been owned originally by a person from Nanhai County. It was at 625 Dupont Street in 1878. By 1882 it had moved to 613 Dupont. It was probably sold to Chen Aida (Oi Dai Chan) from Nanshan Village during this interval. When Chan passed away, his younger brother Lung Chin (Hong Dai Chan) assumed control. According to Lung Chin, he had become connected with the firm in 1882. He became the leading member of the firm no later than 1891 and owned the largest share of the business. He also held the important position of interpreter. According to Yung's interview with Gway Chin, Lung Chin was the sole owner of the store; thus the other individuals were probably either minor partners or merely paper partners, a common practice use by Chinese immigrants during the exclusion era to attain exempt status to gain legal entry into the United States.

On different occasions Lung Chin gave different dates for his first arrival in the United States. His Aug. 16, 1893, affidavit claimed that he had been in the United States for fourteen years, that is, since 1879. His Nov. 9, 1904, statement to Immigration stated that his first arrival was in the seventh year of the Guangxu reign era (1881). But on Jan. 11, 1912, and in subsequent statements the date had been changed to the eighth year of Guangxu (1882). The earlier 1893 affidavit was given when his wife Leong Shee arrived in San Francisco with a young domestic slave girl whom he claimed as her daughter. Although this was Leong Shee's first arrival in the United States, she told the Immigration inspector that she had first immigrated to the United States with her parents. She claimed to have been married in San Francisco in 1885, given birth to the alleged daughter in 1886, and returned with her to China in 1889.

21. Telephone interview with Gordon Chan, Apr. 17, 1996. Referenced hereafter as telephone interview with Gordon Chan.

22. Shanghai Trunk Manufacturing Company Partnership Lists, Apr. 1, June 3, 1921; July 7, 1923; interrogation of Wing Chan, Jan How Chun, and Lung Chin by Immigration, Dec. 15, 1923. The company was started in 1921 with Chan Chun Wing (Chan Chung Wing, also known as C. C. Wing) as

manager and largest shareholder. Lung Chin bought into the company on Jan. 5, 1922.

23. Sucheng Chan, *This Bittersweet Soil,* 206–11; *Chung Sai Yat Po,* Mar. 22, 1911; Sucheng Chan, "Chinese American Entrepreneur: The California Career of Lung Chin," *Chinese America: History and Perspectives, 1987* (San Francisco: Chinese Historical Society of America, 1987), 73–86.

24. Interview with Lawrence Jue, son of Jun You Jew, Sept. 7, 1995. Referenced hereafter as interview with Lawrence Jue.

25. Liu Pei Chi, *A History of the Chinese in the United States of America II* (Taipei: Liming wenhua shiye gufen youxian gongsi, 1981), 307; interview with William Mock, Nov. 13, 1995; William Mock, "Doumenren de huaye" (The flower industry of Doumen people), *Xishan Tang bai zhounian kan* (Publication commemorating the centennial of the Hee Shen Association), 98–99 (referenced hereafter as William Mock, "Flower Industry of the Doumen People").

26. *Chung Sai Yat Po,* Feb. 2, 4, 9, 20, June 10, 1926.

27. "Sanfanshi Huabu 40 nian dashiji" (Important events in San Francisco Chinatown during the past forty years), 74–90, in Liu Weisen, *Meiguo Sanfanshi Huaqiao gongli Donghua Yiyuan 40 zhounian jinian zhuankan* (Special publication commemorating the fortieth anniversary of the Chinese Hospital of San Francisco, U.S.A.) (San Francisco: Chinese Hospital, 1963); interview with Lawrence Jue; *Daguan xiyuan kaimu zhuankan* (Special publication for the opening of Grandview Theater) (San Francisco: Grandview Theater, 1940).

28. Advertisement in *Chinese Times,* Dec. 30, 1977.

29. Huang Lizhi, "Huang Kaiji xiansheng zhuanle" (Short biography of Mr. Kee Wong), in *Doumen wenshi,* 7th collection (Sept. 1988), 26–27 (referenced hereafter as Huang Lizhi, "Short biography of Mr. Kee Wong"); notarized partnership lists dated Aug. 17, 1893; Nov. 6, 1899; 1904 (month and day not listed); Oct. 26, 1905; Oct. 7, 1907; Mar. 16, 1917; interviews with John Mock. According to the partnership lists, Kwong On was at 714 Jackson St. in 1893, at 616 Jackson St. in 1899, and at 735 Clay St. in 1907. The last change of address was probably related to the 1906 earthquake and fire. Although Kee Wong was already listed as a partner in the 1893 partnership list, his name did not appear as manager until 1907. Lung Chin's name first appeared as a partner in 1917. His responsibility was to collect accounts payable and to solicit orders for the firm in rural areas.

30. Interviews with John Mock.

31. Interview with Robert Fong, Dec. 2, 1995.

32. Interviews with John Mock.

33. Sally Jean Dobson, "Dr. Henry Wong Him, His Contributions to Santa Clara County," in *Chinese Argonauts: An Anthology of the Chinese Contributions to the Historical Development of Santa Clara County,* ed. Gloria Sun Hom (Los Altos Hills: Foothill Community College, 1971), 151–55.

34. Collin Quock, *Chinese Hospital Medical Staff Archives: The Dawning* (San Francisco: Chinese Hospital Medical Staff, 1978), 9. According to an interview with Dr. James Hall, Aug. 23, 1970, government authorities periodically "go after" old Dr. Wong Him for practicing medicine without a license. To skirt this requirement, Dr. Wong Him sent his son through medical school. His son did not receive a license in California but was licensed in Nevada, which through reciprocity allowed him to practice in California.

35. Zhao Yujia, "Cong Hefeng shuyuan dao Doumen zhongxue" (From Hefeng academy to Doumen middle school), in *Doumen wenshi* (Doumen literature and history), 1st collection, 43–47; Huang Zhiwen, Tan Fang, "Zhao Shunzhi shilüe" (A short biography of Zhao Shunzhi), in *Doumen wenshi,* 10th collection (Aug. 1990), 34–37.

36. From around the 1880s until the mid-1920s, presidents of the district associations forming part of the Chinese Consolidated Benevolent Association were men of letters from the home districts in China. At that time they were considered assistants to the Chinese consulate and were issued diplomatic visas. During the mid-1920s the U.S. State Department objected to the practice as contrary to international diplomatic practice. In 1923 the Peking government decreed that the presidents should be issued tourist visas and should be forbidden to bring along staff members. The district associations objected strenuously, but after several years of fruitless negotiations, the Chinese government prevailed. In 1927 it was the turn of Hee Shen Association to assume the presidency of Yeong Wo Association, and in January of that year Ging Saan Chan, who had already immigrated, was elected president.

37. H. M. Lai, "The Kuomintang in Chinese American Communities before World War II," in Sucheng Chan, ed., *Entry Denied: Exclusion and the Chinese Community in America, 1882–1943* (Philadelphia: Temple University Press 1991), 170–212; Huang Lizhi, "Huang Baohuan xiansheng shile," (Short biography of Mr. Bou Waan Wong), in *Doumen wenshi,* 5th collection (Oct. 1987), 42.

38. Interview with Shek Ng Mock, Jan. 15, 1977.

39. Interviews by Kenneth Joe, Philip Choy, and the author with Man Quong Fong. 1, 10, 1970.

40. Collin Quock, *Chinese Hospital Medical Staff Archives: Following the Dawn* (San Francisco; Chinese Hospital Medical Staff, 1979), 46–57.

41. Judy Yung, H. M. Lai, Laura Lai, interview with John Mock, former kitchen worker at Angel Island, Dec. 27, 1975.

42. Connie Young Yu, "John C. Young, a Man Who Loved History," *Chinese America: History and Perspectives, 1989* (San Francisco: Chinese Historical Society of America, 1989), 3–14.

43. Interviews with John Mock.

44. Michael D. Brown, *Views from Asian California, 1920–1965: An Illustrated History* (San Francisco: Michael Brown, 1992), 16

45. Mitchell P. Postel, *San Mateo: A Centennial History* (San Francisco: Scottwall Associates, 1994), 139; interviews with John Mock.

46. *Palo Alto Times,* Nov. 3, 10, 1893.

47. *Palo Alto Citizen,* July 29, 1905; Pamela Gullard and Nancy Lund, *History of Palo Alto: The Early Years* (San Francisco: Scottwall Associates, 1989), 105–7; Xixian, "Liang Ji de yisheng" (The life of Kee Leung), *Chinese Pacific Weekly,* Dec. 11, 18, 1958.

48. *Palo Alto Times,* Dec. 29, 1903; interviews with John Mock.

49. Connie Young Yu, *Chinatown, San Jose, USA* (San Jose: San Jose Historical Museum Association, 1991), 21 30.

50. Ibid., viii, 107–10.

51. Interview with John Young, Oct. 19, 1968; Connie Young Yu, *Chinatown, San Jose, USA,* 66–67.

52. *San Francisco Chronicle,* Jan. 5, 1902 (Sunday edition).

53. Interview with Norman Mock and his mother, May 3, 1969. Referenced hereafter as interview with Norman Mock.

54. Interview with J. P. Wong, July 16, 1977.

55. Interviews with John Mock.

56. *1872–1942: A Community* (San Mateo: San Mateo Chapter JACL, 1981); interviews with John Mock; interview with Shek Ng Mock; William Mock, "Flower Industry of the Doumen People." Japanese began to be employed on San Mateo County estates during the 1890s. Some became gardeners and soon gained a reputation for showplace gardens on estates in San Mateo, Burlingame, and Hillsborough. Japanese flower growers, however, were concentrated in Oakland and did not arrive on the peninsula until after the 1906 earthquake. Jim Mock may have learned his horticultural skills from one of the gar-

deners on the estates. According to William Mock, Jim Mock taught his techniques to fellow villager Yee Him Mock.

57. Interview with Mary Wong, daughter of Charlie Wong, Jan. 24, 1996 (referenced hereafter as interview with Mary Wong).

58. Mike Culbertson, "The Chinese Involvement in the Development of the Flower Industry in Santa Clara County," in *Chinese Argonauts: An Anthology of the Chinese Contributions to the Historical Development of Santa Clara County*, 47–59. Ah Sam the flower grower should not be confused with the well-known San Mateo flower shop of the same name. The latter business started with Leong Shun Chew, or Sam Shun Leong, who came to the United States in 1906. He moved to San Mateo in 1928 to help his cousins the Lees with their flower business while he maintained a fruit and vegetable route. In 1933 his son Gordon borrowed $150 to start the Ah Sam Flower Shop and ran it for many years with his brothers Lincoln and Arthur and his sister Mable. The Leong family was from Xinhui. Their Chinese surname is Zhao (Chew). Postel, *San Mateo: A Centennial History*, 162–63; Lisa Zinckgraf, "The Floral Industry of San Mateo County" (student monograph, San Mateo Community College, spring 1980); interview with Mamie Leong at Ah Sam Flower Shop, Nov. 24, 1995.

59. Interview with Norman Mock; interview with Shek Ng Mock; *San Francisco Chronicle*, Jan. 5, 1902; Gordon Chan lecture at Chinese Historical Society of America meeting, Oct. 16, 1981.

60. Lecture by Gordon Chan, Oct. 16, 1981.

61. Interview with J. P. Wong, July 16, 1977.

62. Interviews with John Mock.

63. Thomas B. Carter, "A Blooming Business," *San Francisco*, May 1970, 27–29, 43–45.

64. Mike Culbertson, "The Chinese Involvement in the Development of the Flower Industry in Santa Clara County"; interview with Mary Wong.

65. Catherine Clare Oefinger, "The Flower Industry of San Mateo County" (San Mateo Junior College student paper, Jan. 1941).

66. Lecture by Gordon Chan, Oct. 16, 1981; Lincoln Fong, "Aster Production in San Mateo and Santa Clara County" (Paper, San Mateo Junior College, June 1951); William Mock, "Flower Industry of the Doumen People"; Pei Chi Liu, *A History of the Chinese in the United States of America II*, 307–8.

67. Lecture by Gordon Chan, Oct. 16, 1981; "Interview with Gordon Chan," in John Handley, *Toward the Golden Mountain: A History of the Chinese in the Santa Clara Valley* (Cupertino: Cupertino Historical Society, 1997), 43–45.

68. Lecture by Gordon Chan, Oct. 16, 1981.

69. Ibid.

70. Carter, "A Blooming Business."

71. Lecture by Gordon Chan, Oct. 16, 1981; "Interview with Gordon Chan," in *Toward the Gold Mountain*.

72. William Mock, "Flower Industry of the Doumen People."

73. Interviews with John Mock. In 1970 there were about twenty nurseries owned by Fuzhou people. Most of these nurseries were two to three times the size of the ones operated by many Huangliang Du people.

74. Interviews with John Mock; lecture by Gordon Chan in Santa Clara, June 6, 1970; telephone interview with Gordon Chan, Oct. 16, 1981.

75. Mike Culbertson, "The Chinese Involvement in the Development of the Flower Industry in Santa Clara County," in *Chinese Argonauts: An Anthology of the Chinese Contributions to the Historical Development of Santa Clara County*, 47–59.

76. William Mock, "Flower Industry of the Doumen People"; telephone interview with Gordon Chan; lecture by Gordon Chan, Oct. 16, 1981; "Interview with Gordon Chan," in *Toward the Gold Mountain*.

77. Lecture by Gordon Chan, Oct. 16, 1981.

78. Telephone interview with Gordon Chan.

79. Lecture by Gordon Chan, Oct. 16, 1981; *San Jose Mercury News*, Oct. 20, 1987; June 9, Dec. 27, 1990; "Interview with Gordon Chan," in *Toward the Gold Mountain*.

80. *San Jose Mercury News*, Oct. 20, 1987; Dec. 27, 1990; "Interview with Gordon Chan," in *Toward the Gold Mountain*.

81. *World Journal*, June 13, 1991; *International Daily News*, Mar. 8, 1995.

82. Interview with Kong Chow; telephone interview with Gordon Chan.

83. Huang Lizhi, "Short biography of Mr. Kee Wong"; *Minguo chunian zhi Guomindang shiliao* (Historical materials on the early years of the Kuomintang) (Taipei: Zongyang wenwu gongyingshe,1967), 25, 97, 105; *Zhonghua Gemingdang shiliao* (Historical materials of the Chinese Revolutionary Party) (Taipei: Zhongyang wenwu gongyingshe, 1969), 420, 421; "Zhongguo Guomindang zhu Sanfanshi zongzhibu suo shu jiguan Minguo 13 nian 14 nian zhiyuan mingce" (List of officers for 1924, 1925 of offices under the San Francisco General Branch of the Nationalist Party of China) (San Francisco: San Francisco General Branch of the Nationalist Party of China, 1924), 1, 22; *Guofu quanji* (Complete works of Sun Yat-sen) (Taipei: Zhongguo Guomindang zhongyang weiyuanhui dangshi weiyuanhui, 1973), 4:538.

84. Complete Works of Sun Yat-sen, 4:557; Ou Daquan, "Rong Zhaozhen xiansheng ji qi xianshi jile" (Short account of the lives of Mr. John Young and his forebears), in *Doumen wenshi*, 7th collection, 23–25. Referenced hereafter as Ou, "Short Account of the Lives of Mr. John Young and His Forebears."

85. Feng Ziyou, *Zhongguo geming yundong ershiliu nian zuzhishi* (History of organizations during the twenty-six years of the revolutionary movement) (Shanghai: Commercial Press, 1948), 215; "Chen Yaoyuan," in *Zhuhai shi renwu zhi* (Annals of Zhuhai personages), ed. Zhuhai shi difangzhi ban'gongshi (Zhuhai City gazetteer office) (Guangzhou: Guangdong renmin chubanshe, 1993), 205–7; H. M. Lai, "The Kuomintang in Chinese American Communities before World War II," in *Entry Denied: Exclusion and the Chinese Community in America, 1882–1943*, ed. Sucheng Chan (Philadelphia: Temple University Press, 1991), 170–212.

86. "Zhu Meiguo zongzhibu dangwu yange gaiyao" (Essentials of the evolution of party affairs in the General Branch of the Kuomintang in the United States), *Zhongguo Guomindang zai haiwai* (The Nationalist Party of China abroad) (Taipei: Zhongguo Guomindang zhongyang weiyuanhui disan zu [Group no. 3 of the Central Committee of the Nationalist Party of China, 1961]), 2–39; *Fiftieth Anniversary (1910–1960), "The Young China Morning Paper"* (San Francisco: Young China Morning Paper, 1960), 13, illus. 59.

87. *Meiguo Zhijiage "Sanmin chenbao" zhengxinlu* (Record of income and disbursements of *San Min Morning Paper*) (Chicago: San Min Morning Paper and Publishing Co., 1931), 8; *Zhongguo Guomindang zhu Meiguo zongzhibu Meixi zhibu di'er ci, disan ci daibiao dahui jishi* (Account of the second and third congresses of delegates from the western U.S. and U.S. general branches of the Nationalist Party of China) (San Francisco: n.p., 1933), 22; *Fiftieth Anniversary (1910–1960), "The Young China Morning Paper,"* 13.

88. *Minguo chunian zhi Guomindang shiliao* (Historical materials on the early years of the Kuomintang), 25; *Zhongguo Guomindang zhu Sanfanshi zongzhibu disan ci daibiao dahui jishi* (An account of the third congress of delegates of the General Branch of the Nationalist Party of China in San Francisco) (San Francisco: n.p., 1929), 51.

89. "Chen Yousheng," in *Zhuhai renwu zhuan*, 224; Guangdong kongjun lianyihui (Guangdong air force friendship association),

Guangdong kongjun shiliao. Zhao Rongfang, *Zhongshan wenshi* (Zhongshan literary and historical materials), 16th collection: *Xiangshan hangkong renwu lu* (Annals of aviation personages of Xiangshan) (Aug. 1989), 69–70 (referenced hereafter as Zhao, *Annals of Aviation Personages of Xiangshan*), mentions Chen Shenhu (San Wu Chan) from the same village. Chen allegedly returned to China during the same period as Chen Yousheng. He later successively served military governments in Guangdong, Yunnan, and Sichuan. The two lives are so similar that they may be referring to the same person.

90. Zhao, *Annals of Aviation Personages of Xiangshan,* 130–31.

91. Ibid., 144–45.

92. Ibid., 114–16.

93. *Qiqi kangzhan qi zhounian jinian tekan* (Special publication commemorating the seventh anniversary of the War of Resistance beginning on the seventh day of July) (San Francisco: Chinese War Relief Association in America, 1946), 24. Gam Yee Hong (Garment Workers' Guild), National Dollar Stores, and Joe Shoong shared the top spot, each donating $50,000. The campaign raised more than $300,000.

94. *Fiftieth Anniversary (1910–1960), "The Young China Morning Paper,"* 21; *Sixtieth Anniversary (1910–1970), "The Young China Morning Paper"* (San Francisco: Young China Morning Paper, 1970); Kuang Jinbi, "Huang Huapei xiansheng zhuanle" (Short biography of J. P. Wong), in *Doumen wenshi,* 4th collection (Apr. 1987), 28–34.

95. "Wei shan zui le de Zhao Shusheng xiansheng" (Mr. Shue Sang Jew, who was happiest when doing good deeds), in *Huoyue zai Jinshan qiaoshe de renwu* (Personages active in the San Francisco Chinese community) (San Francisco: Sun Yat-sen News, 1980), 2–3.

96. "Chongman xinxin de Mo Xiangxing xiansheng" (Mr. Cheung Hing Mok, who was full of confidence), in *Huoyue zai Jinshan qiaoshe de renwu,* 3–4.

97. Ou Daquan, "Cong tonggong, qiutu dao laozong, zuojia, Huang Yunji shilüe (From child worker and convict to publisher and author: a short biography of Maurice Chuck," in *Doumen wenshi,* 8th collection (Apr. 1989), 27–34.

98. "Gazetteer of Doumen Overseas Chinese Affairs," 19; *Gazetteer of Geographical Names of Zhuhai,* 222.

99. New China Education Foundation brochure; interview with Kam Hong Kwong, Dec. 8, 1995.

100. "Gazetteer of Doumen Overseas Chinese Affairs," 15; *Zhuhai News,* no. 31 (Aug. 1995), 11–12.

101. *Guangdong Sheng wailai touzizhe biaozhang dahui fangmingce* (Guangzhou: Guangdong sheng renmin zhengfu, 1996).

102. Section 1662 of the Political Code of California called on school districts "to establish separate schools for children of Mongolian or Chinese descent. When such separate schools are established, Chinese or Mongolian children must not be admitted into any other schools." See Victor Low, *The Unimpressible Race: A Century of Educational Struggle by the Chinese in San Francisco* (San Francisco: East/West Publishing House, 1982), 85.

103. *Jinshan Zhengbu Daqing qiaomin gongli xiaoxuetang zhengxinlu* (Record of income and disbursements for the Daqing Qiaomin Gongli Xiaoxuetang) (San Francisco: n.p., 1909), folio 3a, 6a.

104. Ibid., 3a.

105. Zhao, *Annals of Aviation Personages of Xiangshan,* 127.

106. Ou, "Short Account of the Lives of Mr. John Young and His Forebears"; Yu, "John C. Young, a Man Who Loved History"; *Los Angeles Times,* June 2, 1946.

107. Letter from Connie Young Yu, Jan. 25, 1996, with information provided by Vera Leung.

108. Lawrence Sinclair Jue, "My Memoirs: Lifelong Experiences of a Chinese American Engineer" (manuscript, 1995).

109. *San Francisco Independent,* June 1995.

110. *Chinese Times,* Sept. 28, 30, 1994; Apr. 13, 1995.

111. *Chinese Times,* July 2, 1994; *Sing Tao Daily,* July 1, 1995.

112. Connie Young Yu, *Profiles in Excellence: Peninsula Chinese Americans* (Palo Alto: Stanford Area Chinese Club, 1986), 39–41.

113. Résumé of Judy Yung, n.d.

114. *East/West,* June 23, 1988; *World Journal,* July 12, 1991.

115. *Ta Kung Pao,* Oct. 12, 1993; *World Journal,* Feb. 11, 1994; *Sing Tao Daily News,* Aug. 17, 1997.

116. Interview with Gordon Chan.

117. *World Journal,* July 9, 1995.

118. *Sing Tao Daily News,* Nov. 26, 1995.

119. *Asian Week,* Feb. 2, 1996; telephone interview with Gordon Chan.

120. *San Francisco Chronicle,* Mar. 26, 1997.

CHINESE GLOSSARY: NAMES AND TERMS

Baijiao 白蕉
Bao'an Tang 寶安堂
Bay Area Chrysanthemum Growers Association 灣區菊花會
Canton Flower Shop 廣東花店
Chan, C. C. 陳春榮
Chan, Charles Foo 陳富
Chan, Gai Jing 陳界正
Chan, Ging 陳典經
Chan, Ging Saan 陳景山
Chan, Gordon 陳國男
Chan, Hong Dai 陳康大
Chan, Jaak Saam 陳澤三
Chan, Kan Hok 陳勤學
Chan, Mary 陳秀仲
Chan, Oi Dai 陳愛大
Chan, San Wu 陳神護
Chan, Sucheng 陳素貞
Chan, T. S. 陳壽
Chan, Yau Shing 陳有勝
Chan, You Foon 陳耀恒
Chann, George 陳蔭羆
Chengshan Tang 成善堂
Cheu, Henry D. 趙德富
Chew, Edwin 趙樹嵩
Chin, Arnold 陳有琪
Chin, Chew 周濂傳
Chin, Gway 陳貴
Chin, John 陳振熊
Chin, Lung 陳龍
Chin, Ming 陳惠明
Chin, William 周偉廉
China Mail Steamship Co. 中國郵船公司
China War Relief Association of America 旅美華僑統一義捐救國總會
Chinese American Citizens' Alliance 同源會
Chinese Chamber of Commerce 中華總商會
Chinese Consolidated Benevolent Association, Chinese Six Companies 中華總會館
Chinese Flower Growers Association 華人菊花會
Chinese Hospital 東華醫院
Chinese Times 金山時報
Chinese Voice 華聲報
Chishuikeng 赤水坑
Choi, Lai Bik 蔡麗碧
Chow, Kong 周剛

Chuck, Maurice 黃運基
Chun, Jan How 陳續休
Chung Sun Wo 忠信和
Chungshan Association 中山同鄉會
Comfort Shoes 金福鞋店
Dahaochong 大濠涌
Dahuan 大環
Dan'gan 擔杆
Daqing Qiaomin Gongli Xiaoxuetang 大清僑民公立小學堂
Dening Du 德寧都
Deshan Tang 德善堂
Dongguan 東莞
Doumen 斗門
Dunshan Tang 敦善堂
East/West 東西報
Fong, Hiram 鄺友良
Fong, Man Quong 鄺文光
Fong, March 江月桂
Fong, Matthew 鄺傑靈
Fong, Paul 方文忠
Fong, Robert 莫興維
Fushan Tang 福善堂
Gam Yee Hong 錦衣行
Gelü qingchao 歌侶情潮
Grandview Film Co. 大觀聲片公司
Grandview Theater 大觀戲院
Guangxu 光緒
Guishan 歸善
Guishan Tang 歸善堂
Guzi Du 谷字都
Hall, George 余志勇
Hall, James 何廷光
Hang Ah Teahouse 香亞茶室
Hee Shen Association 喜善堂
Hefeng Middle School 和風中學
Hip Cheong Jan 協昌棧
Hip Sen Association 協善堂
Hip Sing Chong 協成昌
Hongqi 紅旗
Hop Yick 合益
Huangliang Du 黃梁都
Huangliang Du Gongsuo 黃梁都公所
Huangliang Du Jilu 黃梁都寄蘆
Huangyang Mountain 黃楊山
huiguan 會館
Huiyang 惠陽
Hushan 虎山
Jew, Fook 趙福
Jew, James 趙樹彪

Jew, Jun You 趙峻堯
Jew, Shue Sang 趙樹生
Jew, Sun Jee 趙順之
Jew, Yin San 趙彥新
Jew Fook Corporation 招福公司
Jing'an 井岸
Jingsheng Primary School 景勝小學
jinshanzhuang 金山莊
Jishan Tang 積善堂
Joe, Kenneth 周堅乃（關春如）
Joe, Shoong 周崧
Jue, Joseph Sunn 趙樹燊
Jue, Lawrence 趙樹材
Kuomintang 國民黨
Kwangtung Corporation 廣東公司
Kwong On and Co. 廣安號
Kwong Wo Jan 廣和棧 號
Kwong Kam Hong 鄺錦洪
Lampacao 浪白澳
Lau, Jou Moon 劉祖滿
Lee, Pius 李兆祥
Leong Shee 梁氏
Leung, James 梁宗耀
li 里
Liang Qinggui 梁慶桂
Lin Shihan 林時漢
Literati, The 文化人報
Liuxiang 六鄉
Liwuwei 李屋圍
Long Du 隆都
Longtan 龍壇
Louie, Dan 呂登
Low, Victor 馮天賜
Lufeng 陸豐
Mee Brothers 譚氏兄弟
Mock, Guong Dung 莫光棟
Mock, Jim 莫載耀
Mock, John 莫松年
Mock, Marshall 梁光桓
Mock, Shek Ng 莫錫五
Mock, William 莫景勝
Mock, Yee Him 莫裕欽
Mok, Chang Hing 莫翔興
Mok, Foon Man 莫煥文
Mok, Yik Ngaa 莫益雅
Mon Ming Hotel 文明旅館
Mushan Tang 慕善堂
Nanmen 南門
Nanshan 南山
Nanshui 南水

New China Education Foundation
新中國教育基金會
Ng Shing Gung 五聖宮
Ning Yung Association 寧陽會館
Niwan 泥灣
Northern California Aster Growers
Association 北加省江南菊同
業會
Oriental, The 東涯新錄
Paishan 排山
Ping Yuen Bakery 平園餅家
Pingsha 平沙
Poo Wo Tong 保和堂
Qianshan 前山
Qianwu 乾霧
qiao ze shilin 僑澤士林
Qing dynasty 清朝
Quock, Collin 郭嘉麟
Quong Wo Chan 廣和棧
Renzi Du 仁字都
Republic Pharmacy 共和藥房
Sam Jo Kong Fong 三灶公房
San Francisco Journal 時代報
Sanzao 三灶
Sanzao Gongsuo 三灶公所
Shang Gongchang Du 上恭常都
Shangce 上柵
Shanghai Noodles 上海麵廠
Shanghai Trunk Company 上海洋
箱公司
Shangheng 上橫
Shew Hing Lung 肇興隆
shi 市
Shidianchenbolu 士店臣波爐
Shima, George 牛島謹爾

Shuangsong Library 雙頌圖書館
Sing Kee 生記
Sizi Du 四字都
Soo Yuen Association 溯源堂
Sun Wen College 孫文學院
Sun Yat-sen 孫逸仙
Sun Zhongshan 孫中山
Tangjia 唐家
Tianxin 田心
Tin Suie Tong 天壽堂
Tong K. Achik 唐廷植
Tongmenghui 同盟會
Tongshan Tang 同善堂
Tuck Wo and Company 德和店
United Flower Growers Association
華聯花會
Wankou 灣口
Wanshan 萬山
Wing Nien 永年
Wing Shun Tai 永信泰
Wing, C. C. 陳春榮
Women's New Life Movement
Association of China 中國婦女
新生活運動會
Wong, Alan 黃作述
Wong, Anna May 黃柳霜
Wong, Bou Waan 黃曝寰
Wong, Charlie 黃炳基
Wong, J. P. 黃華培
Wong, Jook Yee 黃足以
Wong, Kee 黃開基
Wong, Mary 黃美仙
Wong, Siu Gwan 黃兆均
Wong, Wah Git 黃華傑

Wong, Yoey 黃銳
Wong Him, Henry (father) 黃華添
（黃曉霖）
Wong Him, Henry (son) 黃天恩
Wushan 五山
Xiangshan 香山
Xiangzhou 香洲
Xiaolin 小林
Xiaoliqi 小瀝岐
Xiaohaochong 小濠涌
Xiazhou 下洲
Xinhui 新會
Xue Pinggui quan zhuan 薛平貴全
傳
Yaomo zhi yue 妖魔之穴
Yeong Wo Association 陽和會館
Yi'an Tang 義安堂
Young China Morning Paper 少年
中國晨報
Young, George 容兆明
Young, John 容兆珍
Young, Mary 容李如心
Young, Soong Quong 容嵩光
Yu, Connie Young 虞容儀芳
Yu, Jessica 虞琳敏
Yuan Sheng (Asing, Norman) 袁生
Yung, Judy 譚碧芳
Zengcheng 增城
Zhonghua Yizhi Yinghua Gongsi
中華益智映畫公司
Zhongshan 中山
Zhongshan College 孫文學院
Zhuhai 珠海

CHINESE GLOSSARY: ARTICLES AND BOOKS

Chinese Community in New York City (New York: Chinese Community Research Bureau, 1950) 《紐約華僑社會》（紐約：紐約華僑社會研究社，1950）

Chinese of Hawaii (Honolulu: Overseas Penman Club, 1929) 《檀山華僑》（火奴魯魯：檀山華僑編印社，1929）

Chinese of Hawaii, Vol. II (Honolulu: Overseas Penman Club, 1936) 《檀山華僑第二集》（火奴魯魯：檀山華僑編印社，1936）

"Chongman xinxin de Mo Xiangxing Xiansheng," in Ye Lili, *Huoyue zai Jinshan qiaoshe de renwu* (San Francisco: Sun Yat-sen News, 1980), 3–4 《充滿信心的莫翔興先生》見葉莉莉，《活躍在金山僑社的人物》（舊金山：中山報，1980），第3-4頁

Daguan xiyuan kaimu zhuankan (San Francisco, 1940) 《大觀戲院開幕專刊》（舊金山：1940）

"Doumen xian qiaowuzhi" (draft) (Doumen, 1988) 《斗門縣僑務志》（稿）（斗門：1988）

Feng Ziyou, *Zhongguo geming yundong ershiliu nian zuzhishi* (Shanghai: Commercial Press, 1948) 馮自由，《中國革命運動二十六年組織史》（上海商務印書館，1948）

Fiftieth Anniversary (1910–1960), "The Young China Morning Paper" (San Francisco: Young China Morning Paper, 1960) 《少年中國晨報五十周年記念專刊》（舊金山：少年中國晨報，1960）

Guangdong Sheng wailai touzizhe biaozhang dahui fangmingce (Guangzhou: Guangdong sheng renmin zhengfu, 1996) 《廣東省外來投資者表彰大會芳名冊》（廣州：廣東省人民政府，1996）

Guangdong sheng Zhuhai shi dimingzhi (Guangzhou: Guangdong keji chubanshe, 1989) 《廣東省珠海市地名志》（廣州：廣東科技出版社，1989）

Guofu quanji (Taipei: Zhongguo Gomindang zhongyang weiyuanhui dangshi weiyuanhui, 1973) 《國父全集》（台北：中國國民黨中央委員會黨史委員會，1973）

Huang Lizhi, "Huang Baohuan xiansheng shilüe," in *Doumen wenshi*, 5th collection (Doumen: Doumen xian zhengxie wenshi ziliao yanjiu weiyuanhui, Oct. 1987), 42 黃禮之，《黃曝寰先生事略》，見《斗門文史第五輯》（斗門：斗門政協文史資料研究委員會，1987年十月），第42頁

Huang Lizhi, "Huang Kaiji xiansheng zhuanlüe," in *Doumen wenshi*, 7th collection (Doumen: Doumen xian zhengxie wenshi ziliao yanjiu weiyuanhui, Sept. 1988) 黃禮之，《黃開基先生傳略》，見《斗門文史第七輯》（斗門：斗門政協文史資料研究委員會，1988年九月），第26-27頁

Huang Qichen, *Aomen lishi* (Macao: Macao Historical Society, 1995) 黃啓臣，《澳門歷史》（澳門歷史學會，1995）

Huang Zhiwen, Tan Fang, "Zhao Shunzhi shilüe," n *Doumen wenshi*, 10th collection (Doumen: Doumen xian zhengxie wenshi ziliao yanjiu weiyuanhui, Aug. 1990), 34–37 黃志文、譚方，《趙順之事略》，見《斗門文史第十輯》（斗門：斗門政協文史資料研究委員會，1990年　八月），第34-37頁

Jinshan Zhengbu Daqing qiaomin gongli xiaoxuetang zhengxinlu (San Francisco, 1909) 金山正埠大清僑民公立小學堂徵信錄》（舊金山, 1909）

Kuang Jinbi, "Huang Huapei xiansheng zhuanlüe," *Doumen wenshi*, 4th collection (Doumen: Doumen xian zhengxie wenshi ziliao yanjiu weiyuanhui, Apr. 1987), 28–34 鄺金鼻，《黃華培先生傳略》，見《斗門文史第四輯》（斗門：斗門政協文史資料研究委員會，1987年四月），第28-34頁

Li Puzhen, "Liushan jiyao," in *Meiguo Sanfanshi liu huiguan chongxiu Liushan fenchang zhengxinlu* (San Francisco: Chinese Cemetery Association, 1953) 李璞珍，《六山紀要》，見《美國三藩市六會館重修六山墳場徵信錄》（舊金山, 1953）

Liang Zhenxing, Wen Liping, "Sanzao dao jianshi," in *Zhuhai wenshi*, 5th collection (Zhuhai: Zhongguo renmin zhengzhi xieshang huiyi Zhuhai shi weiyuanhui wenshi ziliao yanjiu weiyuanhui, 1987), 63–73 梁振興，溫立平，《三灶島簡史》，見《珠海文史第五輯》（中國人民政治協商會議珠海市委員會文史資料研究委員會，1987年七月），第63-73頁

Liu Pei Chi, *A History of the Chinese in the United States of America II* (Taipei: Liming wenhua shiye gufen youxian gongsi, 1981) 劉伯驥，《美國華僑史續編》（台北：黎明文化事業股份有限公司，1981）

Meiguo Zhijiage "Sanmin chenbao" zhengxinlu (Chicago: San Min Morning Paper and Publishing Co., 1931) 《美國芝加哥三民晨報證信錄》（芝加哥：三民晨報兼印務局通訊處，1931）

Minguo chunian zhi Guomindang shiliao (Taipei: Zhongyang wenwu gongyingshe, 1967) 《民國初年之國民黨史料》（台北：中央文物供應社，1967）

Mock, William, "Doumenren de huaye," in *Hee Shen Benevolent Association Centennial Celebration, 1895–1995* (draft), 98–99 莫景勝，《斗門人的花業》，見《喜善堂百週年刊》（稿）第98-99頁

Ou Daquan, "Cong tonggong, qiutu dao laozong: zuojia Huang Yunji shilüe," in *Doumen wenshi*, 8th collection (Doumen: Doumen xian zhengxie wenshi ziliao yanjiu weiyuanhui, Apr. 1989), 27–34 區達權，《從童工、囚徒到老總：作家黃運基事略》，見

《斗門文史第八輯》（斗門：斗門政協文史資料研究委員會，1989年四月），第27-34頁

Ou Daquan, "Rong Zhaozhen xiansheng ji qi xianshi jilüe," in *Doumen wenshi*, 7th collection (Doumen: Doumen xian zhengxie wenshi ziliao yanjiu weiyuanhui, Sept. 1988), 23–25 區達權，《容兆珍先生及其先世記略》，見《斗門文史，第七輯》（斗門：斗門政協文史資料研究委員會，1988年九月），第23-25頁

Ou Tianqi, "Zhonghua, Sanyi, Ningyang, Gangzhou, Hehe, Renhe, Zhaoqing, Keshang, ba da huiguan lianhe Yanghe xin guan xu," in *Jiushan chongjian Yanghe guan miao gongjin zhengxinlu* (San Francisco: Yeong Wo Association, 1900), folio 25a, 25b 區天驥，《中華、三邑、寧陽、岡州、合和、人和、肇慶、客商八大會館聯賀陽和新館序》，見《金山重建陽和館廟工金徵信錄》（舊金山：陽和會館，1900），對開第25a-25b頁

Qiqi kangzhan qi zhounian jinian tekan (San Francisco: China War Relief Association of America, 1946) 《七七抗戰七周年紀念特刊》（舊金山：旅美華僑統一義捐救國總會，1946）

"Sanfanshi Huabu sishi nian dashiji," in Liu Weisen, *Meiguo Sanfanshi Huaqiao gongli Donghua Yiyuan sishi zhounian zhuankan* (San Francisco: Chinese Hospital, 1963), 74–90 《三藩市華埠四十年大事記》，見劉偉森，《美國三藩市華僑公立東華醫院四十週年專刊》（舊金山：東華醫院，1963），第74-90頁

Sixtieth Anniversary (1910–1970), "The Young China Morning News" (San Francisco: The Young China Morning News, 1970) 《少年中國晨報六十週年紀念專刊》（舊金山：少年中國晨報，1970）

"Wei shan zui le de Zhao Shusheng xiansheng," in Ye Lili, *Huoyue zai Jinshan qiaoshe de renwu* (San Francisco: Sun Yat-sen News, 1980), 2–3 《為善最樂的趙樹生先生》，見葉莉莉，《活躍在金山僑社的人物》（舊金山：中山報，1980），第2-3頁

Xiangshan xian zhi, xubian (Guangzhou: Mobaolou, 1923) 香山縣誌續編（廣州：墨寶樓，1923）

Zhao Fuchong, "Mulong sui zhong," in *Doumen wenshi*, 1st collection (Doumen: Zhengxie Doumen xian weiyuanhui wenshi ziliao gongzuozu, 1985), 59–60 趙富崇，《木龍歲塚》，見《斗門文史，第一輯》（斗門：政協斗門縣委員會文史資料工作組，1985），第59-60頁

Zhao Guoyong, "Xuelei banban de 'yijie' shijian," in *Doumen wenshi*, 2nd collection (Doumen: Doumen xian zhengxie wenshi ziliao yanjiu weiyuanhui, Apr., 1986), 49–51 趙國勇，《血淚斑斑的移界事件》，見《斗門文史第二輯》（斗門：斗門政協文史資料研究委員會，1986年四月），第49-51頁

Zhao Guoyong, "Doumen ge xingzu yuanliu gaikuang," Part 1, *Doumen wenshi*, 4th collection (Apr. 1987), 48-50; Part 2, *Doumen wenshi*, 5th collection (Oct. 1987),

49–55 趙國勇，《斗門各姓族源流概況》，《斗門文史第四輯》（斗門：斗門政協文史資料研究委員會，1987年四月），第48-50頁，《斗門文史第五輯》（斗門：斗門政協文史資料研究委員會，1987年十月），第49-55頁

Zhao Rongfang, *Zhongshan wenshi*, 16th collection: *Xiangshan hangkong renwu lu* (Zhongshan: Zhengxie Guangdong sheng Zhongshan shi weiyuanhui wenshi weiyuanhui, Aug. 1989) 趙榮芳，《中山文史第十六輯：香山航空人物錄》（中山：政協廣東省中山市委員會文史委員會，1989年八月）

Zhao Yujia, "Cong Hefeng shuyuan dao Doumen zhongxue," in *Doumen wenshi*, 1st collection (Doumen: Zhengxie Doumen xian weiyuanhui wenshi ziliao gongzuozu, Sept. 1985), 43–47 趙毓佳，《從和風書院到斗門中學》，《斗門文史第一輯》（斗門：政協斗門縣委員會文史資料工作組，1985年九月），第43-47頁

Zhongguo Guomindang zhu Meiguo zongzhibu Meixi zhibu di'er ci, disan ci daibiao dahui jishi (San Francisco: n.p., 1933) 《中國國民黨駐美國總支部美西支部第二次、第三次代表大會紀事》（舊金山，1933）

Zhongguo Guomindang zhu Sanfanshi zongzhibu suo shu jiguan Minguo shisan nian, shisi nian zhiyuan mingce (San Francisco: San Francisco General Branch of the Nationalist Party of China, 1924) 《中國國民黨駐三藩市總支部所屬機關民國十三年、十四年職員名冊》（舊金山：中國國民黨駐三藩市總支部，1924）

Zhonghua Gemingdang shiliao (Taipei: Zhongyang wenwu gongyingshe, 1969) 《中華革命黨史料》（台北：中央文物供應社，1969）

Zhou Zhangcai, "Xieshantang lishi lüeshu," in *Doumen xiangyin*, no. 23 (fall 1992), 17 周章才，《協善堂歷史略述》，見《斗門鄉音》第23期（1992年秋），第17頁

Zhuhai renwu zhuan (Guangzhou: Guangdong renmin chubanshe, 1993) 《珠海人物傳》（廣州：廣東人民出版社，1993）

Zhuhai shi renwu zhi (Guangzhou: Guangdong renmin chubanshe, 1993) 《珠海市人物誌》（廣州：廣東人民出版社，1993）

The Fake and the True
Researching Chinese Women's Immigration History
by Judy Yung

For a long time I assumed that my mother, Jew Law Ying, was the first in her family to immigrate to the United States in 1941. Only after I began researching our family history did I realize that her grandfather Chin Lung came in 1882, her grandmother Leong Shee arrived in 1893, and her mother Chin Suey Kum was born in San Francisco in 1894. My mother, born in China, was thus a derivative U.S. citizen; yet she could only fulfill her dream of coming to America in 1941 by marrying a Gold Mountain man like my father Yung Hin Sen, who had been in the United States since 1921. Here the story gets complicated, because not only was my father a "paper son," someone who had entered this country illegally, but he was a laborer and according to American law not eligible to bring his wife and family to the United States at all. Yet he evidently found a way to do so. How I figured this all out in the process of reconstructing my mother's family history—by poring over immigration files at the National Archives in San Bruno, California, and interviewing relatives and my mother about her life story—is a lesson in the complications involved in researching Chinese women's immigration history. I learned in the process that no document—whether it be a legal affidavit, an immigration transcript, a letter, or an oral history interview—should be taken at face value; care must be taken to distinguish the fake from the true in piecing together a family history.

Many of the complications stem from the Chinese Exclusion Act of 1882, which barred the further immigration of Chinese laborers and their families.[1] It was not repealed until 1943. Thus for sixty-one years, immigration from China was limited to certain exempt classes, namely derivative U.S. citizens, merchants, scholars, diplomats, and travelers. However, for a certain amount of money (usually $100 per year of age), people like my father—a peasant—could buy papers and come posing as the son of a U.S. citizen or merchant. (The 1906 earthquake and fire in San Francisco, which destroyed all the birth certificates in the city, provided a way by which many Chinese immigrants could step forward and claim native-born status and a number of sons in China, thus creating slots by which their kinsmen could immigrate to the United States.) Although fewer in number than the men, Chinese women also immigrated as "paper daughters." Most, however,

came as wives of U.S. citizens or merchants. Then, after the Immigration Act of 1924 prohibited the immigration of Chinese wives of U.S. citizens, women mainly immigrated as daughters of U.S. citizens or wives of merchants. Both my great-grandmother and my mother immigrated as merchant wives; but whereas my great-grandfather was truly a merchant, my father was not.

Immigration officials, aware of these efforts on the part of the Chinese to circumvent the Exclusion Act, set up an elaborate process by which to keep the Chinese out. The burden of proof rested on Chinese immigrants to prove their legal right to enter the United States. They had to pass a grueling examination about their family history, village life in China, and relatives in the United States, who were in turn asked the same questions for confirmation of identity and relationship. Any discrepancies could mean deportation. "Official" records were kept of all documents and proceedings pertaining to each immigration case, which was linked to file numbers of other related cases. In anticipation of the interrogation, prospective immigrants in China spent months studying "coaching books" that gave answers to questions that immigration officials were likely to ask them.[2] If the immigrant or his or her relatives were "paper sons" or "paper daughters," much of the coaching book would contain "fake" information. Since my father's identity was false but my mother's was true, only half of her coaching book contained false information.

Aware of this immigration history and process, I began researching my mother's family history at the National Archives—Pacific Sierra Region in San Bruno, California, which houses Record Group 85, or Records of the Immigration and Naturalization Service (INS) for the San Francisco and Honolulu districts. Because my great-grandfather Chin Lung was a prosperous farmer and businessman who made a number of trips back to China, it was easy finding his file by his name and the names of his businesses, Sing Kee Company and Shanghai Trunk Company. His file led me to my great-grandmother Leong Shee's file as well as that of their children. Similarly, I located my mother's immigration file through my father's case file, which I found by providing staff at the National Archives—Pacific Sierra Region with the name of the ship he came on and the date of arrival.[3] Contained within each case file were applications, certificates of identity, INS interrogation transcripts and decisions, witness statements and affidavits, photographs, and exhibit letters. Keeping in mind that my father was a "paper son," I used these materials judiciously. Only after interviewing my parents and relatives about their versions of "the truth" was I able to tell what in these files was fake and what was true. In the process, I came to understand how hard it was for Chinese like my parents to immigrate to this country during the Exclusion period, how one lie grew into another, and how one "paper son" could complicate matters for others in the family.

I have selected a number of documents from the INS files of Leong Shee and Jew Law Ying to illustrate the complicated process of immigration for Chinese women as well as the deceit they had to employ in order to circumvent anti-Chinese immigration policies. Because both my great-grandmother and my mother came at times when the Chinese Exclusion Act was still enforced, the burden of proof was on them to show that they were indeed the wives of merchants and therefore exempt from exclusion. Prior to their journey across the seas, their husbands had to declare merchant status with the immigration service. An affidavit in the file of Sing Kee Company dated August 16, 1893, showed that Chin Lung swore before a notary public that he had been a resident of San Francisco for fourteen years and a merchant and member of "Sing Kee & Company, Dealers in General Merchandise" for eleven years, and "that the interest of each of the named members in said firm is $500.00 or more." Another affidavit, dated May 11, 1892, and signed by eight white witnesses, attested to Chin Lung's status as merchant. Furthermore, Document 1, an affidavit dated May 14, 1892, stated that Chin Lung was a merchant and that his wife, a resident of San Francisco, departed for Hong Kong in 1889 with their four-year-old daughter Ah Kum. This was not the case. According to subsequent testimonies by Chin Lung to the immigration service and oral histories I conducted with relatives, Great-grandmother immigrated to the United States for the first time in 1893.

For some reason, Leong Shee felt compelled to claim Ah Kum, the eight-year-old *mui tsai* (domestic servant) who accompanied her from China, as her daughter, which meant she also had to lie about the place and date of her marriage in order to justify having an eight-year-old daughter (Document 2, dated April 18, 1893). This fabrication would come back to haunt her in 1929 when she prepared to leave for China for the second time. In Document 3, dated July 4, 1929, she denied outright that she had ever said that she immigrated to the United States before 1893 and asserted that Ah Kum died soon after they arrived in 1893. Although a major discrepancy, the immigration inspector ignored it, decided that there was sufficient proof that she was a legal resident of the United States, and approved her application for a return certificate as a laborer.

According to Leong Shee's file, the only other time she was confronted by the immigration service was when she returned from China in 1921 after a seventeen-year stay, accompanied by Chin Lung, who by then had made a total of six trips back to China since he first immigrated to the United States in 1882. (Each time he left he had to re-establish his merchant status, and on each return, he was subjected to an immigration interrogation.) To make it easier on her, Chin Lung had an attorney request that "Leong Shee be permitted to land immediately upon the arrival of the steamer and not be sent to the Angel Island Immigration Station."[4] The argument was made by the attorney that she was a "first cabin" passenger and that her status as wife to Chin Lung, a merchant, had been previously established. The very next day, the request was granted on the basis that there was indeed such proof in her immigration records and that, as the immigration inspector noted, "her alleged husband, Chin Lung, is well known to the officers of this Service, having been a merchant of Stockton for many years and is reported to be one of the wealthiest Chinese merchants residing in that vicinity and is commonly known as the 'Potato King.'" Here we see an example of how upper-class status accorded one better treatment on arrival in this country during the Exclusion period.

My mother, Jew Law Ying, would have been born in the United States had Great-grandmother not decided to return to China in 1904 with all her children, or had my grandmother been allowed by her parents to return to the United States as her five brothers were. But that was not to be. Moreover, although my mother was a daughter of a U.S. citizen, immigration as a derivative citizen through the mother was not legally permissible. Thus, she married my father and in 1941 found herself repeating the same immigration process her grandmother had experienced close to a half-century earlier. She immigrated as a merchant's wife.

Documents in my mother's file show that my father Yung Hin Sen, who was actually a poor gardener, had found a way to establish merchant status. This he did by investing $1,000, which he borrowed from various relatives, in the Far East Company, a Chinatown import business. He then had the manager of that company and two white witnesses (a drayman and an expressman who had dealings with the firm) sign affidavits attesting to his active membership in the firm for more than one year past. Next, he had to appear at the Angel Island Immigration Station with the manager. Both were interrogated about details regarding the firm's business and Yung Hin Sen's role as salesman and partner. Then my mother had to apply for a visa as "wife of a domiciled Chinese merchant" from the American Consulate General in Hong Kong. Meanwhile, she memorized the information in the coaching book about my father's "paper" family and village, her own family and village background, and their marriage (Document 4, given to me by my mother). There was a delay when my sister Bak Heong, who was born in Macao a year after my parents' marriage, was diagnosed as having trachoma and my mother had to find a doctor to treat her.

Finally, they arrived in San Francisco on March 13, 1941, and were immediately detained at the temporary immigration station at 801 Silver Avenue (the Angel Island Immigration Station was destroyed in a fire in 1940). They appeared before the Board of Special Inquiry for interrogation on April 2, 1941. Document 5 of the same date is the transcript of the interrogation I found in her immigration file at the National Archives—Pacific Sierra Region. The transcript of close to one hundred detailed questions asked of her seemed intimidating, but in an interview I conducted with her fifty years later, she remembered the interrogation as "easy." Apparently her answers and my father's answers agreed. According to the immigration inspector's summary statement, "Testimony has now been taken from the alleged wife, applicant 11-13 and from YUNG HIN SEN concerning their marriage and subsequent stay together in CHINA. This testimony is [in] very good agreement, both principals testifying freely. No discrepancies worthy of mention were brought out by the testimony."

Although I was unable to interview my great-grandmother or my grandmother, I did two interviews with my mother in the 1980s. The first interview was conducted in 1982 in conjunction with my book *Chinese Women of America: A Pictorial History*.[5] I asked her the same questions that were asked of 273 other Chinese American women, covering her life history and reflections on being a Chinese woman in the United States. The second interview in 1987 was to gather specific information about her grandparents Chin Lung and Leong Shee for author Ruthanne Lum McCunn, who subsequently included Chin Lung's story in *Chinese American Portraits: Personal Histories 1828–1988*.[6] More recently, as I worked on this article, I went back to my mother a number of times with specific questions about her true family history, the fake answers in her coaching book, and the official answers she gave in the immigration transcript. Although it had been over fifty years since she immigrated, she was still able to answer some of my questions in detail.

Despite the problems of bias and unreliable memory, I believe oral history offers me the best shot at the truth, especially when I corroborate her story with that of other relatives, including my father, whom I interviewed twice before he died in 1987. I have included my mother's interviews as Document 6, following the translation of her coaching book and the transcript of her immigration interrogation, so that we might compare the "fake," "official," and "true" versions of my mother's family history and thereby come to a better understanding and appreciation of the complex process of immigration for Chinese women during the Exclusion period.

DOCUMENT 1: CHIN LUNG'S AFFIDAVIT, MAY 14, 1892

My great-grandfather Chin Lung immigrated to the United States for a better livelihood right before the Chinese Exclusion Act of 1882 was passed. He was hardworking and resourceful. Within six years he had learned to speak English and saved enough money—sacking rice at the Sing Kee store

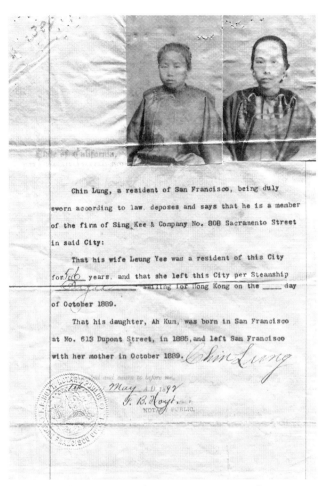

Document 1 (Source: *Leong Shee, case 12017/37232, Chinese Departure Case Files, San Francisco District Office, Immigration and Naturalization Service, Record Group 85, National Archives, San Bruno, California.*)

in San Francisco Chinatown and, later, engaging in tenant farming with fellow villagers in the Sacramento–San Joaquin Delta—to go home and be arranged in marriage to Leong Kum Kew (a.k.a. Leong Yee, her maiden name; and Leong Shee, her married name).[7] But he could not bring her back with him to the United States because he was still considered a laborer, and the Chinese Exclusion Act did not allow family members of Chinese laborers to immigrate to this country. Upon his return, therefore, Chin Lung invested wisely in the Sing Kee store in order to establish merchant status; he was finally able to send for Leong Shee in 1892.

This notarized affidavit, attesting to Chin Lung's merchant status, was intended to pave the way for Leong Shee to immigrate as a merchant's wife. Although Leong Shee had never lived in the United States, Chin Lung, for some reason, felt compelled to vouch that she had lived in San Francisco for five or six years before leaving for Hong Kong in October 1889 with their "daughter" Ah Kum, who supposedly was born in San Francisco Chinatown in 1885. The photographs attached to the affidavit are of Leong Shee and seven-year-old Ah Kum.

From interviews with my mother and two of Chin Lung's sons, I learned that Ah Kum was really a *mui tsai* whom my great-grandmother wanted to bring to America. But why did Chin Lung and Leong Shee have to fabricate the story about Ah Kum's birth in San Francisco, when the treaty of 1880 stipulated that Chinese merchants could bring their household servants with them? I think it may be because they feared that slavegirls would not be permitted entry or that they might be accused of bringing in a potential prostitute, since there was a scarcity of Chinese women and Protestant missionary women like Donaldina Cameron were making an issue of Chinese prostitution. Whatever the reason, Leong Shee's testimony upon arrival (Document 2) not only confirmed the story but elaborated on the fabrication.

DOCUMENT 2: LEONG SHEE'S TESTIMONY, APRIL 18, 1893

This testimony was given by Leong Shee upon arrival in San Francisco. The original document was handwritten and in a narrative rather than a question-and-answer format. The cover sheet described Leong Shee as "female (small feet)," an important signifier of genteel or merchant class. However, descriptions of her in the immigration files of her family members after 1917 indicate that she had "natural feet." Also, whereas a 1904 photograph showed her with bound feet, photographs taken in the 1920s showed her with natural feet. I surmise that Great-grandmother most likely unbound her feet after the 1911 Revolution in China, along with many other women who were encouraged to do so by the new government. By her signature mark, we know that Leong Shee was illiterate. In 1929, however, she told the immigration inspector that she could read and write Chinese, and indeed signed her own name on the document. Relatives told me that she converted to Christianity and learned to read and write at church after her return to China in 1904.

Her testimony confirmed Chin Lung's affidavit that she had lived in San Francisco before and had returned to China with their four-year-old daughter Ah Kum on October 17, 1889, on the *Belgic*. Probably in response to Interpreter Huff's questions, she elaborated on Chin Lung's story by saying that she first came to America with her parents and later married Chin Lung in San Francisco in 1885. After their marriage, they lived upstairs of the Sang [Sing] Kee store at 808 Sacramento Street, where Ah Kum was born on December 28, 1886. (Chin Lung had said in his affidavit that Ah Kum was born at 613 Dupont Street in 1885, but Interpreter Huff evidently did not catch this discrepancy.) She further testified that she returned with her brother-in-law and daughter to China in 1889. "Who else was on that ship?" she was probably asked. In response, she said that "Lee Moon's wife and child" were on the same steamer with her. As to what she remembered of San Francisco Chinatown, she ended with the statement that she did not know the city except for a few

street names "as I have small feet and never went out." The immigration inspector evidently believed her story and landed her and Ah Kum the next day. This testimony would come back to trouble Great-grandmother in 1929, when she appeared before immigration authorities again, this time for permission to leave for China (Document 3).

Document 2

San Francisco, April 18th, 1893.
Kind of Certificate, or Paper, Certificate of Identification   Ticket No. 388.
Name of Passenger, Leong Yee & Ah Kum, child.
Sex, Female.
Where born? China.
Here in U.S.? Yes.   Place of former residence in U.S. San Francisco.
Date of departure from U.S.? Oct. 17/89.
Name of Vessel departed on, Belgic . . .
Do you speak English? No.   Destination, San Francisco
Place of stopping in City, #808 Sacramento St.
Who bought your ticket to China? My brother-in-law.
With whom connected, Gurm Wo Jan–Jackson St., don't know number.
When did you first arrive in U.S.? 1879.

I was married in San Francisco on Dec. 15, 1885 to Chong [Chin] Lung of the firm of Sang Kee wholesale dealers in tea & rice #808 Sac. St. San Francisco. When I first came to this country I came with my father Leong Hoong Wum and my mother Lee Shee and lived at #613 Dupont St. My father was formerly connected with the firm of Sang Kee #808 Sac. St. My father died in this city Nov. 25, 1887. My mother died in this city 1883 so long ago I have forgotten the date. I went home to China with my brother-in-law Chun Gwun Dai and my daughter Ah Kum who was 4 years of age the time of departure. After I was married I lived on the 2nd floor over the store of Sang Kee #808 Sac. St. where my daughter Ah Kum was born on the 28 day of December 1886. My daughter is 8 years old now. My brother-in-law Chun Gwun Dai returned to S.F. in the later part of year 1891. Lee Moon's wife went home in the same steamer with me. I do not know her name. There was also a woman named Sam Moy and a child Ah Yuck on board. I do not speak English and do not know the city excepting the names of a few streets as I have small feet and never went out.

H. S. Huff, Interpreter
Leong X (her mark) Yee

(*Source:* Leong Shee, case 12017/37232, Chinese Departure Case Files, San Francisco District Office, Immigration and Naturalization Service, Record Group 85, National Archives, San Bruno, California)

DOCUMENT 3: LEONG SHEE'S TESTIMONY, JULY 24, 1929

While Great-grandfather Chin Lung farmed in the Sacramento Delta on hundreds of acres of leased land, amassing a fortune growing potatoes with borrowed credit and hired help, Great-grandmother Leong Shee lived in San Francisco Chinatown, where she gave birth to five children, two girls and three boys. The oldest child was my grandmother Chin Suey Kum, born in 1894. Even though she had the means to live well and the help of a *mui tsai*, Leong Shee found life in America inconvenient, alienating, and harried. So unhappy was she that in 1904 she insisted that Chin Lung take the entire family back to China. Chin Lung returned alone and continued farming in the Sacramento Delta. Periodically, he would visit the family in China, siring two more sons in the process.

Although Chin Lung's children all had the right to return to America, only the boys were permitted to do so by their parents. The two girls—my grandmother Suey Kum and my grandaunt Mee Ngon—did not have a say in the matter. They were married into wealthy families in China. According to the Act of 1907, they automatically lost their U.S. citizenship by marrying foreigners. Mee Ngon's husband died soon after their wedding, and she was able to return to America in 1920 by lying about her marital status. My grandmother ended up staying in China and having five daughters and two sons, the oldest being my mother Jew Law Ying. In 1921 Chin Lung persuaded Leong Shee to return to the United States. This time she stayed for eight years before returning to China in 1929.

Under the Exclusion laws, each time a Chinese person wanted to leave the country temporarily, he or she had to apply for a Return Permit to ensure that he or she would be allowed back into the United States. In 1904, when the entire family returned to China, they were covered under Chin Lung's permit and Leong Shee did not have to make a separate application. But in 1929 Leong Shee was returning to China without Chin Lung, which necessitated her appearance and testimony before the immigration service at the Angel Island station. Because her husband's merchant status was under investigation at the time, she had to apply for a Laborer's permit. According to the Immigration Act of 1924, as a "laborer departing," she would be permitted reentry only if she had a relative who was a U.S. resident, such as her husband or one of her sons. And as the immigration officer further warned her, if she should be away for more than six months and her husband or child not be a resident of the United States, she must "be able to read in some language or dialect" in order to be readmitted (in accordance with the Immigration Act of 1917). In answer to an earlier question, "Can you read and write?" she had responded, "I can read and write Chinese, but not English." Unlike her affidavit of 1893 (Document 2), where she made an "X" mark as her signature, she was able to write her name Leong Shee in Chinese characters at the end of this document.

During the interrogation Leong Shee was confronted with earlier statements she had made in 1893 about her immigration history, her marriage, and her eldest daughter Ah Kum. At first she stumbled and said that she had two daughters, the oldest child who died being Chin Suey Kum (the name of

my grandmother who was born in San Francisco in 1894). She then changed her answer and said, "My oldest daughter is Chin Gum, who died shortly after she and I came to this country K.S. 19 (1893)."[8] (A family photograph taken in 1904 showed Chin Gum or *mui tsai* Ah Kum to be alive and well. My mother thinks Ah Kum was married off before Leong Shee returned to China in 1904. She would have been about eighteen years old, the right age to be married off.) Leong Shee also said that Chin Gum was born in China. The inspector then asked her to state again when she first arrived in the United States and where she was married. Leong Shee evidently forgot about her earlier testimony in 1893 and replied with the truth—she first came in 1893 and she was married in China. The inspector then cited the testimony she gave in 1893 (Document 2), setting forth that she had been in the United States "five or six years prior to October, 1889," and that her daughter Ah Kum was born in the United States. Leong Shee repeatedly denied ever giving such testimony even after the inspector reminded her that she was making statements under oath. Fortunately for her, the inspector did not pursue the discrepancies or use it against her, probably because she was departing and not entering the country. As it turned out, Leong Shee never returned to the United States. She died in Macao in 1962 at the age of 94.

Document 3

U.S. Immigration Service
Port of San Francisco

12017/37232	Angel Island Station
Leong Shee	July 24, 1929
Laborer Departing	Exam. Inspector, H. F. Hewitt
	Interpreter, Yong Kay

Applicant, sworn and admonished that if at any time she does not understand the interpreter to at once so state. Also advised of the crime of perjury and the penalty therefor. Speaks the Heung Shan dialect.

Q: *What are all your names?*
A: Leong Shee; Leong Yee was my maiden name.

Q: *How old are you?*
A: 61.

Q: *Where were you born?*
A: Kay Boo village, H.S.D.,[9] China.

Q: *When did you first come to the U.S.?*
A: K.S. 19/3 (1893, April) ss "China."

Q: *Were you accompanied when you came to the U.S. in K.S. 19 (1893)?*
A: By my daughter, Chin Kum, and a clansman, Leong Wai Kun, a clansman of mine.

Q: *Under what status were you admitted to the U.S. at that time, K.S. 19 (1893)?*
A: I do not know; I came here to join my husband, Chin Lung, who was a merchant of Sing Kee Co., San Francisco.

Q: *Who is this (showing photo attached to affidavit of Chin Lung,[10] contained in file 20437/2-6, Leong Shee, Wife of Mer.,*

"Shinyo Maru," 7/14/29—affidavit referred to attached to landing record April 18, 1893, Leong Yee & child, Ah Kum, ss "China")?
A: That is my photo.

Q: Who is represented in the photo of the child next attached to the photo which you claim is of yourself?
A: My daughter, Ah Kum.

Q: Have you ever left the U.S. since you arrived here in K.S. 19 (1893)?
A: Yes, one trip to China; departed K.S. 30/2 (1904, Mar.)? ss "China." I returned to the U.S. C.R.10/7 (Aug. 1921),[11] ss "Shinyo Maru," at San Francisco, and was admitted as the wife of a merchant, wife of Chin Lung, who was then a merchant of Sing Kee Co., San Francisco.

Q: Have you a cer. of identity?
A: Yes. (There is contained in the present file CI No. 36086, Leong Shee, Mer. Wife returning, ss "Shinyo Maru," 20437/2-6, 8.14.21. Same is retained in file and contains photo of the present applicant.)

Q: Why do you appear here today?
A: I want to depart for China on a laborer's return certificate.

Q: Are you married at this time?
A: Yes.

Q: How many times have you been married?
A: Once only.

Q: Will you name your husband?
A: Chin Lung—Chin Hong Dai.[12]

Q: Where is he at this time?
A: He is here today, with me.

Q: What is your present address?
A: 1210 Stockton St., S.F., Calif.

Q: With whom do you live there?
A: My husband and my children—one of my children lives there with me, a son, Chin Sow; also my husband lives there with me.

Q: What is your husband's occupation?
A: Merchant, Shang Hai Trunk Co., 1210 Stockton St., S.F., where I live.

Q: What is your present occupation?
A: Housewife.

Q: Do you follow any other occupation?
A: No.

Q: Can you read and write?
A: I can read and write Chinese, but not English.

Q: What will be your foreign address:
A: C/o Dok Jan Co., Macao, China; I don't remember the street or number. (Alleged husband states this applicant's address will be No. 16 Hung Shung San Street, Macao, China, Dok Jan Co.).

Q: Will anyone accompany you to China?
A: Yes, my son, Chin Sow, who lives with me in San Francisco (12017/37115).

Q: How many children have you ever had?
A: 5 sons and 2 daughters.

Q: Name all your children, their ages, date of birth and whereabouts.

A: My oldest child is Chin Suey Kum, who died (changes). My oldest daughter is Chin Gum, who died shortly after she and I came to this country K.S. 19 (1893).

Q: Is Chin Gum whom you have just mentioned as your oldest daughter, the child who accompanied you to the U.S. in K.S. 19 (1893)?
A: Yes.

Q: Was that daughter born in China?
A: Yes.

Q: How many daughters have you had born to you, altogether?
A: Three.

Q: Name your second daughter?
A: Chin Suey Kum, about 35 or 36; I don't remember her birth date; she is now in China; she was born in the U.S., at San Francisco. Chin Suey Kan, 29; she is now in San Francisco, living in the Yet Sin Building, Stockton St., near Broadway; she is not married; she was born in San Francisco; she works on Market St., I don't know for whom; she embroiders handkerchiefs. I don't remember the date of her birth.

Q: Name your sons, the ages, dates of birth and whereabouts and where born?
A: Chin Wing, 34 or 35; I don't remember the date of his birth; he was born in San Francisco. He is now in San Francisco, in my husband's store, he is a member of the firm; he lives on Powell Street, with his wife. Chin Wah, 32, he is in the East; he is in New York city; he was born in San Francisco. Chin Foo, 26; he was born in San Francisco; I don't remember the date of his birth; he is now in my husband's store; he is a member of the firm; he is married and lives in the Yut Sin Building; my daughter who lives in that building lives there with him. Chin Gway, 26, born K.S. 30/4-11 (May 25, 1904), in San Francisco, and is now a member of my husband's firm; he lives on Powell Street, with his wife. Chin Sow, 23, born K.S. 33/10-13 (1907, Nov. 17); he was born in China, in Nom Song village, China. He is not married; he lives with me in San Francisco.

Q: Are you the mother of any other children?
A: No.

Q: On what do you base your right to depart for China and to return to the U.S.?
A: On the ground that my son Chin Sow is a resident of the U.S. and that I can return to him in this country.

Q: When did Chin Sow come to the U.S.?
A: C.R. 13 (1924), ss "Korea," at San Francisco.

Q: Did you testify for him at that time?
A: Yes.

Q: Under what status was he admitted at that time?
A: As the son of a merchant.

Q: Did your husband testify for him at that time?
A: Yes.

Q: Did you state that Chin Sow will accompany you to China?
A: Yes.

Q: Is Chin Sow here today?
A: No.

Q: Have you a photograph of Chin Sow with you at this time?
A: No.

Q: Who is this (showing photo of applicant, Chin Sow, attached to affidavit contained in file 23303/12-7, Chin Sow, mer. Son, ss "Korea Maru," May 4, 1924)?
A: My son, Chin Sow.

Q: Who is this (showing photo attached to same affidavit next to that of applicant in above mentioned case)?
A: My husband, Chin Lung.

Q: Is your husband Chin Lung going to remain in the U.S.?
A: Yes.

Q: Do you expect that he will be a resident of the U.S. upon your return to this country?
A: Yes, I expect that if he is living he will be in the U.S.

Q: Will you again state when you first arrived in the U.S.?
A: K.S. 19/3 (1893, April).

Q: Where were you married?
A: I was married in Nom Song village, HSD, China.

Q: Do you remember the date of your marriage?
A: No, I can't remember that.

Q: Do you recognize this affidavit and the photos attached thereto (showing affidavit of Chin Lung, dated May 14, 1892, which contains photo of the present applicant, and which affidavit is attached to arrival record of Leong Yee and child, Ah Kum, ss "China," April 18, 1893)?
A: Yes, that is the paper I had when I first came to the U.S.

Q: You are advised that that affidavit sets forth that you had been in the U.S. five or six years prior to October, 1889—9th month, K.S. 15, and you now state that you first came to the U.S. in K.S. 19 (1893). Can you explain why that affidavit should set forth such information?
A: I first came to the U.S. in K.S. 19 (1893). I don't know why that information is in the affidavit that I was in this country before K.S. 19 (1893).[13]

Q: Do you know that that affidavit also sets forth that your daughter, who accompanied you in K.S. 19 (1893) to the U.S., was born in the U.S., and you have stated today that she was born in China?
A: I don't know why; the fact is that that daughter was born in China.

Q: Had that daughter ever been in the U.S. before K.S. 19 (1893)?
A: No.

Q: Do you realize that you are making your statement today under oath?
A: Yes.

Q: Were you ever in the U.S. before K.S. 19 (1893)?
A: No.

Q: Do you ever recall being questioned by this Service, before, as to when you came to the U.S. the first time, and also that it was called to your attention that the affidavit just referred to sets forth that you were in the U.S. before K.S. 19 (1893)?
A: Yes, and I said that I had first come to the U.S. in K.S. 19 (1893).

Q: Do you remember when you testified to that effect?
A: Yes, in the case of Chin Sow.

Q: Do you remember being asked at that time where you were married?
A: Yes, and I said I had been married in China.

Q: You are advised that in order to permit your re-entry into the U.S. it will be necessary that your son, Chin Sow will have to return to the U.S. with you or prior thereto, in order that the grounds upon which you are basing your application shall then be existent. Do you understand?
A: Yes.

Q: You are further advised that should you remain away from the U.S. for a period longer than six months should your husband or your child not be a resident of the U.S. in the event of your reapplication for admission it would be necessary, in order to entitle you to admission to the U.S., that you be able to read in some language or dialect. Do you understand?
A: Yes.

Q: Who is this (showing photo of applicant, Chin Sow, 12017/37115, attached to Form 432)?
A: Chin Sow, my son.

Q: Have you anything further to state?
A: No.

Q: Who is this (indicating Chin Lung, alleged husband, who has been called into the room)?
A: My husband, Chin Lung.

Q: (to Chin Lung, alleged husband) Who is this woman?
A: My wife, Leong Shee. (Alleged husband dismissed.)

Q: Did you understand this interpreter (through interpreter J. Q. Moy)?
A: Yes.

Signed: [Leong Shee in Chinese characters] I certify that the foregoing is a true and correct record of testimony taken direct on the typewriter at the above described hearing.

H. F. Hewitt, typist.

> (*Source:* Leong Shee, case 12017/37232, Chinese Departure Case Files, San Francisco District Office, Immigration and Naturalization Service, Record Group 85, National Archives, San Bruno, California)

DOCUMENT 4: JEW LAW YING'S COACHING BOOK

As a result of Great-grandmother Leong Shee's decision to return to China with all her children in 1904, my grandmother Chin Suey Kum, a native-born U.S. citizen, ended up marrying Jew Hin Gwin, an herb doctor in China, and forfeiting her right to return to the United States. My mother Jew Law Ying was thus born in Dai Chek Hom village, Heungshan [Zhongshan] District, Guangdong Province, in 1915. The eldest child and the favored grandchild of Chin Lung and Leong Shee, she lived with them in Macao from age seven until she was arranged in marriage to my father, Tom Yip Jing, in 1937. My father, born in Pai Shan village, Heungshan District, in 1903 had immigrated to the United States in 1921 as Yung Hin Sen, the paper son of Yung Ung of Sin Dung village, Sunwui (Xinhui) District, which was adjacent to Heungshan District. At the age of thirty-three, he had finally saved enough money to come home to marry. The marriage

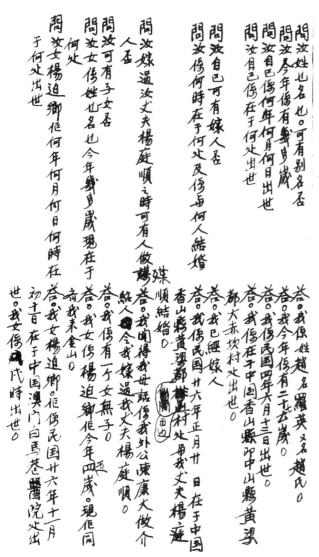

Document 4 figure. First page of my mother's coaching book.

home village. As was the case for most other Chinese immigrants coming during the Exclusion period, my father had multiple copies prepared by someone experienced in the business.[14] Father kept the carbon copy and sent the original copy to my mother to study. I would later inherit both copies.

The point was that when interrogated by the immigration inspector my parents' answers to the same questions had to match in order to prove their relationship as husband and wife. Answers also had to cross-check with answers given by relatives who had immigrated earlier. Moreover, as many of the old-timers I interviewed attested, one was never sure which and how many of the questions in the coaching book would be asked. They all spent months memorizing these coaching books. True sons were as likely to fail the examination as paper sons. In my mother's view, however, she had an easier time preparing for the interrogation because she kept her true identity. "I didn't have to study it too long," she told me. "I just read it through and answered whatever question they asked me one by one. It was really quite simple." As it turned out, of the one hundred questions asked of my parents, only twenty-seven resembled those in my mother's coaching book.

Most immigrants I interviewed said they destroyed their coaching books before their arrival in San Francisco, but a few like my mother kept theirs. When asked why she did that, my mother replied, "For a souvenir." My father also kept his carbon copy through the years. In comparing the two copies, I can see that my father only bothered to make changes and additions to my mother's copy. I have thus translated my mother's copy in its entirety, inserting notes whenever necessary for clarification and to distinguish the fake parts from the true. In general, because my father was a paper son but my mother's identity was true, the description of his family background in the coaching book is fake, while my mother's family background is true.

A few of the answers were written in my father's handwriting, probably because the compiler didn't have all the answers at hand. At one point, my father teased my mother that she should be able to describe his appearance without his prompting. At other times, he warned her to omit certain information to avoid complications or contradictions in their stories. For example, he told her not to say that his mother and brother were at their wedding since according to his fake identity, his mother was deceased and his brother was in the United States at the time of the wedding. The section in the coaching book about witnesses was left blank, probably because he was not sure who they might be at the time. As it turned out, no other witnesses were called besides my father.

One major change my father made in the coaching book was the village where he and my mother supposedly got married. According to the coaching book, the wedding took place in Hin Bin village, Heungshan District, when by custom it should have taken place at his fake birthplace, Sin Dung village in Sunwui District. In actuality, it took place in my father's true birthplace, Pai Shan village in Heungshan

to my mother was arranged by my great-grandfather Chin Lung, at the suggestion of his eldest daughter-in-law, Wong Shee Chan, who had befriended my father in San Francisco. As my mother later admitted in an interview with me (Document 7), she agreed to the marriage only because it offered her a way to leave war-torn China and come to America.

After the wedding my father returned to the United States alone to make arrangements for my mother to immigrate as the wife of Yung Hin Sen, a bona fide merchant. In preparation for the immigration interrogation, my father sent her a coaching book to study. Hand-written in Chinese with blue ink on 8½ x 11 inch parchment paper folded in half and stapled together, the book was fifteen pages long and contained 155 questions and answers about my mother's family history, my father's family history, their arranged marriage and wedding, where they lived together in China, their stay in Hong Kong before his departure to the United States, correspondence between them, mutual acquaintances, and a map of his

District. He probably set his wedding and their new home in Heungshan District because he and my mother were more familiar with the region. In an interview with me in 1977, he told me that he was prepared to say that his family had to move to Heungshan District because of the Sino-Japanese War in the 1930s. But why did he not use Pai Shan village if he was going to relocate to Heungshan District anyway? My mother thinks it may have been because there were more Yungs in Hin Bin village than in Pai Shan village. Indeed, that was the case, according to one of the answers given in the coaching book. Regardless of the reason, the decision to use Hin Bin village was evidently made after the coaching book was written, since my father had to change Pai Shan village to Hin Bin village throughout the book. The map, however, was the layout of Pai Shan village. Later, upon return to the United States in 1937, he slipped and said that his wife was living in Sin Dung village instead of Hin Bin village. When confronted with this discrepancy in 1941, he replied, "I am a native of Sin Dung village and possibly I was thinking of my own home."

In a number of places the compiler gave helpful advice, indicating he thoroughly understood the interrogation process. At one point, he noted that it was important for my mother to say she was literate because then my father could produce letters she wrote him as evidence of their relationship.[15] As another example, the compiler advised my parents to pay close attention to questions about their living arrangements in Hin Bin village: "This is the most important part of the interrogation so be careful with your answers." When in doubt, he wrote in a number of places, answer truthfully to avoid mistakes. He evidently also wanted to keep current of any changes that needed to be made by any of the parties involved, instructing them that they should notify him first.

According to my aunt Tom Ngun Dai, who lived in Pai Shan village from 1924 until 1948, the map that appears at the back of my mother's coaching book is a simplified version of the actual village as she remembered it: There were at least eighty houses, not just the ten shown on the map. There were many more children in the households than indicated. Missing from the map were a second ancestral hall, two watchtowers near the village gates, and a ball field. She also said there were no bamboo groves to the west, no outhouse for the women, and my father's family actually owned two houses, not just the one given on the map. My father may have remembered certain things incorrectly, but most likely he wanted to keep things simple for my mother and himself.

Document 4

Q: *What is your name? Do you have any other names?*
A: My surname is Jew, name Law Ying. My other name is Jew Shee.

Q: *How old are you?*
A: I am twenty-seven years old.

Q: *What is your birthdate?*
A: I was born on C.R. 4th year [1915], 6th month, 13th day.

Q: *Where were you born?*
A: I was born in China, Heungshan District, Wong Lung Doo section, Dai Cheuk Hom village.

Q: *Are you married?*
A: I am married.

Q: *When, where, and to whom were you married?*
A: I married my husband Yung Hin Sen on C.R. 26th year [1937], 1st month, 20th day, in China, Heungshan District, Wong Lung Doo section, Hin Bin village.

Q: *Who was the matchmaker?*
A: My mother said that my maternal grandfather Chin Hong Dai was the matchmaker.

Q: *Do you have any children?*
A: I have one daughter, no son.

Q: *What is your daughter's name, what is her age, and where is she now?*
A: My daughter is Yung Bak Heong. She is four years old. She came to the United States with me.

Q: *What is your daughter Bak Heong's birthdate and birthplace?*
A: My daughter Bak Heong was born on C.R. 26th year [1937], 11th month, 11th day, the *she* hour [between 7:00 and 9:00 P.M.], at the Bock Ma Hong Hospital in Macao, China.

Q: *Was your husband present in China when your daughter Bak Heong was born?*
A: My husband was not in China when our daughter was born. He had left for the United States three months before the birth of my daughter.

Q: *How long was it after your daughter's birth before you wrote to inform your husband in the United States?*
A: Two days after my daughter's birth, I immediately sent a letter to inform my husband Yung Hin Sen in the United States.

Q: *Did you or your husband name your daughter?*
A: I named my daugher Yung Bak Heong[16] and wrote my husband about it.

Q: *Do you have any schooling? Can you read and write letters?*
A: I went to school. I can read and write simple letters.

NOTE: This is an important issue that will help shorten the interrogation and help the new immigrant Jew Shee get landed. Because if she knows how to write and send letters to her husband Yung Hin Sen in the United States, he can keep these letters and present them to the immigration inspector as evidence when Jew Shee arrives.

Q: *When and where did you marry your husband Yung Hin Sen and by what custom were you married?*
A: I was married on C.R. 26th year [1937], 1st month, 20th day, in China, Heungshan District, Wong Lung Doo section, Hin Bin village, according to the old Chinese custom of "riding the bright red sedan."[17]

Q: *Can you describe the wedding ceremony?*
A: (Be sure to describe the traditional ceremony as it happened, but do not mention that my [true] mother and brother were there.)[18]

Q: As a bride on the wedding day, what did you wear? Did you wear the red wedding skirt and veil?
A: (Describe the wedding as it happened and your husband should do the same.) (Do not say that my mother, brother, or relatives were there.)

Q: Who officiated at your wedding?
A: There was only one *seungtau gung*, older brother Hin Biew.[19]

Q: How many times did you see your husband before you married him?
A: I saw him twice before we married. Once in Nam San village and once at the Dow Moon Market.

Q: The two times that you saw one another, who introduced you and who was there with the two of you? What were the dates and times and how long did you talk?
A: (Reply as it happened to avoid mistakes.) The first time was at maternal great-grandfather's home in Nam San village. Great-grandfather introduced us. Great-grandfather and great-grandmother were there, as well as a slavegirl. It was on C.R. 25th year [1936], 12th month, 25th day, about 10 A.M. We talked for about two hours. We had tea and lunch. The second time was on C.R. 26th year [1937], 1st month, 14th day, at 9:00 A.M. I met my husband in the Dow Moon Market, upstairs of Wong Jeet Mun [a distant relative of my mother's]. We talked for about an hour. There was no one there with us. My husband told me my grandfather had recommended me to him for a wife.

Q: The two times you met your husband before your marriage, what clothes did he and you have on?
A: (Reply as it happened to avoid mistakes.) At our meeting in Nam San, my husband wore a light red Chinese outfit. I wore a white dress with blue trim. At the Dow Moon Market meeting, he wore a black Western suit and I wore a light red *cheongsam*. (Note: Aside from the two of us, to prevent complications, don't mention there was a third person present.)

Q: How far is your native village Dai Chek Hom from the village where you were married? What bridges, rivers, and villages do you pass?
A: My village is about eight or nine miles from Hin Bin village. There is one bridge and no river near the village. You pass about six or seven villages of varying sizes. (If asked for the names of the villages, answer Lei Ok, Lik Kei, Sek Jue, Sum Tum, Dow Moon Market, See Ji Hou, Ngau Bing Tong, then you arrive at Hin Bin village.)

Q: How many people carried your bridal sedan chair?
A: Four people carried my sedan chair.

Q: When did you exchange engagement gifts? What was the bride price? How many wedding cakes and roast pigs?
A: (Both of you should answer as it happened to avoid mistakes.) On C.R. 26th year, 1st month, 16th day, we set the date for the 20th to exchange engagement gifts. The bride price was $1,600. There were wedding cakes but no roast pigs.

Q: What dowry did you present your husband?
A: (Both of you should answer as it happened to avoid mistakes.)

Q: What time did you arrive at your husband's home by sedan chair from your home?
A: (Both of you should answer as it happened to avoid mistakes.) It was approximately 6:00 P.M.

Q: What did your husband wear on the day of the wedding?
A: (Both of you should answer as it happened to avoid mistakes.) A black Western woolen suit.

Q: Did you invite three "fraternity brothers" for the wedding? Did you observe the custom of "knocking on the sedan door?"[20]
A: Yes, we observed the custom of "knocking on the sedan door" and invited three "fraternity brothers." Their names were Jun Hei, Ging Kau, and Wun Tong.

Q: What were their surnames, where were they from, and how old were they?
A: Yung surname, from Hin Bin village. Jun Hei was twenty-six years old, the second one was about twenty years old, and the third one was about thirty years old.

Q: How many days of celebration and how many wedding banquets?
A: Two days of celebration and one banquet.

Q: How many guests attended the wedding banquet?
A: About thirty people.

Q: Where was the wedding banquet held?
A: At the Yung ancestral hall in Hin Bin village.

Q: Did your husband put a gold wedding ring on your finger in the presence of the wedding guests?
A: No.

Q: Did your husband present you with any jewelry, clothes, or gifts before or after the wedding?
A: Nothing before. (Answer about after the wedding as it happened.)

Q: Did your husband build a pavilion for the banquet on the day of the wedding?[21]
A: No.

Q: Were there any musicians hired for the wedding celebration?
A: Five musicians were hired.

Q: Were there any firecrackers and teasing of the bride?
A: Yes.

Q: Who served as seungtau gung at the wedding?
A: Yung Yip Ghin.[22]

Q: As the groom, did your husband wear a red sash?
A: I didn't see him with a red sash (in other words, you don't know).

Q: As the bride, did you kowtow to the ancestors, toast three cups of wine with the groom, and offer tea and betel nuts to the elders?
A: I kowtowed to the ancestors. Did not toast wine or offer tea. Offered betel nuts to the *seungtau gung* and *seungtau po*. (If the interrogator asks you the ages of the *seungtau gung* and *seungtau po*, say that the *seungtau gung* was about sixty years old and the *seungtau po* Jew Shee was about sixty years old, had natural feet, and was from Dai Chek Hom.)

Q: Were the three "fraternity brothers" related to your husband?
A: No.

Q: Who owned the house in Hin Bin village that you and your husband lived in and was it an old or new house?
A: The house that we lived in was an old house belonging to Yung Yip Ghin. My husband rented it from him. The monthly rent was $10. My husband took care of paying the rent so I didn't pay any attention to it.[23]

NOTE: Be sure to agree on your answers regarding your living arrangements in Hin Bin village. This is the most important part of the interrogation, so be careful with your answers.

Q: What was the house in which you and your husband lived made of and in what style?
A: (Answer according to the interior and exterior of my house. Do not say there were any livestock or ancestral tablets and pictures hanging inside.)[24]

Q: What is the floor of the house made of? How many bedrooms, balconies, parlors? How many entrances altogether? In which direction does the front entrance face?
A: (Both of you must describe the house in the village the same way to avoid mistakes.)(Do not say there was livestock or ancestral tablets. Say that the ancestral picture was on red paper and hung on the altar.)

Q: Did anyone else live with the two of you?
A: Just us one couple. No one else lived with us.[25]

Q: How long did the two of you live in Hin Bin village?
A: We lived there for three months.

Q: Did you follow the custom of returning to the bride's family three days after the wedding? Did your husband go with you to see your parents?
A: After the wedding, we did not follow the custom of returning to the bride's family together. I returned home alone to see my family four times after the wedding. The first time was on the one-month anniversary of the 2nd month, 5th day, when I stayed for four days. The second time was in the 3rd month, 11th day, and I stayed about ten days. The third time was in the 3rd month, 29th day, when I stayed only a few hours to talk before returning to my husband's home. The fourth time was in the 4th month, 20th day, when I stayed for three days. All four times I went home alone without my husband.

Q: Did your husband ever go visit your parents and family alone after you were married?
A: No.

Q: Where did you live after you left Hin Bin village?
A: We were married on C.R. 26th year [1937], 1st month, 20th day, in Hin Bin village and lived in our home there until the 5th month, 10th day of that same year, when my husband and I moved to Macao to live in the house of my maternal grandfather Chin Hong Dai.

Q: How long after you both moved to Macao to live with your maternal grandfather Chin Hong Dai before your husband returned to the United States?
A: After my husband accompanied me from Hin Bin village on C.R. 26th year [1937], 5th month, 10th day, to my maternal grandfather's home, my husband did not stay there because he had important business in Hong Kong. On the same day—5th month, 10th day—at 4:00 P.M. he took the boat from Macao to Hong Kong. Thus he never stayed overnight or had a meal at my family's home. He only had some tea. It wasn't until the 5th month, 5th or 6th day, that my husband returned alone from Hong Kong to Macao and took me from my grandfather's home to Hong Kong. We lived in Hong Kong until my husband returned by boat to the United States. Then I returned to live at my maternal grandfather's home in the 8th month until I left for the United States with my daughter.[26]

Q: After you both left your maternal grandfather Chin Hong Dai's home for Hong Kong, where did you live and eat in Hong Kong? How long before your husband took a boat to return to the United States?
A: We lived at the Look Hoy Hung Hotel and ate at Wing Hung Cheong for about three months before my husband returned to the United States. (If you're asked about the Wing Hung Cheong Company, say that it belongs to your husband's friend, Tom Share Dew [a.k.a. Tom Yip Pooh].)

Q: What time did your husband leave to take the boat to the United States? What luggage did he take? Did he have anyone help him carry the luggage? Where did you and your husband part? Did you accompany your husband to the dock?
A: (Be sure that you both answer the above questions the same as it happened.)(Note that besides you, all who came to say farewell were just friends. Be sure not to mention that Foo Wing is my true brother.)

Q: What furniture did you have in your home at Hin Bin village? Whose furniture was it?
A: There was a big bed and my dowry. Everything else belonged to the landlord.

Q: When you both lived in Hin Bin village, who did the cooking and who fetched the water?
A: I did it myself.

Q: When you both lived in Hin Bin village, were there occasions when you had a servant help with the housework or cooking?
A: No.

Q: When you both left Hin Bin village to go to your maternal grandfather Chin Hong Dai's home to live, what household furniture and bedding did you take with you?
A: When we went to Macao to my maternal grandfather's, we only brought three pieces of luggage. Everything else, including my bed, dresser, and chairs, we left to the landlord to take care of.

Q: Do you know which direction Hin Bin village faces? How many rows of buildings are there? Is there a temple or ancestral hall? Any gates, fish ponds, village shrine, and wells?
A: I know that Hin Bin village faces east. The houses are arranged in six rows. There are five main lanes and one side lane, one ancestral hall, no temples or fish ponds. There are ten houses and one ancestral hall, making a total of eleven buildings. No fish ponds. There are two gates. One village shrine is on the left side of the village, to the left of the ancestral hall. There is a round well in front of the village.[27]

Q: Are there any walls, trees, or bamboo around Hin Bin village?
A: There are trees behind Hin Bin village, a wall in front, no bamboo.

Q: What is the predominant surname in Hin Bin village?
A: Mostly people with the surname Yung live in Hin Bin village.

Q: Do you know why your husband chose to get married and rent a house in Heungshan District, Hin Bin village?
A: My husband told me it was because his parents had passed away and he had no more relatives in Sunwui Sin Dung village. He was not planning to stay in China long and would be returning to the United States so he rented that house.

Q: Do you know who are your husband's closest friends or relatives in Hin Bin village?

A: I don't know because my husband never talked about them.

Q: *Do you know which family have members who have gone to the United States or have relatives there now?*
A: I don't know aside from my husband what other villager has relatives in the United States.

Q: *Which house in Hin Bin village did you both live in?*
A: The second house, fourth row from the north.

Q: *Do you know how many people live in Hin Bin village?*
A: There are over thirty people.[28]

Q: *Which room and on which side of the house did you sleep in, cook in, and dine in?*
A: We slept in the north wing on the left side. The kitchen was to the left. The dining room was in the middle.

Q: *During meal times, did the two of you eat together or did you eat after your husband?*
A: We ate together at the same table at the same time.

Q: *Do you know the age of your husband Yung Hin Sen and when he was born?*
A: My husband is thirty-nine years old. He was born in K.S. 29th year [1903], 7th month, 15th day.[29]

Q: *Do you know where your husband Yung Hin Sen was born?*
A: My husband was born in China, Sunwui District, Sin Dung village.

Q: *Do you know when your husband Yung Hin Sen first left China for the United States and after he came to the United States how many times he returned to China?*
A: My husband first came to the United States when he was nineteen years old. He returned to China once, in C.R. 25th year [1936], the last month, to marry me. After that, he returned to the United States from Hong Kong in C.R. 26th year [1937], 8th month, 20th day. He has been in the United States since then.

Q: *Do you know the names, ages, and present location of your husband's parents or your father-in-law and mother-in-law?*
A: My husband's father is Yung Ung and his mother is Wong Shee. Both are dead. I don't know their ages.[30]

Q: *Do you know when and where your father-in-law and mother-in-law passed away?*
A: My father-in-law died in the United States eleven years ago and is buried in a cemetery in San Francisco. My mother-in-law died in Sunwui Sin Dung five years ago.[31]

Q: *Do you know if your father-in-law and mother-in-law ever came to the United States?*
A: My father-in-law was in the United States. My mother-in-law never came to the United States.

Q: *Do you know what kind of work your father-in-law did when he was in the United States?*
A: He was a businessman in the United States.[32]

Q: *If you saw a picture of your father-in-law and mother-in-law, would you recognize them?*
A: I've never seen a picture of them so I wouldn't be able to recognize them.

Q: *Do you know if your husband Yung Hin Sen has any brothers and sisters?*
A: My husband has an older brother in the United States.[33]

Q: *Do you know the name, age, location, and work of your husband's siblings?*
A: My husband has one older brother and no sisters. His name is Yung Hin Biew. He is forty years old and works in the United States.[34]

Q: *Have you ever seen this brother in person or in a photograph?*
A: I've never seen him before.

Q: *Do you know if your husband visited Sunwui District, Sin Dung village, after the wedding?*
A: He went before the wedding but not after the wedding.

Q: *Do you know how far your husband's home village is from the village where you were married?*
A: I have never been there so I do not know.

Q: *Do you know which direction and how far Hin Bin village is from your ancestral village Dai Chek Hom? How far is it from Dow Moon Market and Macao?*
A: From Hin Bin village to Dow Moon Market, you go left to the north about three and a half miles. From Hin Bin village to my ancestral village Dai Chek Hom, it is an eight- or nine-mile walk. To go to Dai Chek Hom you must pass Dow Moon Market, then from there it's a five-hour boat ride to Macao.

Q: *Which direction does Dai Chek Hom face? How many rows of houses? How many houses?*
A: (Answer according to the actual situation in Dai Chek Hom.)
(If you are asked about your parents' house in Dai Chek Hom, answer according to what you know.)

Q: *What is your father's name, age, residence, and line of work?*
A: Jew Sun, also Hin Gwing, forty-eight years old, doctor.

Q: *What is your mother's name and age? What kind of feet? Where is your mother now and what kind of work does she do?*
A: My mother is Chin Shee. Her birth name is Chin Suey Kum. She is forty-eight years old. She has natural feet. She is in China living with her husband. She is a housewife.

Q: *Do you know where your parents were born?*
A: My father was born in China, Dai Chek Hom village. My mother Chin Shee was born in San Francisco, California, United States. My mother told me this.

Q: *Do you know when your mother returned from the United States to China? Did she ever go back to the United States after she returned to China?*
A: My mother came back to China when she was eleven years old to live. She has not returned to the United States since.

Q: *Do you know the birthdate of your father Jew Sun?*
A: (Answer according to the truth.)

Q: *Has your father ever been to the United States or abroad?*
A: No.

Q: *Do you know when your mother Chin Shee or Chin Suey Kum was born?*
A: (The new immigrant must find out what her mother reported to immigration as her birthdate when she returned to China.) She was born on February 13, 1894. She returned to China from the United States on March 23, 1904, by SS *Siberia.*

Q: *Does your father Jew Sun or Hin Gwing have any brothers and sisters?*

A: (Answer according to the truth.)

Q: *Does your mother Chin Shee or Chin Suey Kum have any brothers or sisters?*
A: My mother has five younger brothers and one younger sister.

Q: *Does your mother have any brothers or sisters who died?*
A: No.

Q: *What are the names and ages of your mother's brothers and sisters? Where are they and what kind of work do they do?*
A: My oldest uncle is Chin Wing, forty-six years old, married. His entire family is in the United States. I don't know how many children he has because we haven't corresponded. Second uncle Chin Wah is forty-three years old, unmarried, in the United States. Third uncle Chin Foo is thirty-nine years old, married, in the United States. He has children but I don't know their names or ages because we have not corresponded. Fourth uncle Chin Gway is thirty-seven years old, married, in the United States. His wife, Leong Jew Shee, who is twenty-three years old, is in Macao. They have one son named You Tien, who is four years old. Fifth uncle Chin Show is thirty-four years old, in the United States. His wife Lau Shee is thirty years old. They have two sons—Gwok Cheong, five years old, and Gwok Nam, four years old. Fifth aunt and their two sons are in Macao. I don't know where my uncles live or what work they do. Aunt Chin Mee Ngon is forty years old and is in the United States.

Q: *Do your uncles have wives and children?*
A: (See above.)

Q: *Is your aunt married and where does she live now?*
A: Unmarried, living in the United States but I don't know the address.[35]

Q: *What are the names of your maternal grandfather and grandmother? Are they still alive?*
A: My maternal grandfather is Chin Lung, also Chin Hong Dai. He is seventy-seven years old. My maternal grandmother Leong Shee is seventy-three years old, unbound feet. They both live in Macao, China, at 73 Haw Lon Yin Street.

Q: *Do you know if your maternal grandfather Chin Hong Dai and maternal grandmother Leong Shee have ever been to the United States?*
A: My maternal grandparents have been to the United States many times but I don't know exactly how many times.

Q: *Do you know where they were born?*
A: My maternal grandfather Chin Hong Dai was born in China, Heungshan District, Nam San village. My maternal grandmother Leong Shee was born in Heungshan, Kee Mo village.

Q: *Did your maternal grandmother unbind her feet?*
A: Yes.

Q: *Do you know when your maternal grandfather Chin Lung or Chin Hong Dai made his last trip to the United States from China? When was his last trip to China from the United States?*
A: (Ask maternal grandfather.)

Q: *Do you know when your maternal grandmother Leong Shee made her last trip to the United States from China? When was her last trip to China from the United States?*
A: (Ask maternal grandmother.)

Q: *Do you know what kind of work your maternal grandfather Chin Lung or Chin Hong Dai did while in the United States?*
A: When my maternal grandfather Chin Lung was in the United States, he did business at the Sang Kee rice store and later, the Shanghai Trunk Company. He also grew potatoes.

Q: *If you saw pictures of your maternal grandparents, your mother, your uncles and aunts, would you be able to recognize them?*
A: I could recognize all of them.

Q: *Who owned the house at 73 Haw Lon Yin Street in Macao in which your maternal grandfather Chin Lung or Chin Hong Dai and family lived?*
A: It was my maternal grandfather Chin Hong Dai's property.

Q: *What was this building made of? How many stories? Any garden?*
A: (Answer according to the truth to avoid mistakes.)

Q: *Did your husband Yung Hin Sen ever live or have a meal at your maternal grandfather Chin Lung's house?*
A: He had a meal there and tea.

Q: *Do you know if your maternal grandfather Chin Lung or Chin Hong Dai owned any other properties or land besides the house in which he and his family lived?*
A: (You and your husband must answer according to the truth.)

NOTE: Whenever the interrogator asks questions not in the coaching book, you must both answer according to the truth to avoid mistakes.

Q: *When you married your husband Yung Hin Sen, did you exchange genealogies going back three generations?*[36]
A: We did not.

NOTE: If you say you exchanged genealogies, then both of you must be prepared to name the generations. It is best if the new immigrant could bring her husband's genealogy to the United States and present it as evidence when interrogated. It will be easier if you said you did not exchange genealogies. The two of you must agree on this answer to avoid mistakes.

Q: *During or after the wedding, did you take any pictures together?*
A: (If you took a picture together, it is best that the new immigrant present the picture to the interrogator as evidence. If you didn't take any picture together, say you didn't.)[37]

Q: *When you were married in the village, did your husband change his name and post that name in the house?*[38]
A: (Your and your husband's answers must agree.)

Q: *Do you have any brothers and sisters?*
A: Three younger sisters and three younger brothers, seven of us altogether. Sister Wun Jee is my same age. Third sister Jin Dai, twenty-five years old. Fourth sister Ngan Bun, twenty-three years old. Sing Haw, twelve years old.[39]

Q: *Do you have any brothers and sisters who died?*
A: No.

Q: *Do you have any brothers or sisters who ever came to the United States?*
A: No.

Q: What are the names of your brothers and sisters? Their ages, birthdates? Where do they live and what kind of work do they do?
A: (Answer according to the truth.) Two brothers Jew Sing Haw, twelve years old, and Jew Sing Lurt, nine years old, are in school. Third brother Sing Jun is seven years old.

Q: Has your husband Yung Hin Sen ever seen your brothers and sisters?
A: My husband saw my two sisters, Ah Dai and Ah Ngan, and younger brother Haw about five times in my husband's house.

Q: After your wedding, the three times that you went home to visit your family from your husband's village, did someone accompany you or did you go alone?
A: I went home to my family alone. When I returned to my husband's home, often I was accompanied by a brother or a sister.

(The last time Yung Ung returned to China was in C.R. 10th year [1921], 12th month, 10th day, on the SS *Golden State*. My father Yung Ung passed away in C.R. 18th year [1929], 7th month, at Chinese Hospital. Funeral services at Kwong Fook Sang. My mother Wong Shee passed away in C.R. 25th year, 1st month, 15th day, in Sunwui.)

Regarding correspondence and arrangements for the new immigrant to come to the United States.

Q: After your husband returned to the United States, how often and how much money did he send you for household expenses?
A: After my husband returned to the United States, he would send me about HK $200 four times a year, also ten or more letters.

Q: When he sent you money from the United States for household expenses, whom did he address it to and at what address?
A: He sent the money in my name Jew Law Ying to 73 Haw Lon Yin Street in Macao.

Q: When you sent letters to your husband in the United States, what address did you use?
A: In [C.R.] 26th, 27th year [1937, 1938], I sent letters to my husband at 1107 Stockton Street, care of Wah Ching.[40] After my husband said in his letters that he had become a partner in a Chinatown firm, Far East Company, I began sending my letters to him at 760 Sacramento Street.

Q: Do you have any schooling? Can you read and write letters?
A: I can read and write simple letters.

Q: Did you write the letters you sent your husband in the United States or did you have someone else write them for you?
A: All the letters I sent my husband I wrote myself. I did not have to ask anyone to write them for me.[41]

Q: Do you know what kind of work your husband does in the United States?
A: He is presently doing business at the Far East Company, located in San Francisco Chinatown at 760 Sacramento Street.[42]

Q: Do you know what your husband's position is at the Far East Company?
A: He is a salesman at the Far East Company.

Q: Do you know how long he has been with the Far East Company and how long he has held this position?
A: He has been there for over a year.

Q: Do you know what kind of work your husband did before he joined the Far East Company?
A: Before my husband joined the Far East Company, he worked for other people. (If you are asked where your husband worked, say you do not know.)

Q: Who financed your and your daughter's trip to the United States?
A: My husband sent the money to cover our traveling expenses to the United States.

Q: Whose decision was it for you and your daughter to come to the United States? Yours or your husband's?
A: It was my decision. I wrote and asked him to find a way for us to come to the United States.

Q: When did you write your husband to ask him to bring you two to the United States?
A: In C.R. 28th year [1939], the 9th month of the lunar calendar.

Q: When and who sent the photograph of you and your daughter to the United States to be used on the immigration documents?[43]
A: I sent the photograph of us to my husband in the 2nd month according to the lunar calendar.

Q: Aside from that photograph of you and your daughter for the application, what other photographs did you send your husband in the United States?
A: (You sent pictures four or five times. Best to give the dates you sent them. If not, just answer what really happened. Also mention that you sent them to me care of your uncle's address.)

Q: When did your husband Yung Hin Sen send you the visa papers and the money for the boat fare?
A: We were to leave on the 9th month, 18th day, on the SS President Garfield. He sent $800, care of Wing Hung Cheong Company.

Q: Whom did your husband write to in Hong Kong to arrange for your and your daughter's trip to Hong Kong and the boat trip to the United States?
A: My husband wrote Wing Hung Cheong Company and instructed Tom Share Dew in Hong Kong to make the arrangements for us.

Q: Before embarking for the United States, who wrote your husband about the name of the boat and dates of travel?
A: Before embarking for the United States, I wrote a letter to my husband informing him of the boat and dates of travel. (Describe the voyage as it happened.)

Q: Did your husband meet you and your daughter when your boat arrived at the San Francisco wharf?
A: (Answer according to the truth.)

Q: After you and your daughter arrived in the United States and were detained at the Immigration Station for interrogation, did your husband send you any money, letters, food, or clothing? Did you send any letters to him in San Francisco?
A: (Note that if you wrote letters, be sure not to mention any coaching notes.)

Q: How would you describe your husband Yung Hin Sen? His character, appearance, birth marks, gold teeth, etcetera?
A: (Dear Ying, I trust you remember what I look like so I need not write it down for you. Just tell the truth and there will be no mistakes.)

Q: *After you were married in China, did any Gold Mountain guests visit the two of you whom you knew or talked with?*[44]
A: None.

Q: *Besides your husband in the United States, is there anyone else in the United States who can testify that you are the wife of Yung Hin Sen?*
A: Besides my husband, there are my uncles in the United States who can testify. (In regard to your uncles, answer according to the truth.)

Q: *Who else can serve as your witnesses besides your husband Yung Hin Sen and the two named witnesses in the United States?*[45]
A: No one else.

Q: *When and where did you first meet the named witnesses? And for what reasons?*
A: [no written answer]

Q: *How many times did you see the named witnesses in China? Where and for what reasons?*
A: [no written answer]

Q: *How old are the named witnesses? Where were they born? Do they have wives and children?*
A: [no written answer]

Q: *Besides your husband Yung Hin Sen and the two named witnesses, whom else do you know in the United States?*
A: [no written answer]

Q: *When your uncles and their families who are now in the United States were in China, did they see you and can they act as your witnesses?*
A: Before I married and when I was young, I saw my uncles and their families. But when I married my husband, they were not in China to witness the marriage.

NOTE: If the interrogator asks the new immigrant when your uncles and their families went to the United States from China, and if they ever returned to China, be sure to check on the dates and answer accordingly.

Q: *What villages surround the village where you and your husband were married?*
A: [no written answer]

Q: *Are there any mountains, rivers, or bridges around the village?*
A: [no written answer]

The following is a map of Hin Bin village.[46] The new immigrant and all witnesses must not change anything in their answers in order to avoid discrepancies. If there's anything you do not understand or must change in this coaching book, you must notify me in writing before the new immigrant begins her voyage to the United States by boat.

Key to map:

1. Pai Shan village sits west and faces east. Trees are at the south end. [47]
2. The brick wall is approximately five feet tall.
3. North is to the left.
4. East is in front of the village.
5. South is to the right.
6. West is behind the village.
7. The woods at the rear are about ten yards away.
8. Behind Pai Shan village is a bamboo grove.

9. Trees.
10. Village gate (six feet).
11. Men's outhouse.
12. Women's outhouse.
13. Village shrine.
14. Vertical lane.
15. Horizontal lane.
16. Yung family ancestral hall.[48]
17. Tom Share Dew house. Two daughters named Ngun Dai and Wun Ching. Wong Shee (wife).[49]
18. Tom Yip Ghin house. He has three sons named Choi Kwong, Dat Kwong, You Gong, and one daughter named Ngun Ho.[50]
19. Tom Fat Yuet house. His son died. He has daughter Ngun Dai, one grandson named Ging Kau, and two granddaughters named Ah Gee and Ah Mei.[51]
20. Tom Mai Ming has one son named Yee Yeen and a daughter named Chin Oy.
21. Myself, Yung Hin Sen's house.
22. Yung Hin Gum has a wife Lee Shee and no children. The couple is in their thirties.[52]
23. Tom Kwong Yuan. One son Ah Mon, younger brother Choy Bun, and younger sister Ngun Gee.[53]
24. Tom Wing house. Two sons Bing Sun and Wun Tong. Daughter Kau Dai.[54]
25. Tom Yip Sou house. Has two sons named Wah Yuet and Wah You and a daughter Jwun Ho.[55]
26. Tom Yip Yee house. Has three sons Jun Hei, Yee Wun, and Tong Sing.
27. Village well.
28. If the interrogator asks about Pai Shan village, answer according to this map.
29. If he asks about your maternal grandmother's house in Macao, answer according to the truth.
30. I didn't ask about the names of the people in Hin Bin village.[56]

DOCUMENT 5: JEW LAW YING'S TESTIMONY, APRIL 2 TO 3, 1941

On March 13, 1941, after a month long journey by ship, my mother, Jew Law Ying, and my eldest sister, Bak Heong, arrived in San Francisco and were detained at the temporary immigration station at 801 Silver Avenue. My mother and my father were separately interrogated on April 2 and 3. According to the official transcript that follows, my mother was asked a total of 98 questions and my father, 102 questions. Although only a small percentage of the questions they were prepared to answer were asked, the line of questioning was similar to that in the coaching book. Both were asked to describe how they met and to give details about their wedding day, their respective family histories, the village where they were married, the house where they lived, and their stay in Hong Kong before my father returned to the United States. Many of the intimate questions asked, such as about the hotel room they shared in Hong Kong and their sleeping and eating arrangements at home, could only be answered by a truly married couple. They were also asked to identify three photographs and five letters my mother had sent my father as

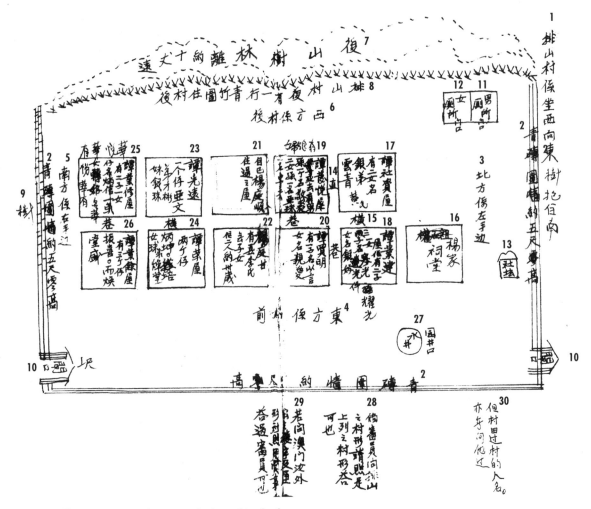

Map of Pai Shan village as it appeared in my mother's coaching book.

proof of their relationship. (So the coaching book compiler gave my mother the right advice to say she was literate and was therefore capable of writing letters to my father herself.)

Neither of my parents had to appear for questioning more than once, which meant there were no major discrepancies between their testimonies. Fortunately, the Sunwui dialect that my father was supposed to speak was very similar to the Heungshan dialect that he actually spoke, as noted by the interpreter in the transcript.[57] Thus, no suspicion was raised by his speech. As I have noted throughout the transcript, most of my mother's answers were true except for those involving my father's family background as Yung Hin Sen. In those incidences, she answered largely according to the coaching book. When she was not sure, as in the question about why my father would marry someone in another district, she said she did not know. Her one big lie regarding her own family background was to say that she had a third brother, Jew Sing Jun. Years later, she admitted to me that my father had instructed her to do so in order to create a slot by which he could help bring another relative over.

Because my father was a paper son and had testified twice before, upon arrival at Angel Island in 1921 and again in 1936 when he departed for China from Seattle, there was more reason for him to know his paper family history well and to lie in order to cover his tracks. But he obviously had not studied the coaching book as carefully as my mother. For example, he could not remember which direction the head of his village faced or whether my mother's grandparents were living in Macao or Dai Chek Hom village when he was introduced to my mother. He was also more cocky than my mother, as when he chose to focus on the teasing of the bride when describing their wedding day. But each time the interrogator tried to bait him with answers my mother had given, he was always quick with a retort. When he was confronted with a different answer my mother had given about the covering to the kitchen skylight at home, he replied, "If she said that she must be right because I was very seldom in the kitchen and paid very little attention to it." In contrast, my mother answered all the questions with assurance, even volunteering information at times. She felt she had every right to enter the United States. "Why should I be afraid?" she said to me fifty years later. "I wasn't a crook or a robber. If they let me land, fine. If not, too bad. Nothing to be scared about." Both of my parents' ease during the interrogation was noted in the summary and that, combined with their agreeable answers, contributed to their passing the test.

Document 5

RECORD OF BOARD OF SPECIAL INQUIRY HEARING

U. S. DEPARTMENT OF JUSTICE
Immigration and Naturalization Service
San Francisco, California

Manifest No. 40766/11-13 & 14   Date: April 2, 1941.

IN THE MATTER OF:	At a meeting of a BOARD OF SPECIAL INQUIRY held at San Francisco, Calif.
11-13: JEW SHEE (JEW LAW YING), Merchant's wife.	
11-14: YUNG BAK HEONG, Merchant's daughter.	PRESENT: Inspector R. F. VAUGHN, Chairman " H. W. CUNNINGHAM Member Clerk W. T. POSEY, Member
ex SS PRESIDENT COOLIDGE, 3/13/41 (vessel and date of arrival)	Interpreter J. Q. MOY

Travel documents presented, if any: For 11-13: American Consular Visa issued in the name of JEW SHEE (JEW LAW YING) as wife of domiciled Chinese Merchant under Sec. 3(6) of Immigration Act of 1924 issued at HONG KONG 2/4/41. The above also covers the accompanying daughter YUNG BAK HEONG, traveling as the daughter of domiciled Chinese Merchant.

Applicant(s) 11-13 is sworn and is informed of nature of perjury and penalty therefor. (If not sworn, state reasons: Applicant 11-14 is not sworn because of age; also too young to testify.

TO APPLICANT(S): If at any time you should fail to understand the interpreter or to understand the meaning of any statement or question in the course of these proceedings, you should so state at once. Do you understand? A. Yes.

Q: What are all the names you have ever used or have ever been known by? A: JEW SHEE nee JEW LAW YING; no others.

Mother (11-13) speaks for daughter (11-14): My daughter's name is YUNG BAK HEONG.

Q: What is your native dialect? A: WONG LUNG DOO Dialect of the HEUNG SHAN District.

Q: Is that the dialect in which you will testify at this hearing? A: Yes.

(IF NOT) Q: In what dialect will you testify, and why will you testify in a dialect other than your native one? A: _____

Q: Your right to enter the United States will be considered by this Board. The burden is upon you to prove that you are not subject to exclusion under any provision of the Immigration Laws, and all evidence in your behalf must be submitted at this hearing. There are present as witnesses your alleged husband YUNG HIN SEN. Are there any other persons anywhere in the United States who know of your claimed right to enter the United States? A: Yes.

(IF SO) Q: What are their names and addresses? A: CHUN WING and his wife WONG SHEE, now in San Francisco, address unknown; CHUN WAH, now in New York, address unknown; CHUN FOO, now in San Francisco with his wife LEONG SHEE; CHUN SHEOW, now in San Francisco, address unknown; CHUN MAY NGON, address unknown.

Q: What knowledge have those persons of your claimed right to enter the United States? A: They are my maternal relatives and have seen me in China.

Q: Do you wish to present such persons as witnesses, either here or at any immigration office nearer their residence? A: No.

Q: Have you any letters, documents or photographs which you wish to offer in support of your application for admission? A: No.

Q: At this hearing you may have a relative or an actual acquaintance present, who, if a witness, must have finished testifying. Do you wish to use this right? A: No.

PHYSICAL DESCRIPTION OF APPLICANT: 11-13. (Height in slippers).

Height 5 ft. 2½ in., complexion medium, hair black, eyes brown, marks or scars: Large flat scar upper left bridge of nose; ears pierced; four vaccination scars on upper left arm and three vaccination scars on upper right arm; flesh mole on right side of neck at collar line; mole underside of right wrist.

APPLICANT QUESTIONED, GIVES FOLLOWING MANIFEST DATA:

Age: 27 years, Chinese reckoning   Sex: Female
Race: Chinese

Date and place of birth: CR 4-6-13 (July 24, 1915) at DAI CHEUK HOM Village, WONG LUNG DOO Section, HEUNG SHAN District, China.

Marital status: Married.   Calling or occupation: Housewife.

Ability to speak, read, and write: Chinese only.

Last permanent residence: 73 HAW LON YIN JIN Street, MACAO, China.

Resided there how long: From CR 26 (1937) to CR 29-9 (Oct. 1940)

Name and address of nearest relative in country whence applicant came: My father JEW HIN GWING, DAI CHEUK HOM Village, HEUNG SHAN District, China.

Destined to (Name and address): My husband YUNG HIN SEN, Far East Company, 760 Sacramento Street, San Francisco, Calif.

Purpose for which coming to United States: To join my husband.

Length of intended stay in United States: Indefinite.

Whether ever arrested: No.

<u>Whether ever excluded and deported or arrested
and deported</u>: No.

(Other manifest questions and answers where applicable):

Q: When and where were you married? A: CR 26-1-20 (March 20, 1937) at HIN BIN VILLAGE, WONG LUNG DOO Section, HEUNG SHAN District, China.

Q: What are all the names you know for your husband? A: YUNG HIN SEN or YUNG NGIP JICK; no others.

Q: On what grounds do you seek admission to the United States? A: As the wife of a merchant.

Q: Of what country do you claim nationality? A: China.

Q: How many children have you ever had? A: One daughter, no sons.

Q: Did you ever have a child that died? A: No.

Q: Did you ever adopt a child? A: No.

Q: Do you have any documentary evidence showing your marriage to YUNG HIN SEN? A: No.[58]

Q: By what custom were you married? A: Old Chinese custom.

Q: When did you first see your husband? A: In CR 25-12-26 or 27 (Feb. 7 or 8, 1937), in NOM SAN Village, WONG LUNG DOO Section, HEUNG SHAN District, China.

Q: Did you see your husband before the actual marriage ceremony? A: Yes. My maternal grandparents CHUN HONG DAI and LEONG SHEE returned to the NOM SAN Village, our ancestral village, from MACAO in the latter part of CR 25 (1936) to spend the New Year holiday there. Shortly after their arrival there from MACAO I also went to that village at my maternal grandfather's request from the DAI CHEUK HOM Village. On CR 25-12-26 or 27 (Feb. 7 or 8, 1937), or the day after my arrival in the NOM SAN Village, my husband called at our home there and my maternal grandfather introduced us to each other.

INSPECTOR R. B. JONES REPLACES H. W. CUNNINGHAM AS MEMBER OF THE BOARD.

BY MEMBER R. B. JONES: I have familiarized myself with the evidence thus far adduced in this case.

Q: Where was the marriage ceremony actually held? A: The marriage took place in a house in the HIN BIN Village rented by my husband from YUNG YIP GHIN.[59]

Q: Is YUNG YIP GHIN any relative of yourself or your husband? A: No. He is a resident of the HIN BIN Village.

Q: On the day of the ceremony, how did you arrive at the house of YUNG YIP GHIN? A: By sedan chair.

Q: Did you walk into the house then or were you carried in? A: After I alighted from the sedan chair, my husband and I walked together to the threshold of the house. My husband then entered the house, after which a woman attendant who came with me carried me across the threshold into the house.

Q: Will you describe your marriage ceremony? A: My husband preceded me into our bedroom; then I was carried into that room by a woman attendant. Next my husband left our bedroom to mingle with the guests who had gathered in the house. I remained in the bedroom and occasionally I left the bedroom to appear before guests at their request and served tea to them; occasionally guests would come into our bedroom to look at me. This lasted until a very late hour that night. The following morning at about 11 AM my husband and I went to the ancestral hall in the HIN BIN Village, and there I served tea to some guests who had gathered there. After having done this, we returned to our house, and at about 1 PM I returned to my native village accompanied by two women attendants who had accompanied me from my native village; this return trip to my native village was made in a sedan chair owned by two men. There was a feast held on the day of my marriage but before my arrival in the HIN BIN Village. That was the only feast held in connection with my wedding.

Q: At any time was there any ancestral worship in connection with the ceremony of your marriage? A: No.

Q: Where did your husband stay after you returned to your home village following the ceremony? A: He remained in the HIN BIN Village and I returned to the HIN BIN Village the same day that I returned to my home village.

Q: Did you present your husband with any dowry? A: Yes, bedding, a bureau, a table, two basin stands, two basins, two chairs and two wooden tubs.

Q: Did your husband present you or your family with any gift at the time of your wedding? A: On my first trip to my native village after my marriage, I brought home to my parents some cakes from my husband. That is all.

Q: How long did you remain in the HIN BIN Village after your wedding took place? A: We made our home there for about three and one-half months; we lived in the house rented from YUNG YIP GHIN.

Q: After you left the HIN BIN Village where did you go to then? A: Then my husband and I went to MACAO where I remained with my maternal grandfather.

TO INTERPRETER J. Q. MOY:
    Q: In what dialect has the applicant testified? A: WONG LUNG DOO.

AT THE DIRECTION OF THE INSPECTOR IN CHARGE, INTERPRETER EDWAR LEE REPLACES J. Q. MOY.[60]

THROUGH INTERPRETER EDWAR LEE:

Q: Have you understood the previous interpreter? A: Yes.

Q: Have you ever visited the native village of your husband, the SIN DUNG Village? A: No.

Q: How does it happen that your husband married you, your home being in the HEUNG SHAN District, rather than someone from or nearer to his native village in the SUN WUEY District? A: I was introduced to my husband by my maternal grandfather. I don't know how they knew each other.[61]

At this point, because of constant interruptions by applicant 11-4 [Bak Heong], board is moved to Matrons' quarters and hearing is recorded in shorthand.

Q: Was the home in MACAO to which you went after leaving the HIN BIN Village in CR 26 (1937) at the same address as that at which you lived just before you came to this country? A: Yes, after living at the HIN BIN Village for three and one-half months I went to my maternal grandfather's house in Macao and lived there until I left for HONG KONG (Changes) After I and my husband left the HIN BIN Village together for MACAO, then on the same day we arrived in MACAO my husband left MACAO by himself for HONG KONG, but he came back five days later and took me to HONG KONG, and we lived in HONG KONG together for a little over three months; then my husband left to return to the United States, and after he left I returned to my maternal grandfather's house in MACAO and I lived there until I left for the United States.[62]

Q: What are the names of your maternal grandparents? A: My maternal grandfather is CHUN HONG DAI or CHUN LUNG, 70 odd years old, now living in MACAO. My maternal grandmother is LEONG SHEE, 70 odd years old, living in MACAO.

Q: What are the names of your paternal grandparents? A: I don't know my paternal grandfather's name. He died when I was very young. My paternal grandmother is LEONG SHEE, 70 odd years old and now living in the DAI CHEUK HOM Village.

Q: Describe your parents. A: My father is JEW HIN GWING or JEW SUN, 48 years old, living at DAI CHEUK HOM Village. My mother is CHUN SHEE or CHUN SUEY KUM, 48 years old, living at DAI CHEUK HOM Village.

Q: How many brothers and sisters have you? A: Three brothers and three sisters.

Q: Describe them. A: My brothers are—

JEW SING HAW, 12 years old;
JEW SING LUT, 10 years old;
JEW SING JUN, 8 years old.[63]

My sisters are—
JEW NGOON JEE, 27 years old; she is my twin;
JEW JIN DAI, 25 years old;
JEW NGAN BUN, 23 years old.

All are living in the DAI CHEUK HOM Village except JEW NGOON JEE, my twin sister, who is married to a WONG family man of the SIU CHEUK HOM Village.

Q: Have you ever met any of your husband's relatives? A: None, except the wife of my husband's brother YUNG HING BEW.

Q: Where did you meet her? A: At the HIN BIN Village at the time of my marriage.

Q: Describe the wife of your husband's brother. A: JEW SHEE, about 39 years old; she lives at the SIN DUNG Village, SUN WUEY District.[64]

Q: Is she the only one of your husband's relatives, through marriage or otherwise, who attended your wedding? A: Yes.[65]

Q: Who of your own relatives attended your wedding? A: None of my maternal relatives were present at my marriage. My husband had invited the HIN BIN Villagers to attend the wedding and there were about 30 odd guests at the wedding feast.

Q: Had JEW SHEE, the wife of YUNG HING BEW, made the trip to the HIN BIN Village just to be present at the marriage ceremony? A: According to my husband, she came the day before my marriage to help attend to the details of the wedding and entertain the guests, and she remained at the HIN BIN Village for about ten days and then returned to the SIN DUNG Village.

Q: Do you know if she traveled alone from the SIN DUNG Village to the HIN BIN Village? A: As far as I know she was alone.

Q: Where was her husband at that time? A: He was in the United States.

Q: What are the names of your alleged husband's parents? A: His father was YUNG AH DUNG. He died before my marriage. I don't know when. His mother was WONG SHEE. She also died before my marriage but I don't know when she died.[66]

Q: How many brothers and sisters that you know of does your husband have? A: One brother and no sisters.[67]

Q: Please describe the house of your maternal grandparents in which you were living at MACAO? A: It is a two story residential building, constructed of brick and faced with cement, and that entire house is occupied by my maternal grandfather's family. The ground floor contains a parlor, three bedrooms, a kitchen, two toilets, a bathroom and also a back yard. The second floor contains three bedrooms, a hallway and a sun deck.

Q: Did your husband pay a visit to your maternal grandparents' home in MACAO before proceeding on to HONG KONG the first time? A: Yes. We arrived at my maternal grandfather's house together in the morning from the HIN BIN Village and my husband stayed there with me until the afternoon of the same day when he left for HONG KONG.

Q: After your husband's first visit to HONG KONG how long did your husband remain in MACAO before you both went to HONG KONG? A: He returned from HONG KONG to my maternal grandfather's house at about 12 Noon and then he explained to my maternal grandfather that he was taking me to HONG KONG to stay for a while, and we left at about 2 AM of that same day for HONG KONG.

Q: What was the reason for this sudden departure for HONG KONG? A: I don't know.[68]

Q: Did you know in advance of the day you departed for HONG KONG that it was anticipated you would go there? A: Yes, he wrote to me while he was in HONG KONG and said he was coming back on the 15th of that month, and that he would then take me to HONG KONG.

Q: Did you know at that time that you were going to live in HONG KONG for an extended period of time? A: That letter did not say how long but he said that he would take me to HONG KONG to live.

Q: Where did you stay while in HONG KONG? A: We stopped at the LOOK HOY HUNG Hotel, which is near the waterfront, and we stayed at that hotel the entire period of about three months.

Q: Do you know the address of that hotel? A: No.

Q: Which floor of that hotel did you live on? A: The second floor.

Q: How tall was that hotel building? A: I don't know for certain but I think it is about four stories high.

Q: Did you occupy one or more rooms in that hotel? A: Only one room.

Q: Did you sleep together in the same bed or in separate beds? A: In one bed.

Q: Was water obtainable in your room at that hotel? A: Yes.

Q: What was your husband doing in HONG KONG during that three month period? A: He had no occupation.

Q: How did you spend your time then? A: Sometimes we went out walking and sometimes we went to a show.

Q: Did you attend motion picture theaters in HONG KONG? A: Yes, and to a Chinese show once.

Q: Did you make any special trips to a place just outside of HONG KONG for a day's journey? A: Yes. My husband and I rode on the ferry across the Bay to WONG GOCK, and on another occasion we took the train up to the peaks.

Q: Did your husband have any business associations that you know of while in HONG KONG? A: No, not to my knowledge.

Q: Did you return to your maternal grandparents' home in MACAO alone after leaving HONG KONG? A: Yes.

Q: Where did you last see your husband when he left for the United States? A: At the pier in HONG KONG after he had taken me down to the steamer which he took to return to the United States.

Q: About what time of day did your husband board the steamer for the United States? A: I don't remember the exact time but it was in the afternoon. He took me down to the steamer about 12 Noon or 1 PM and I was with him at the steamer for about one or two hours, and then he took me back to the pier and I bade him goodbye there. The steamer was supposed to have sailed at 4 PM but actually it did not sail at that hour because the time was changed and I understand it did not sail until the next morning. In the meantime, I returned to the WING HUNG CHUNG Company, which is my husband's headquarters in HONG KONG. At the time my husband and I left for the steamer we had already taken our baggage out of the LOOK HOY HUNG Hotel to the WING HUNG CHUNG Company. Then on the afternoon of that same day I returned to MACAO by myself.

Q: Did you have any photographs taken while you were in HONG KONG? A: Yes, one; that was when I and my husband were photographed together.

Q: (Showing Exhibit "A") Is this the picture which was made in HONG KONG? A: Yes.

Q: Who are the persons shown in this picture? A: Myself at the left and my husband at the right.

Q: (Showing photographs marked Exhibits "B" and "C") Who are these people and when was this picture taken? A: Both of them are pictures of myself and my daughter. Exhibit "B" was taken when my daughter was about one hundred days old, and that photo was taken in MACAO. Exhibit "C" was taken just when my daughter was beginning to learn to walk, and that photo was also taken in MACAO.

Q: (Showing letter marked Exhibit "D") Do you recognize this letter? A: Yes, that is a letter written by me to my husband acknowledging receipt of the affidavits which he had sent to me and also the money which he sent along with the

Exhibit A. Jew Law Ying and Yung Hin Sen [Tom Yip Jing] in 1937.

affidavit which was sent in care of a friend at the WING HUNG CHUNG Company.

Q: (Showing letter marked Exhibit "E") Do you recognize this letter? A: Yes. This is also a letter written by me to my husband acknowledging receipt of the letter which he sent on the 23rd instant through my maternal grandfather. I also informed him that I had arrived in HONG KONG with our daughter and together we went to see the American Consul regarding my papers, and that I would again inform him as to the date of sailing for the United States.

Q: (Showing letter marked Exhibit "F") Do you recognize this letter? A: Yes. This is a letter which I wrote to my husband informing him that our daughter YUNG BAK HEONG had been undergoing treatment for her eyes by a doctor and that everything is all right now and that we would be permitted to sail and that we would board the PRESIDENT COOLIDGE for the United States.

Q: (Showing letter marked Exhibit "G") Do you recognize this letter? A: Yes. This is also a letter written by me to my husband informing him definitely that we were coming aboard the PRESIDENT COOLIDGE on the 22nd day of this month.

Q: (Showing letter marked Exhibit "H") Do you recognize this letter? A: Yes. This is also a letter written by me to my husband, sent by airmail, and in which I acknowledged the letter which he sent to me through my maternal grandfather by airmail and mailed together with $100, and in his letter to me he mentioned something about that if I should run short of money to borrow it from his friend HOM SHARE JOO, the man who looked after my transportation, and in this letter I told him I had spoken of this matter to his friend.

Q: During your stay in MACAO did your husband send regular remittances to support you while you were living with your maternal grandparents after your husband's return to the United States? A: Yes. He sent me some about three or four times a year and in regular sums and amounting to some $200 or $300 a year.

Q: How large a village is the HIN BIN Village where you were married? A: It is a village of about ten houses.

Q: Which way does the village face? A: East, and the head is at the north.

Q: How many rows of buildings are there in the HIN BIN Village? A: The houses are arranged in six rows. The ancestral hall is the first building at the north, and each of the other rows has two dwellings. Including the ancestral hall, there are 11 houses in that village.

Q: Where is the house located which you rented from YUNG YIP GHIN? A: The second house, fourth row from the north.

Q: Please describe the house in which you lived in the HIN BIN Village? A: It is a one story adobe house containing two bedrooms, two kitchens, a parlor and an open court, and the house has a front entrance which opens into the open court.[69]

Q: Where did you and your husband sleep while you were living in the HIN BIN Village? A: In the north bedroom.

Q: Did anyone else occupy this house with the two of you? A: No, except for that ten days when my husband's brother's wife stayed with us. During that period she slept in the south bedroom.[70]

Q: Where were the meals prepared? A: In the north kitchen.

Q: Are there any lofts or balconies in the bedrooms? A: There is a loft running crosswise in each of the bedrooms but no balconies or sundecks.

Q: Were there outside windows in this house? A: There is a small opening in the outside wall of each bedroom and it has a little wooden door, but it could hardly be called a window.

Q: Were there skylights in that house? A: One in each of the bedrooms and one in each of the kitchens. Those in the bedrooms are covered with glass and so is the skylight in the south kitchen, but the one in the north kitchen has no covering and is used for smoke to escape.

Q: Is the stove in the north kitchen portable or built-in? A: The north kitchen is equipped with a permanent stove but not the south kitchen.

APPLICANT VOLUNTEERS: During the period that we lived in this house, some of my younger brothers visited me in this house.

Q: During your stay in this house were there any special dinners or feasts or celebrations held during that three and one-half month period? A: No.

Exhibit B. *Daughter Yung Bak Heong and mother Jew Law Ying in 1938. Chinese message at bottom reads: To Bak Heong's daddy, from wife Law Ying and daughter Bak Heong.*

Q: When your younger brothers visited you did they remain overnight at all or did they always return the same day? A: They had to stay overnight.

Q: Did you and your husband make any visits overnight or longer away from the HIN BIN Village during the time you were staying there? A: No, but the third day after my marriage I returned to my home at the DAI CHEUK HOM Village, but I returned on the same day, and one month after my marriage I made another trip back to my home village and I was there for about three or four days.

Q: How far is the DAI CHEUK HOM Village from the HIN BIN Village? A: Eight or nine *li*[71] to the north of the HIN BIN Village.

Q: Where did you do your marketing while you were at the HIN BIN Village? A: I did not do any marketing during the period I was at this village, but my husband did the marketing at this time and he said he marketed at the DOW MOON Market.

Q: Have you ever been to the DOW MOON Market? A: When I returned to my native village I passed by the DOW MOON Market.

Q: How large is that market? A: It is a very large market but I don't know the number of stores there.

Q: Was your husband with you when you last said goodbye to your relatives in the DAI CHEUK HOM Village before departing for MACAO and HONG KONG? A: About a month before he finally left the HIN BIN Village I made one visit back to my native village and I was there for four days. I went by myself on that trip.

Q: Do you know your husband's occupation in this country? A: He is a merchant and salesman at the YUEN TUNG Company (Far East), 760 Sacramento Street, San Francisco, Calif.[72]

Q: If you are admitted to this country where will you live? A: I will live with my husband. He will provide the place for me but I don't know exactly where.

Q: (Showing photographs of YUNG HIN SEN and JEW LAW YING attached to the affidavit of the alleged husband and father in present file) Who are these people? A: My husband YUNG HIN SEN and myself.

Q: (Showing photographs of applicants on Foreign Service Form No. 257) Who are these persons? A: My daughter YUNG BAK HEONG and myself.

Q: (Showing photograph of YUNG HIN SEN attached to Form 432, dated 10/28/36 in file 12017/51188) Who is this? A: My husband YUNG HIN SEN.

Q: (Showing photograph of YUNG UNG attached to Form 432, dated Nov. 30, 1921 in file 22447/3-20) Who is this person? A: I don't know.

NOTE: Throughout the hearing, although unable to testify, YUNG BAK HEONG (11-14) evidenced that she considered applicant 11-13, JEW SHEE (JEW LAW YING) to be her mother by clinging to the mother and resisting any attempt to part them even momentarily.

TO OTHER BOARD MEMBERS:
    Q: Do you wish to question the applicant?
    A: BY MEMBER R. B. JONES: No.
        BY MEMBER POSEY: No.

TO APPLICANT:
    Q: Have you anything further you wish to state? A: No.

THROUGH INTERPRETER M. J. LEE:
    Q: Have you understood the interpreter? A: Yes.

TO INTERPRETER EDWAR LEE:
    Q: In what dialect has the applicant testified? A: WONG LUNG DOO.

SIGNATURE OF APPLICANT 11:13 [Jew Law Ying in Chinese characters] DISMISSED.

I hereby certify that the foregoing is a true and correct transcript of shorthand notes taken on April 2, 1941, notebook 18015.

Stenographer

HEARING RESUMED APRIL 3, 1941. (Board Room)
    Interpreter H. K. TANG.

ALLEGED HUSBAND AND FATHER SWORN AND ADMONISHED THAT IF AT ANY TIME HE SHOULD FAIL TO UNDERSTAND THE INTERPRETER TO IMMEDIATELY SO STATE; ADVISED AS TO THE NATURE OF AND PENALTY FOR THE CRIME OF PERJURY.

INSPECTOR H. F. DUFF REPLACES R. B. JONES AS MEMBER OF THE BOARD.

BY MEMBER DUFF: I have familiarized myself with the evidence thus far adduced in this case.

Q: What are all your names? A: YUNG HIN SEN or YUNG NGIP JICK. I am also known as Tommy; no others.[73]

Q: What is your natural dialect? A: SUN WUEY Dialect.[74]

Q: Will you use that dialect throughout this examination? A: Yes.

Q: What is your age and place of birth? A: 39 years old, Chinese reckoning, born at SIN DUNG Village, SUN WUEY District, China.[75]

Q: What is your birthdate? A: KS 29-7-15 (Sept. 6, 1903).

Q: How many times have you been out of the United States? A: Just once.

Q: Will you describe that trip to China? A: I departed from Seattle on January 8, 1937 and returned to Seattle Oct. 14, 1937.

Q: What papers have you to show your right to remain in the United States? A: I forgot to bring my Certificate of Identity.

NOTE: Witness is subject of SF file 12017/51188 which shows his initial arrival and departure through port of Seattle as claimed. He is also subject of Seattle file 7032/3392, which shows his return through that port as claimed. Letter from this office to Seattle dated Jan. 6, 1937, indicates that witness is subject of C.I. No. 35835 but no receipt for such C.I. appears to be in witnesses' file.

Q: What are your present occupation and address? A: I am a merchant and member of the YUEN TUNG Company, 760 Sacramento St., San Francisco, Calif., and I live at No. 50-A Beckett Street, San Francisco.[76]

Q: What is your position in that firm? A: Salesman and Stock Clerk.

Q: Since your hearing on Sept. 6, 1940 in which you applied for preexamination of your status in anticipation of the arrival of your alleged wife and daughter, have you daily been occupied in your business at the firm above mentioned? A: Yes.

Q: Why are you appearing here today? A: To testify for my wife JEW LAW YING and my daughter YUNG BAK HEONG, applicants for admission.

Q: Will you please describe your parents? A: My father was YUNG DUNG or YUNG JING YIN. He died in the Chinese Hospital in San Francisco in CR 18 (1929). My mother was WONG SHEE; she died in my native village in China in CR 25-1-15 (Feb. 7, 1936).[77]

Q: Do you have in your possession the Certificate of Identity which was issued to your father and which he presumably had at the time of his death? A: No. If my father had a Certificate of Identity it might be in my older brother's possession.

Q: Do you have regular contact with your older brother? A: No, not in recent years. I have not seen him for the past five years and I don't know where he is at the present time.

Q: Then you have no means that you know of of ascertaining whether or not he has that Certificate of Identity in his possession? A: No, I have not.

Q: It is necessary for the completion of the records of this Service that there be on file a death certificate and the certificate of identity which belonged to your father. It appears that neither has been submitted to this Service as yet. Will you arrange to have a death certificate prepared and forwarded through your attorney and if possible make an effort to procure the Certificate of Identity belonging to your father and submit it also to your attorney that both documents may become a matter of record at this station? A: Yes, I understand and will do so.

Q: Of what country do you claim nationality? A: China.

Q: Have you registered under the Alien Registration Act? A: Yes.

NOTE: Witness presents Alien Registration receipt card bearing No. 2549494; same is returned.

Q: How many brothers or sisters have you ever had? A: One brother, no sisters.[78]

Q: Describe your brother. A: YUNG HING BIEW, 41 years old, now in the United States, but I don't know at what place. He is married.[79]

Q: What is his wife's name? A: JEW SHEE, now living in my native village in China.

Q: Where did you first meet your wife JEW LAW YING? A: I first met her in her maternal grandfather's home in NOM SAN Village, WONG LUNG DOO Section, HEUNG SHAN District, China, in CR 25, the latter part of the 12th month (January 1937).

Q: Were your wife's maternal grandparents living in the NOM SAN Village before your arrival there? A: No, (Changes) Yes.[80]

Q: Where was your wife living at that time? A: In DAI CHEUK HOM Village, WONG LUNG DOO Section, China.

Q: Where was the marriage ceremony actually held? A: In HIN BIN Village, WONG LUNG DOO Section. I rented the house to get married there and lived there several months.[81]

Q: Who did you rent that house from? A: YUNG YIP GHIN.

Q: Is YUNG YIP GHIN any relative of yours? A: No.

Q: On the day of the ceremony how did your wife arrive at the house in HIN BIN Village owned by YUNG YIP GHIN? A: In a sedan chair.

Q: What took place immediately after your wife alighted from the sedan chair? A: She went into the house and into the bride's chamber—she was carried into the house by a woman. She went into her chamber and sat there in the presence of some women who accompanied her from her home

village and also some of my own friends who were invited to come there to see the bride. Those persons in the bride's chamber were teasing the bride by asking her for tea, cakes, lucky money, etc.

Q: Did your wife occasionally leave the bedroom and visit in the other part of the house? A: Yes, she went out to the parlor and to the kitchen and served tea.

Q: What occurred the following morning that was a part of the ceremony? A: The next morning some old people of the village came to the house to tease her again and then she went out to the well to fetch water; when she came back they again teased her. After that she returned to her parents' home and came back to my home that same evening.

Q: Your wife describes an event which took place in the ancestral hall of the village on that morning. Do you have any recollection of such an event? A: Yes, she did go to the ancestral hall in the company of her women attendants, but she was there for only a short time. I did not go there.

Q: Were there any feasts held in connection with your marriage? A: Yes. There was only one banquet and that took place on the day of the marriage at about 5 PM or 6 PM and the banquet tables were set in the ancestral hall.

Q: At what time of the day did your wife first arrive at the house of YUNG YIP GHIN? A: About 6 PM.

Q: Was there at any time any ancestral worship in connection with your marriage ceremony? A: No.

Q: Did your wife present you with any dowry? A: Yes, one wardrobe, two chairs, one table, one letter trunk, one suitcase, one wash basin stand, one wash basin, some clothes, one gold bracelet and one gold necklace, one spittoon (Changes) two spittoon.[82]

Q: Did you present a gift either to your wife or any members of her family at the time of your marriage? A: No.

Q: How long did you remain in the HIN BIN Village after your wedding took place? A: About three and one-half months.

Q: How large is the HIN BIN Village? A: Ten houses and one ancestral hall.

Q: Which way does the village face? A: East.

Q: Where is the head? A: I don't know.[83]

Q: How many rows of buildings are there in the HIN BIN Village? A: There are five rows of dwelling houses with two houses in each row, occupying the first and second house spaces; the ancestral hall stands in a row by itself at the north end of the village.

Q: Will you please describe the house in which you lived in the HIN BIN Village? A: That house is the second house, third row of dwellings counting from the north. It is a regular five room house, built of dirt, tile floors in all rooms, the open court is paved with stone; it has one outside entrance, located on the east side or front.

Q: Which bedroom did you occupy in that house in the HIN BIN Village? A: The bedroom on the north side.

Q: Did anyone else occupy this house with the two of you at any time? A: No, except my brother's wife who stayed there for ten days and sometimes my wife's young relatives came there and stayed with us for a day or two.[84]

Q: Did JEW SHEE, your brother's wife, make the trip to the HIN BIN Village from the SIN DUNG Village just to be present at the marriage ceremony? A: Yes.

Q: Did she make that trip to HIN BIN Village and back again alone? A: Yes, except when she came I went to the boat landing to meet her, and when she returned home I also took her to the boat landing.

Q: Where were the meals prepared in your home in the HIN BIN Village? A: In the kitchen on the north side of the house.

Q: Are there any lofts or balconies in that house? A: Each bedroom has an L-shaped loft and the parlor has an ancestral loft.

Q: Was anything kept in the loft in the parlor during your stay there? A: Yes, there is a piece of red paper with writings representing the YUNG family ancestors, and in front of it is a lamp and an incense burner.

Q: Are any of your ancestors commemorated by that piece of red paper? A: No.

Q: Are there any outside windows in that house? A: Yes, on the outside wall of each bedroom there is a window.

Q: What covers the windows you mentioned? A: It is closed by a wooden door.

Q: Where there any skylights in that house? A: Each bedroom has one skylight and each kitchen has one and they are all covered with glass.

Q: Is the cooking stove in the north kitchen portable or built-in? A: That kitchen has a stationary double stove and two portable stoves, one large and one small.

Q: How does the smoke escape from the permanent stove or built-in stove? A: The smoke rises to the ceiling and through the side openings on the roof.

Q: Are you sure that there is a glass covering over the skylight in the north kitchen? A: Yes.

Q: Your wife states that the north kitchen skylight is not equipped with glass and that the smoke from the stove goes out through that skylight. What do you say to that? A: If she said that she must be right because I was very seldom in the kitchen and paid very little attention to it.[85]

Q: How did you occupy your time while you were in the HIN BIN Village for that three months? A: I visited around in the neighboring villages, in DOW MOON Market and on the hills nearby, and at night quite often I went to the ancestral hall and chatted with people there.

Q: Did your wife go with you to DOW MOON Market at any time? A: No.

Q: Who did the marketing while you were in the HIN BIN Village? A: I did.

Q: During your stay in the HIN BIN Village did you and your wife make any visits together to any other village? A: No.

Q: What trips, if any, did your wife make that you know of without you during that three and one-half months period? A: She made four or five trips to her native village. That is all.

Q: How far is the DAI CHEUK HOM Village from the HIN BIN Village? A: About 8 or 9 lis.

Q: What are the names of your wife's maternal grandparents? A: Her maternal grandfather is CHUN HONG DAI and her maternal grandmother is LEONG SHEE. They are now living in MACAO.

Q: Do you know the names of her paternal grandparents? A: No.

Q: What are the names of your wife's parents? A: Her father is JEW HIN GWING, about 49 years old, now living in his home village in China or my wife's native village. Her mother is CHUN SHEE, 49 years old, now living with her parents in MACAO.

Q: How many brothers and sisters does your wife have that you know of? A: She has three brothers and three sisters.

Q: Describe them. A: Her brothers are—

> JEW SING HAW, 13 years old;
> JEW SING LUT (LEK), 11 years old;
> JEW SING JUN, 9 years old.[86]

Her sisters are—

> JEW JEE, 27 years old;
> JEW DAI, 25 years old;
> JEW NGAN, 23 years old.

I know her three brothers are now in MACAO as refugees. JEW JEE, twin sister of my wife, is married to a man in SIU CHEUK HOM Village. I don't know where JEW DAI and JEW NGAN are living at present.

Q: After leaving the HIN BIN Village, where did you and your wife go? A: We went to MACAO and a few hours later I went to HONG KONG, but my wife stayed with her maternal grandparents in MACAO for a few days. Afterwards I returned to MACAO to take her to HONG KONG with me.

Q: When you returned from HONG KONG to get your wife, had she been previously notified that you anticipated taking her back to HONG KONG with you? A: Yes.

Q: How was she notified? A: I sent her a letter.

Q: Where did you stay when you were in HONG KONG with your wife? A: At the LOOK HOY HUNG Hotel.

Q: Do you know the address of that hotel? A: It is on HOY PONG Street, but I don't know the number.

Q: How far is that from the waterfront? A: HOY PONG Street is the waterfront street.

Q: What floor of that hotel did you live on? A: Second floor.

Q: How many rooms did you occupy in that hotel? A: Just one.

Q: Did you have twin beds or one bed in that room? A: Just one bed.

Q: How did you spend your time while you were in HONG KONG? A: I took my wife to visit different places, such as show houses, top of the HONG KONG Mountain, KOWLOON and other places of interest.

Q: How long did you remain in HONG KONG? A: A little over three months.

Q: Did you accompany your wife back to MACAO before you departed for the United States? A: No. My wife returned to MACAO alone.

Q: Where did you last see your wife before leaving HONG KONG? A: At the wharf at KOWLOON when I boarded the steamer for San Francisco.

Q: Did you have any photographs taken while you were in HONG KONG of yourself and your wife? A: Yes.

Q: (Showing Exhibit "A"): Who are the persons shown in this photograph? A: My wife JEW LAW YING and myself.

Q: (Showing Exhibits marked "B" and "C"): Who are these persons? A: Exhibit "B": My daughter YUNG BAK HEONG and my wife JEW SHEE. Exhibit "C": My daughter YUNG BAK HEONG and my wife.

Q: (Showing letter marked Exhibit "D"): Do you recognize this letter? A: Yes. It is a letter written to me by my wife.

Substance of letter by Interpreter H. K. TANG:

This letter is dated Oct. 9, 1940 and addressed to husband HIN SEN from wife LAW YING acknowledging the receipt of a letter sent her by airmail containing $100 HONG KONG money. She says she was happy to know that affidavits were being prepared for her and her daughter to come to the United States. She was also glad to know that $800 HONG KONG money had been sent to WING HUNG CHUNG Company in HONG KONG asking HOM SHARE DEW to make arrangements for her and her daughter to come to the United States. She said that everything was so high in China and asked that her husband send her $200 HONG KONG money for her expenses.

Q: Showing letter marked Exhibit "E"): Do you recognize this letter? A: Yes. This letter was also written to me by my wife.

Substance of letter by Interpreter:

This letter is dated Nov. 3, 1940, written to HIN SEN by his wife LAW YING stating that she had received his letter sent to her through her maternal grandfather. She says she and her daughter BAK HEONG were staying at the WING HUNG CHUNG Co. in HONG KONG; that she had already written to him about the affidavits. She said that she had been to the American Consulate and secured the approval of the American Consul, but the doctor says that BAK HEONG's eyes had to be treated first; so for that reason they had to wait in HONG KONG for a little while longer.

Q: (Showing letter marked Exhibit "F"): Do you recognize this letter? A: Yes. This letter was written to me by my wife.

Substance of letter by Interpreter:

This letter is dated Feb. 3, 1941, written to HIN SEN by his wife LAW YING acknowledging the receipt of his letter from the United States under date of Jan. 8. She says that her daughter BAK HEONG has had her eyes re-examined, and that the doctor has passed her, but the American Consul says that the affidavits were not quite ready and asked her to go and see him a week later. Mr. HOM SHARE DEW has tentatively engaged passage for her and her daughter on the SS PRESIDENT COOLIDGE sailing at the end of the month, so when the date of sailing is definitely known she will let him know by letter again.

Q: (Showing letter marked Exhibit "G"): Do you recognize this letter? A: Yes. This letter is dated Feb. 21, 1941 and was written to me by my wife.

Substance of letter by Interpreter:

This is a letter written by LAW YING to her husband YUNG HIN SEN, dated Feb. 21, 1941. The letter says that her daughter BAK HEONG's eyes have been cured and that the American Consul has given them permission to sail on Feb. 22 for the United States on the SS PRESIDENT COOLIDGE. She says that Mr. HOM SHARE DEW has made all arrangements for them and she asks that when she and her daughter arrive he will meet them on this side.

Q: (Showing letter marked Exhibit "H"): Do you recognize this letter? A: Yes. This letter was written to me by my wife.

Substance of letter by Interpreter:

This letter is dated Jan. 1, 1941, written by LAW YING to her husband HIN SEN acknowledging the receipt of a letter from him through her maternal grandfather in MACAO and two air mail letters received on Dec. 15, together with $100 HONG KONG money. She says that she and her daughter BAK HEONG were then staying at the WING HUNG CHUNG Co. in HONG KONG and that as soon as arrangements were completed she and her daughter would leave for the United States. She says that she had engaged another doctor to treat the daughter's eyes guaranteeing cure for $100. She has taken treatments for several weeks, but the doctor says that in another week she will be cured. She says that the husband's friend has told her that if necessary he was willing to advance her some money for her expenses. As soon as BAK HEONG has passed her eye examination and as soon as a definite date of their sailing for the United States is known she will let you know by letter again, so don't be anxious about them.

Q: When you were last in China did you visit your home village, SIN DUNG? A: Yes, once.

Q: At what time during your stay in China did you visit your home village? A: I visited that village as soon as I arrived in HONG KONG.

Q: Has your wife ever been to SIN DUNG Village? A: No.

Q: When you returned through Seattle in 1937, you gave the name of your wife, her age and your marriage date and showed her as residing at the time of your re-entry into this country in the SIN DUNG Village, SUN WUEY District. How do you suppose that information got into the record? A: I made a mistake and I cannot explain it.

Q: Would it not seem a little unusual to tie the thought of your marriage which took place in the HIN BIN Village with the name of a village utterly different? A: I am a native of SIN DUNG Village and possibly I was thinking of my own home.[87]

Q: If your wife is admitted to this country where will she live? A: She and our daughter will live with me in San Francisco, but perhaps for a short time we will have to stay in a hotel until we find a place to live.

Q: Do you intend then to continue to support them as your wife and daughter as you have in the past? A: Yes.

Q: (Showing photos of YUNG HIN SEN and JEW LAW YING attached to husband's affidavit, in present file): Who are these persons? A: Myself and my wife JEW LAW YING.

Q: (Showing photo on reverse of Consular Precis of Investigation in the present file): Who are these persons? A: My wife JEW SHEE and my daughter YUNG BAK HEONG.

Q: (Showing photo of YUNG BAK HEONG taken at this station in file 40766/11-14): Who is this? A: That looks like my daughter YUNG BAK HEONG.

Q: (Showing photos of YUNG HIN SEN and YUNG BAK HEONG on affidavit of present witness in file 40766/11-14): Who are these persons? A: Myself and my daughter YUNG BAK HEONG.

TO OTHER BOARD MEMBERS:
    Q: Do you wish to question the witness? A:
    BY MEMBER DUFF: No.
    BY MEMBER POSEY: No.

TO WITNESS:
    Q: Have you anything further you wish to state? A: No.

THROUGH INTERPRETER LEE PARK LIN:
    Q: Have you understood the interpreter? A: Yes.

TO INTERPRETER H. K TANG:
    Q: In what dialect has the witness testified? A: SUN WUEY Dialect, very similar to HEUNG SHAN WONG LUNG DOO Dialect.

SIGNATURE OF ALLEGED FATHER AND HUSBAND [Yung Hin Sen and Yung Ngip Jick in Chinese characters; Yung Hin Sen] DISMISSED

I hereby certify that the foregoing is a true and correct transcript of testimony taken at the above described hearing.

——————————————
        Clerk

SUMMARY BY CHAIRMAN:

1. JEW SHEE (JEW LAW YING), 11-13 and YUNG BAK HEONG, 11-14, are applying for admission as the wife and minor daughter of a lawfully domiciled Chinese merchant, YUNG HIN SEN. The alleged husband and father was originally admitted to the United States as a son of a Merchant on June 13, 1921. He subsequently departed from this country through Seattle on January 8, 1937 under a Laborer's status and returned through that port on October 14, 1937, thus placing himself in China at a time to make possible his marriage, and paternity to the alleged daughter, as claimed. On September 6, 1940 there are conducted a preinvestigation of YUNG HIN SEN's claimed status as a Merchant and active member of the YING CHUNG COMPANY or the FAR EAST COMPANY. His status then conceded and used as a basis for the issuance of a Sec. 3(6) non-immigrant visa to the alleged wife and daughter does not appear altered since the time of said preinvestigation.

2. Testimony has now been taken from the alleged wife, applicant 11-13 and from YUNG HIN SEN concerning their marriage and subsequent stay together in CHINA. This testi-

mony is [in] very good agreement, both principals testifying freely. No discrepancies worthy of mention were brought out by the testimony. Applicant 11-14 was too young to testify but gave evidence of regarding JEW LAW YING as her mother. Both applicants appear to be about the claimed ages.

(*Source:* Jew Law Ying, folder 40766/11-13, Chinese Departure Case Files, San Francisco District Office, Immigration and Naturalization Service, Record Group 85, National Archives, San Bruno, California)

DOCUMENT 6:
ORAL HISTORY INTERVIEW WITH JEW LAW YING

My parents were always reluctant to talk about their past. I now understand why. Like many other Chinese who came during the Exclusion years, they were illegal immigrants always fearful of discovery and deportation. It was enough that I knew our real surname was Tom, not Yung, and that my ancestral village was in Chungshan District. I was repeatedly told never to divulge this information to any *lo fan* (whites); otherwise we would all be in trouble.

It was not until I began interviewing old-timers about the Angel Island immigration experience that my parents finally opened up to me. My father, who had been detained at Angel Island for two months in 1921, actually allowed me to interview him for our book. Then after *Island* was published and I had established my reputation as a historian and writer, my mother allowed me to interview her for my second book, *Chinese Women of America*. By then she had become a naturalized U.S. citizen and was more willing to talk about her immigration history.

The following interview is a combination of two interviews that I did with my mother, one in 1982 and the second in 1987. Both interviews were conducted in Chinese at her home on the outskirts of San Francisco Chinatown. As the historian, I had my agenda; as my mother, she had hers. While I was interested in finding out about her family history and her experiences as a Chinese immigrant woman, she was more interested in impressing me, her fifth daughter, with the lessons of her life: work hard, suffer for the sake of your family and children, and above all else, accept Jesus Christ into your life. Although I have taken certain liberties in translating, editing, and reorganizing the interviews for clarity and flow as well as relevancy to the subject matter at hand, I have tried to stay true to her voice and speech pattern throughout.

Assuming that her version of her life story is closer to the truth than the coaching book or immigration transcript, I have noted discrepancies between the three sources as a way to distinguish the fake from the true in her immigration history. For example, I believe her story about Ah Kum over my great-grandmother's story to the immigration inspector in 1893; the number of brothers and sisters she told me she had over what she reported to immigration officials in 1941; and likewise, her story about my father's true family over what my father said in the coaching book. Knowing full well she has biases and lapses in memory, whenever possible, I tried to corroborate what she told me with information from interviews I did with other relatives. And to round out her story I have included cultural and historical references in the endnotes whenever appropriate.

Aside from serving as a lie detector, my mother's interview helps to flesh out and fill in gaps in the immigration documents. Her interview provides a fuller picture of what happened to my great-grandmother in America and in China between and after her appearances before the immigration service. Similarly, it explains what life was like for my mother in China, how and why she chose to marry my father and immigrate to America, and how the Chinese Exclusion Act complicated the process of immigration for women like her. It describes both the hardships she endured in America and her sense of fulfillment in her golden years. The following is the story of my mother's life as told in her own words.

Document 6

There were seven of us and I was the oldest of five girls and two boys.[88] I had a twin sister who died soon after I was born [in 1915 in Dai Chek Hom village, Heungshan District].[89] All the previous generations in my family farmed, so we also farmed. We owned land and planted rice. My mother was born in America. But grandmother couldn't take the harried life in Gold Mountain. She knew that in China she could have servants and a life of leisure. She took all the children home with her [in 1904]. My mother was eleven years old then. She wasn't very smart. Just did what she was told to do. Never had anything to say. She was arranged in marriage to Jew Yee Yuet [a.k.a. Jew Hin Gwing], a Chinese herb doctor. His grandfather left him fifty *mou* of land in Dai Chek Hom. When my mother married him, they had land, a big house, and two *mui tsai*. It was a good match. But then his older brother squandered it all on opium, gambling, and women. After they lost all their land, Grandfather [Chin Lung] supported them. Mother would periodically go visit them in Macao and come back with food and new clothes.

When I was seven I went to live with my maternal grandparents in Macao because my grandmother loved me best (chuckles). She treated me like her own daughter. She supported my schooling so you could say I grew up eating the Chin family's rice. They had four *mui tsai* and a head cook so I didn't have to do any housework. Once a year during vacation time, I would return to Dai Chek Hom [village] to visit the family. I usually stayed with an aunt who was a widow in the Girls' House,[90] where we sang, talked stories, joked, and learned about Chinese customs. After I finished elementary school, I had to quit because although my grandparents were wealthy, they were very stingy. They said girls became a part of another family when they married, so what was the use of educating them? That's the way it was so what could I do?

After I stopped going to school, I was sent to collect rent. Grandmother and grandfather had over ten buildings in Macao and about twice a month I went with Fifth Aunt [the wife of Chin Lung's fifth son, Chin Sow] to collect the rent. Whenever I was out collecting rent, Grandmother would tell the *mui tsai* to be sure to save me some food. I especially liked

red bean congee, and when the weather was hot, she would tell the *mui tsai* to cook me some. When I was home, I would sew clothes for myself on Grandmother's old-fashioned foot-pedal machine, the kind that rocked back and forth. On Sundays I would go to church with Grandmother. Both she and Grandfather were baptized at the local Church of Christ. I wasn't baptized until I came to America and had six children.

When it was time for me to marry, Grandfather made the arrangements. Your father was very active in those days and he often shopped at [Grandfather's] Shanghai Trunk Company [in San Francisco Chinatown]. He also knew Wah Ching [Chin Lung's oldest daughter-in-law], who had a bath house and beauty parlor on Stockton Street. He played *mah jongg* with her. When your father returned to China for a bride at the age of thirty-two, Wah Ching had him bring some head scarves, needles, and slippers to Grandmother and wrote home to recommend your father. At that time I was studying to become a midwife in Canton and was not interested in getting married. Grandmother wrote me and told me to accompany her back to Nan Shan village [Chin Lung's native village]. She fooled me into going back to the village to marry your father. Your father's village Pai Shan was not far from Nan Shan and she had agreed to give me away in marriage. I agreed to it because I wanted to come to America.

In marriage, a bamboo door should be paired with a bamboo door, a wooden door with a wooden door.[91] Ours was not a good match because your father was poor. He had an uncle lend him $300 to come home for a bride. But he was a Gold Mountain man and that's what mattered. He still had a younger brother who was married with three children in the village to support. His father had died when he was fourteen and he had borrowed money from his uncle to come to America. I knew he was just a laborer who worked on a flower farm.[92] He told me I would have to work hard in America, but I still wanted to come. Your father was older than me by eight years, but that was not unusual for marriages to Gold Mountain men. Despite the age difference, I liked him. He told me that he would go back to America and try to bring me over. He made it clear that he wasn't sure he could do it. I wanted to come to America to open a new road for myself and your two uncles. It was one step at a time.

We were married in 1937 in your father's village. We had a simple but traditional wedding. Just a couple of banquet tables. Your mother rode in a red sedan chair. Your father stayed in China for a few months and then returned to America to take care of the paperwork so I could come. I lived with your paternal grandmother for six months in Pai Shan.[93] She was mean to me and your mother suffered.[94] Everyone called her Kau Ma because she was always arguing with people.[95] She had an evil heart and worshiped money. She insisted your father buy her all this stuff so she could eat well and dress well. She had pigs and grew yams, taro, melons, and vegetables. I had to work in the fields, carry manure and urine out to fertilize the crops, and help with the harvesting. I never worked so hard. Even after I became pregnant with your eldest sister, I still had to work hard. If I didn't she would complain. When I cooked rice, she was so afraid I would cook too much she rationed the rice out herself. When the rice bin got low, she accused me of stealing. She was even meaner to my sister-in-law, who came from a poor family. After six months of that, I couldn't take it anymore. I wrote your father and said I had to go to Macao to have the baby. He sent me some money and I never went back to live with his mother again. Your sister was born at the Bak Ma Hong Hospital in Macao.

In Macao I rented a room from Grandfather because I was now married to someone else. Your father sent money home to support us and his mother and brother in the village. He was only making $80 a month as a gardener on a private estate [in Menlo Park, California]. Practically his whole pay-check was sent to support two households in China. After I came to America during the war [World War II], my mother-in-law died and then my own parents. We couldn't get money to them because of the war and they died of starvation. It was unfortunate that no one helped my mother return to the United States. My uncles said that my mother was like a buddha [sat around all day]. She couldn't work and was too used to having servants. If she came back to America, they would have to find someone to take care of her. Mother was also very frail and near-sighted, unlike my aunt [Mee Ngon], who was smart enough to return to the United States with a brother.

My grandparents preferred living in Macao than in the village. It was safer and more comfortable. We had a front and back garden and two outhouses. The *mui tsai* would help us flush the toilets by pouring water. There was no tap water but we had two wells that had water in them all year round. We also had a bathroom. No bathtub but we used buckets of water to wash ourselves. It was a big house. Two stories tall until Grandfather added a third floor. The Japanese were always bombing the villages, but not Macao. We were safe there.

Everyone said life in America was good, except Grand-mother, but I didn't believe her. She warned me that life would be hard there. Before I left for America, she said to me, "Ying, when you go to America, don't be lazy. Work hard and you will become rich. Work and be frugal. Your grandfather grew potatoes [in Stockton] and although I was busy enough at home [in San Francisco], I sewed on a foot-treadle machine, made buttons, and weaved loose threads [did finishing work]. I only had one *mui tsai* to help with the children and housework. But I saved enough so that when I returned to Macao, I was able to buy property." Not only did Grandfather have a house built in Macao, but he also built a house in Nan Shan that was two stories tall with concrete walls and balconies. After Grandmother died, all the property went to the sons. Since my mother had married out, we weren't entitled to any of the inheritance.

Finally your father arranged for me and your sister [Bak Heong] to immigrate on merchant papers. He was [supposedly] doing business at an import company. I went to Hong Kong and your father sent money to us via the *gam saan jong* run by Uncle Dew [a.k.a. Tom Yip Pooh]. He helped us make the necessary arrangements to come by boat. Your sister was four and I was twenty-seven years old when we came to Gold Mountain on the SS *President Coolidge*. It was 1941.

*   *   *

I heard people say that Gold Mountain was a good place. Like going to heaven. But you really don't know until you've been there. It's been a hard life for your mother all the way.

We were on that boat for over a month. Others got seasick and threw up, but neither I nor your sister got seasick. We came by steerage with lots of people. Slept in separate bunk beds. The food was good except I didn't like any of the meat the way they cooked it. They usually served Western food— lamb chops, beef, chicken. Your sister [Bak Heong] ate just about everything, but I couldn't.

When we arrived in San Francisco, Angel Island had burnt down and we were detained at 801 Silver Avenue for three weeks. We had to wait our turn to be interrogated. Our name was Yung so alphabetically we were last.[96] We shared a large room with other women. It was quite comfortable. The air was good and it was spacious. We each had our own bed. Meals were taken downstairs in the dining hall with men on one side and women on the other. We had three meals a day and the food was pretty good. For breakfast we had toast, oatmeal, eggs. The children had milk and the adults, tea. There was coffee but we didn't like coffee then. Lunch and dinner consisted of a variety of Chinese dishes with rice, like vermicelli and dried shrimp, steamed fish, chicken, and soup. I ate everything except for some of the meat, which I found too "wild." That's how I got fat coming to America. Your father sent barbecued duck to us at least four times. Once he sent soy sauce chicken. We must have finished three jars of fermented bean cakes while we were there. Bought them at the little store that sold all kinds of snacks. My grandmother had also given us a box of food to take on the trip—cookies, salted plums, oyster sauce, canned fish, fermented black beans. The two of us finished it all before we were landed.

The interrogation was quite simple. They asked me when I married. They asked about my mother and father, where they were born. They asked how many brothers and sisters I had. That was it.[97] It took no more than an hour. I just answered what they asked. Why should I be afraid? I wasn't a crook or a robber. If they let me land, fine. If not, too bad. Nothing to be scared about. Your sister kept crying throughout, she was so shy. As soon as I signed my name, they allowed us to land. Yelled out our names and said it's time to go. Everyone was happy for us. The women who were coming in as paper daughters and had made mistakes in their interrogations cried when they saw us leave. They cried and said: "You're lucky Heong Ma (that's what they called me because your sister's name was Heong) to be landed so soon. We don't know when we'll be allowed to leave this place." You remember Feng Goon's mother? She was stuck there after I left. Her husband was trying to get her in as a paper daughter and she had made mistakes. She wasn't landed until three months after me. Then there was Ng Feng, who also came posed as a paper daughter. She cried when she saw me leave. Burnt incense to scare away the evil spirits. She said, "Let's get rid of the evil spirits so that we can follow Heong Ma." I still remember what she said. There was Mui, Lee, Seeto, many who couldn't land. Some waited for over a year. Then the war came and they released all these women.[98]

After we were landed, your father met us and took us to the Yee Wo Hotel in Chinatown. We stayed in San Francisco for a few weeks, waiting for the immigration papers while visiting relatives. Then your father took us to live in Menlo Park [California], where he had been working with your granduncle as gardeners on a private estate. The wealthy white boss lived in San Francisco and sent us a check every month for taking care of her flowers and fruit orchards. Your granduncle got $100 and your father, $80. That was considered good wages. We were given a shack to live in. There were no bathrooms, no ice box. Just a wood-burning stove and a broken-down bed with a used mattress. I got a job picking suckers [off flowers] for relatives. Started at six in the morning and returned at six. Twelve hours a day, twenty-five cents an hour. If the relative had a good year, I would be paid at the end of the season. If not, he would owe me the money, sometimes for as long as a few years. Your father drove me there in the morning and picked me up at the end of the day. Then I would go get firewood and cook dinner.

When your second sister was born in the shack, there was only a kerosene lamp. We didn't have money to go to the hospital.[99] We didn't have a phone so your father went to the next farmhouse to call this old demon of a midwife to help. She took a long time to come. She was in her eighties and shaking. She felt my womb and said it felt normal even though my water bag had broken the day before and the baby still refused to come out. Your father lit the kerosene lamp and burned wood in the stove. It was a cold, rainy day in March when I gave birth to your second older sister. Your father helped by boiling water and cutting the umbilical cord. There was a lot of bleeding. I almost died. After a month of rest, I went back to work. Left the two girls at home. Your father and granduncle took turns looking after them. Fed them milk and changed the baby's diapers.

I cried a lot when I first came to Menlo Park. So this was what Gold Mountain was all about! So this was heaven! No bathtub, no ice box, a wood-burning stove, no hot water. I wanted to go back to China, where we had servants to cook and serve us, where I was happy eating my grandfather's food and wearing my grandfather's clothes. Here I had to do everything myself, including washing the laundry by hand and fetching the firewood. It was a sorrowful three years.

When I became pregnant with your third sister, I said no matter what, I was not going to have the baby in Menlo Park. It was a matter of life and death. I told your father, "Even if you don't want to go to San Francisco, I am leaving." There were two Chinese woman obstetricians in the city and I was determined to have my next child in a hospital. I would find work sewing or doing something. I just didn't want to continue working and living like that in Menlo Park. Besides, we were worried that your father would be drafted.

After we moved to San Francisco, he found a good-paying job working at the shipyard, which exempted him from the draft, and I sewed at home. Your third sister was born at the beginning of 1943, your fourth sister at the end of 1943, you in 1916, and your brother in 1948. Not until you were all in school did I sew in the factory, but I would bring work home at night. I couldn't speak English so I couldn't work anywhere else but Chinatown. The Chinese always cheated you. You worked all day for low wages. There were no set hours, so you could come and go. When you worked for whites, you were paid by the hour so you had to work fast but the wages were higher. The Chinese paid you by the dozen. If you worked fast, you made more. If you were slow, you made less. I was so-so. I was never let go. I usually quit. All those years, I worked at only three factories. I joined the union sometime in the 1950s. Worked until I was sixty-two. Your father didn't make enough to feed all six of you. And I had to send money home four times a year to my sisters and brothers. Grandfather refused to support them after our mother died.

After sewing all day, I still had to come home to cook and take care of the housework. It was harder than working in China. For eight years, we lived in this two-room apartment on Stockton Street with no private bathroom, kitchen, or hot water. All of you crammed into two bunk beds. Had to cook and boil water by the window on a three-burner stove. That's how I raised you all. Then we moved to a flat in the North Beach and things got better.

But things were cheap then. You could buy a heavy bag of groceries for twenty-five cents. You could even buy five cents worth of pork. Now it's at least one dollar. Green onions, ginger, garlic, black beans were free. Innards were given away. Sure I was only making a dollar or two sewing twelve hours a day, but food and rent were cheap. That two-room apartment [on Stockton Street] was only $18, water included. Rent, telephone, and electricity cost us a little over $20 a month. Now we talk about needing $1,000 a month to cover expenses. And Chinatown wasn't so crowded and unsafe. No one got mugged or robbed. We kept our doors unlocked. People would stay out in the streets until one or two in the morning. Now Chinatown closes down after dark.

Have my hopes been fulfilled in America? I would say yes. I wanted a better future for myself. That has been fulfilled. And all five of my daughters have finished school and have good jobs. [My brother—her only son—was in an accident when he was nine years old and has since been institutionalized and confined to a wheelchair.] I feel satisfied with life, especially after I accepted Jesus Christ into my life. Now I'm retired with a good pension and am more active in church affairs. I've traveled around a bit and have concluded that America is the best country to live in. Why? Because we have freedom here, the weather's mild, and food is cheap and plentiful. No matter where I go, there's no better place to call home than San Francisco.

(*Source:* Jew Law Ying, interview with author, September 7, 1982, and January 14, 1987)

NOTES

My special thanks to the following people for their assistance with this article: Marlon Hom, Madeline Hsu, Jew Law Ying, Him Mark Lai, Erika Lee, Haiming Liu, Waverly Lowell, Ruthanne Lum McCunn, Wing Lew Tom, Tom Ngun Dai, Tom Yip Sung, and Ellen Yeung.

1. For historical background on the causes and impact of the Chinese Exclusion Act of 1882, see Elmer Clarence Sandmeyer, *The Anti-Chinese Movement in California* (Urbana: University of Illinois Press, 1973); Alexander Saxton, *The Indispensable Enemy: Labor and the Anti-Chinese Movement in California* (Berkeley and Los Angeles: University of California Press, 1980); and Sucheng Chan, ed., *Entry Denied: Exclusion and the Chinese Community in America, 1882–1943* (Philadelphia: Temple University Press, 1991).

2. For a fuller discussion of the Chinese immigration process during the Exclusion period, see Him Mark Lai, Genny Lim, and Judy Yung, *Island: Poetry and History of Chinese Immigrants on Angel Island, 1910–1940* (Seattle: University of Washington Press, 1991).

3. Record Group 85, which contains all documents relating to the enforcement of the Chinese Exclusion Act from 1882 to 1943, can be found in most of the regional archives and the National Archives in Washington, D.C. The National Archives—Pacific Sierra Region has a microfilm copy of the index to INS case files of the San Francisco District Office for all immigrants to San Francisco. The Chinese files are grouped into three major files: Chinese Arrival Case Files (1882–ca. 1950), which document first-time immigrant arrivals; Chinese Departure Case Files (1913–ca. 1950), which document the departure of Chinese

Americans for China; and Chinese Partnership Files, which relate to individual merchants and merchant firms (1890–ca. 1940). There is also a partial index by name to certificates of identity that could lead to a specific file. Other ways to access a case file are by the name of the ship the immigrant came on and its date of arrival, or the names of any business firms he might have been connected to. See Daniel Nealand, "Chinese American Historical Studies: A Summary of Resources at the National Archives—Pacific Sierra Region," *Chinese America: History and Perspectives 1991* (San Francisco: Chinese Historical Society of America, 1991), pp. 121–134; and Waverly Lowell, "Historical Resources for Chinese Americans at the National Archives, Regional Archives System," *Gum Saan Journal* 18, no. 1 (June 1995).

4. From 1910 to 1940 Chinese immigrants upon arrival in San Francisco were detained at the Angel Island Immigration Station and subjected to physical examinations and interrogations to determine their legal right to enter this country. See Lai, Lim, and Yung, *Island*.

5. Judy Yung, *Chinese Women of America: A Pictorial History* (Seattle: University of Washington Press, 1986).

6. Ruthanne Lum McCunn, "Chin Lung's Gold Mountain Promise," in *Chinese American Portraits: Personal Histories 1828–1988* (San Francisco: Chronicle Books, 1988), pp. 88–97.

7. Chin Gway, interview with author, July 29, 1979; Chin Shou and John Chin, interview with author and Sucheng Chan, October 12, 1979; Jew Law Ying, interview with author, September 7, 1982, and January 14, 1987; Sucheng Chan, "Chinese American Entrepreneur: The California Career of Chin Lung," *Chinese America: History and Perspectives 1987* (San Francisco: Chinese Historical Society of America, 1987), pp. 73–86; and McCunn, "Chin Lung's Gold Mountain Promise."

8. The reckoning of dates by the reign of Emperor Kuang Su (Guangxu 1875–1908).

9. Heungshan [Zhongshan] District.

10. See Document 1.

11. The reckoning of dates since the establishment of the Chinese Republic (1911).

12. Chin Hong Dai was the name taken by Chin Lung when he became married.

13. Great-grandmother obviously does not remember that she had to lie in 1893 in order to get *mui tsai* Ah Kum into the United States.

14. In an interview conducted in 1977, a Mr. Yuen recounted how his uncle made a living writing coaching books: "He work with a lawyer, and he would certainly receive some compensation for it. The case is this: you got my case, then if you don't have a book already made, then uncle would help you to make them. He had enough of the basis to make a good book out of it, just by talking to you and your relatives, your father and mother, your grandfather. He might have to take a trip to Hong Kong. So make sure everything is recorded. Then also, he'll draw a house where you live in the village, showing every room, dimensions, bedroom, kitchen, where you cook. Maybe two, maybe three, and you better remember it. It's just fantastic. Just like an architect." See "Angel Island Immigration Station: Interviews with Chris Chow, Mr. Yuen, Ira and Ed Lee" (oral history conducted in 1977 by the Combined Asian American Resources Oral History Project, Bancroft Library, University of California, Berkeley), 21.

15. In another case related to me by Professor Haiming Liu of California Polytechnical State University, Pomona, a husband told his wife to hide her literacy to better her chances of passing the interrogation. Liu's source is a collection of correspondence belonging to Sam Chang, a Chinese agribusinessman in Southern California. See Haiming Liu, "The Trans-Pacific Family: A Case Study of Sam Chang's Family History," *Amerasia Journal* 18, no. 2 (1992):1–34.

16. My eldest sister's true name is Tom Bak Heong, literally, "forced to leave the village."

17. This is the most honorable way for a woman to be married in China. The "bright red bridal sedan," usually carried by four men, can only be occupied by a bride who is a virgin from a good family background.

18. My father's true mother Lee Shee and brother Tom Yip Kuen were at the wedding. My father's paper mother Wong Shee was deceased and his paper brother Yung Hin Biew was in the United States at the time of the wedding.

19. *Seungtau gung* was an older married man who was responsible for combing the groom's hair and assisting him on his wedding day. The female counterpart, *seungtau po,* was an older married woman who performed the ritual of combing the bride's hair and helping her dress before she left her parents' house for her husband's. For some reason my father wrote in his paper brother's name, Hin Biew, as the *seungtau gung* even though he was in the United States at the time of the wedding.

20. Similar to ushers at a Western-style wedding, "fraternity brothers" were close friends of the groom who served as hosts at the wedding. They usually protected the groom from well-wishers who wanted to get him drunk. When the bride arrived at her husband's home, it was customary for the groom to knock on the door of the bridal sedan to claim his spouse.

21. It was customary for the women and children to eat in a separate area from the men, in this case in a makeshift pavilion built with bamboo poles and palm leaves.

22. Here my father wrote in Yung Yip Ghin for the *seungtau gung* instead of Yung Hin Biew, as he did earlier (see note 19).

23. According to the interviews I did with my mother in the 1980s, my parents lived with my father's mother, brother, sister-in-law, and nephew in my father's ancestral home after the wedding.

24. Here my father is instructing my mother to describe his house in Pai Shan village that they actually lived in after they married.

25. See note 23 above.

26. According to the interviews I did with my mother in the 1980s, my mother returned to live with my father's mother for another three months. When she could no longer endure her mother-in-law's tyranny, my mother went to live with her grandparents in Macao.

27. This description correlates to the simplified map of Pai Shan village at the back of the coaching book.

28. Aunt Tom Ngun Dai remembers that there were over one hundred people who lived in the village.

29. My father was actually born in 1905 and was two years younger than his paper identity.

30. According to interviews with my father, his true father was Tom Fat Kwong and his true mother was Lee Shee. Tom Fat Kwong was smuggled across the Mexican border sometime before 1911.

31. Tom Fat Kwong was killed in an automobile accident in Redwood City, California, around 1920. Lee Shee died in China in 1947.

32. According to my father, his father farmed in Redwood City, California, and served in the U.S. Army during World War I.

33. My father actually had one younger brother and one older sister. Both remained in China and were farmers.

34. Yung [Tom] Hin Biew was actually my father's cousin. The two immigrated to America posed as the sons of merchant Yung Ung in 1921.

35. Grandaunt Mee Ngon's husband died soon after their wedding. She was only able to return to the United States in 1920 by lying about her marital status.

36. It was customary to exchange genealogies as proof of the marriage.

37. See Exhibit "A" to Document 5.

38. An individual maintained the same surname throughout his life but could adopt a different given name when he started school, entered business, or became married. My father's birth name was Tom Share Gow. When he married, he adopted the name Tom Yip Jing.

39. As my mother told me recently, my father told her to report an additional brother—Sing Jun—so that they could later help a kinsman immigrate. She actually had three sisters and two brothers. She also made the mistake of reporting Wun Jee as her twin sister. My mother did have a twin sister, but she died at childbirth.

40. Wah Ching, the eldest daughter-in-law of Chin Lung, was the person who introduced my father to Chin Lung as a prospective husband for my mother.

41. Many Chinese women were illiterate at this time and relied on professional letter writers to write for them. My mother was capable of writing her own letters, but she told me that she preferred having a professional letter writer compose the letter for her and then copying it in her own writing. She deliberately addressed all the letters to my father's paper name, Yung Hin Sen.

42. As I explained earlier, my father had to claim merchant status in order for my mother to immigrate to this country. This he did by investing $1,000 in the Far East Company. He said he worked there as a salesman, but he was actually working as a gardener on a private estate.

43. See Exhibit "B" to Document 5.

44. A "Gold Mountain guest" was someone who had been to America.

45. As the blanks that follow indicate, my parents were not sure who the two witnesses were going to be yet.

46. As I explained earlier, this is a simplified map of Pai Shan village intended to represent Hin Bin village. As noted below, certain changes were made to the map in my mother's copy of the coaching book that were not made in my father's copy.

47. The following was added to my mother's copy: "Trees are at the south end."

48. "Kuen Shek ancestral hall" was changed to "Yung family ancestral hall" in my mother's copy.

49. The following was added to my mother's copy: "Wong Shee (wife)."

50. The following was added to my mother's copy: "Son, You Gong."

51. The following was added to my mother's copy: "Daughter, Ngun Dai."

52. The surname Tom was changed to Yung in my mother's copy.

53. The following was added to my mother's copy: "Younger brother, Choy Bun, and younger sister, Ngun Gee."

54. "Chung Pui" was changed to "Wun Tong" and "daughter, Kau Dai" was added to my mother's copy.

55. The two sons' names were changed from Bing Kun and Yut Wing to Wah Yuet and Wah You on my mother's copy.

56. The following was added to my mother's copy: "I didn't ask about the names of the people in Hin Bin village."

57. The Chinese dialect of the immigrant was always noted because it was a way to determine whether he or she was indeed from the village he or she claimed.

58. As a rule, the Chinese did not have birth or marriage certificates.

59. The wedding actually took place in my father's house in Pai Shan village.

60. To make sure that the Chinese interpreters remained honest, it was common to change interpreters at least once during the course of an interrogation.

61. Here my mother deviated from the coaching book answer. She should have said that "it was because his parents had passed away and he had no more relatives in Sunwui Sin Dung village."

62. See note 26.

63. See note 39.

64. Yung Hin Biew's wife was Jew Shee, but she lived in Pai Shan village.

65. As my father indicated in the coaching book, his true mother and brother were at the wedding.

66. See notes 30 and 31.

67. See note 33.

68. According to the coaching book, my mother should have answered, "He had important business in Hong Kong."

69. This actually is a description of my father's house in Pai Shan village.

70. See note 23.

71. A Chinese measure of distance; one *li* is equal to one-third mile.

72. See note 42.

73. See note 38.

74. My father actually spoke the Wong Leung Do dialect, which is very close to the Sunwui dialect.

75. My father was actually thirty-seven years old then. He was born in Pai Shan village, Heungshan District, in 1905.

76. See note 42.

77. See notes 30 and 31.

78. See note 33.

79. See note 34.

80. According to my mother's testimony, my great-grandparents were living in Macao at the time.

81. See note 59.

82. This is one time in which my father provided a more detailed answer than my mother, who had replied, "Bedding, a bureau, a table, two basin stands, two basins, two chairs and two wooden tubs."

83. According to the coaching book, my father should have answered, "North."

84. See note 23.

85. Here is an example of baiting by the interrogator and of my father's quick wit.

86. See note 39.

87. Another example of baiting by the interrogator and of my father's quick wit.

88. She had responded three brothers and three sisters when interrogated in order to create a slot to bring over another relative later.

89. As she told me later, she made a mistake during the interrogation when she said Wun Jee was her twin sister and that none of her siblings had died.

90. Quite common in the Guangdong area of China, a Girls' House was a separate residence for adolescent girls in the village, where they spent the evenings talking, sewing, playing games, telling stories, singing ballads, and learning Chinese customs and etiquette. See Janice E. Stockard, *Daughters of the Canton Delta: Marriage Patterns and Economic Strategies in South China, 1860–1930* (Stanford: Stanford University Press, 1989), chapter 2.

91. A Chinese saying meaning that a husband's and wife's class backgrounds should match.

92. Here is further evidence that my parents did not tell the truth to immigration authorities about my father's siblings, my grandfather's death, and my father's occupation in the United States.

93. So my mother did not stay in Macao with her grandparents after my father returned to America, as she had reported to immigration authorities. She lived in Pai Shan village for three months, not six months, as she said in the interview.

94. Mistreatment of daughter-in-laws by mother-in-laws in China was common. See Margery Wolf, "Chinese Women: Old Skills in a New Context," in *Women, Culture, and Society,* ed. Michelle Zimbalist Rosaldo and Louise Lamphere (Stanford: Stanford University Press, 1974), 157-72

95. I later found out from my uncle in Pai Shan village that she was called Kau Ma because her daughter's name was Kau.

96. The order in which immigrants were called for interrogation was based on order of arrival and availability of witnesses, not alphabetical order.

97. Actually, as Document 5 shows, the interrogation was not that easy. My parents were asked close to one hundred questions about their wedding day, respective family histories, the village and house where they lived, and their stay in Hong Kong before my father returned to America.

98. Not all the women were released because of the war. Some were deported. See Mrs. Chan, interview with author, December 14, 1975, Angel Island Oral History Project, Asian American Studies Library, University of California, Berkeley.

99. My second sister Sandy remembers that my father said he was also afraid of being mistaken for a Japanese American and arrested for breaking curfew and relocation orders.

CHINESE GLOSSARY

Ah Kum 亞琴
Bak Heong 迫鄉
Bock Ma Hong Hospital 白馬行醫院
cheongsaam 長衫
Chin Foo 陳社富
Chin Gway 陳社貴
Chin Hong Dai 陳康大
Chin Lung 陳龍
Chin Mee Ngon 陳美顏
Chin Shee 陳氏
Chin Sow 陳社壽
Chin Suey Kum 陳瑞琴
Chin Wah 陳社華
Chin Wing 陳社榮
Choy Bun 才彬
Chung Pui 從培
Dai Chek Hom 大赤坎
Dow Moon Market 斗門墟
Far East Company 遠東公司
Feng Goon 鳳冠
Foo Wing 富榮
gam saan jong 金山莊
Ging Kau 敬裘
Guangxu 光緒
Gwok Cheong 國祥

Gwok Nam 國南
Haw Lon Yin Street 荷蘭園街
Heong Ma 鄉媽
Heungshan District 香山縣
Hin Bin village 田邊村
Jew Hin Gwin 趙天炯
Jew Law Ying 趙羅英
Jew Shee 趙氏
Jew Sun 趙申
Jew Yee Yuet 趙以越
Jin Dai 轉娣
Jun Hei 振喜
Kau Dai 球娣
Kee Mo village 乾務村
Kwong Fook Sang 廣福生
Lau Shee 劉氏
Lee Shee 李氏
Lei Ok village 李屋村
Leong Jew Shee 梁趙氏
Leong Kum Kew 梁琴嬌
Leong Shee 梁氏
Leong Yee 梁余
Lik Kei village 瀝歧村
lo fan 老番

Look Hoy Hung Hotel 陸海通旅館
mah jongg 麻將
mou 畝
mui tsai 妹仔
Nan Shan village 南山村
Ng Feng 伍鳳
Ngan Bun 雁賓
Ngau Ban Tong village 牛潾塘村
Ngun Gee 銀珠
Pai Shan village 排山村
See Ji Hou village 師子猴村
Sek Jue village 石嘴村
seungtau gong 上頭公
seungtau po 上頭婆
Shanghai Trunk Company 上海洋箱公司
Sin Dung village 仙洞村
Sing Haw 成賀
Sing Jun 成振
Sing Kee Company 生記
Sing Lurt 成律
Sum Tum village 深氹村
Sunwui District 新會縣
Tom Fat Kwong 譚發光

Tom Ngun Dai 譚銀娣
Tom Share Dew 譚社資
Tom Share Gow 譚社教
Tom Yip Ghin 譚業建
Tom Yip Kuen 譚業強
Tom Yip Jing 譚業精
Tom Yip Pooh 譚業培
Wah Ching 華清
Wah You 華有
Wah Yuet 華悅
Wing Hung Cheong 永同昌
Wong Jeet Mun 黃捷文
Wong Leung Do 黃梁都
Wong Shee 黃氏
Wong Shee Chan 黃氏陳
Wun Jee 煥珠
Wun Tong 煥堂
Yee Wo Hotel 頤和旅館
You Gong 耀光
You Tien 有田
Yung Hin Sen 楊庭順
Yung Hin Biew 楊庭標
Yung Ung 楊棟
Yung Yip Ghin 楊業建

"The Inconveniences Resulting from Race Mixture": The Torreón Massacre of 1911

by Larissa N. Schwartz

In dire need of food and clothing,
I took my chances and came to Mexico alone.
Savages rob and loot with frequent violence.
I ask Heaven: Why is there hatred against the
  yellow race?
On a journey,
It's hard to go anywhere without money.
With deep sorrow we Chinese sojourners must
  face many calamities,
Wondering when we can expect to go home in
  triumph and in grace.

> Marlon K. Hom, *Songs of Gold
> Mountain: Cantonese Rhymes from
> San Francisco Chinatown*

On March 15, 1911, a band of Maderista revolutionary soldiers entered the town of Torreón and began to search out and massacre the town's Chinese population.[1] Three hours later 303 Chinese and five Japanese lay dead. Before the massacre, Torreón had been the most prosperous Chinese community in Mexico. In 1903 the Chinese of Torreón had formed the largest Baohuang Hui (Protect the Emperor Society) in Mexico, and in 1906 the famous Chinese revolutionary Kang Youwei had arrived to invest personal and organizational funds in the booming economy. And yet, the northwestern states of Mexico, and particularly the city of Torreón, were also the sites of the most virulent anti-Chinese movements.

Recent scholarship has attempted to explain the relation between these events, demonstrating that in the northern states of Mexico, particularly in Sonora, Chinese immigrants and settlers burst the bonds of their prescribed social position of contracted laborers and rapidly created a petit bourgeois class.[2] This argument attributes the popularity and violence of the anti-Chinese movements in these areas to manifestations of tensions resulting from economic disparity between the Chinese and the indigenous people, both lower-middle-class and middle-class Mexicans. Instead, this paper suggests that the perceived economic and racial threat of the Chinese helped to define Mexican national identity by enabling elites to include the indigenous population in their definition of the new Mexican.[3] Understanding the linkages between anti-Chinese prejudice and the emerging idea of "el Mexicano" first requires a brief history of the racial prejudice against the Chinese in the popular culture of northern Mexico.

PROPONENTS OF CHINESE IMMIGRATION

In 1910 the Maderistas began what would eventually become the successful overthrow of the Porfirian elite, whom the lower classes viewed as remnants of the colonial past, affiliated with European culture, and as cultural compradors selling Mexico to the *Americanos del Norte*. Under the Porfirian dictatorship, from 1876 to 1910, these elites supported and benefited from a cheap labor pool of Chinese immigrants. Thus anti-Chinese propaganda became one method of undermining the development program of the Porifiato without overtly attacking the central governing structure. Toward this end, the expression of anti-Chinese sentiment was, if not from its inception then quickly thereafter, cloaked in and enveloped by exclusionary formulations of "the Mexican." "*El Mexicano*" as celebrated by the Maderistas included indigenous peoples of all classes. This emerging consciousness of national identity was a radical challenge to the reigning ideology of the Porfiriato, which strove to construct national identity in terms of cultural capital and economic pragmatism. From the early 1870s onwards, the debate concerning the signing of a treaty with China to facilitate trade in laborers and silver pesos was part of a larger struggle waged in popular culture with "paper bullets," that is, in the popular press.[4]

Proponents of the Porfiriato development program were the creole elites, who had recently won independence from Spain and strove to develop the nation by encouraging white immigration from Europe. Their plan for modernization depended upon a source of cheap laborers to exploit Mexico's natural resources.[5] White, Catholic Europeans were judged the most desirable; however, in spite of various attempts by the government to entice them, poor, white Europeans did not emigrate to Mexico. Nonetheless, opening "uncivilized" lands and exploiting the natural wealth of the nation necessitated a large labor force, and the educated elites who had ties to foreign business looked to Asia. The need for an alternative source of immigrants was clear to some Mexicans even before the Porfiriato. Maximilliano established the Mexican Pacific Navigation Company in 1865 to import Asian laborers, who sailed on ships crammed with over a thousand immigrants per voyage, to work on railroads, in mines, and on haciendas. Businesses in the United States had already begun importing Chinese to work on the Central National Railway line in 1864. The Cuban fight for independence in 1871 resulted in a new wave of Chinese immigrants, already bearing Spanish names, to Mexico's eastern shores. In 1874, impelled by the desire for more laborers, the Mexican Astronomical Commission to China and Japan went to those countries with explicit instructions to reconnoiter the populace and report their potential for emigration. In 1875 the *Revista Universal* published the following opinion piece, written by the leading proponent of Chinese immigration, Matías Romero:

> It seems to me that the only colonists who could establish themselves or work on our coasts are Asians, coming from climates similar to ours, primarily China. The population of that vast empire, the fact that many of them are agriculturalists, the relatively low wages they earn, and the proximity of our coast to Asia mean that Chinese immigration would be the easiest and most convenient for both our coasts. This is not an idle dream. Chinese immigration has been going on for years, and wherever it has occurred prudently, the results have been favorable.[6]

This portion of Romero's article is frequently cited as describing the pragmatic position of the *científicos,* which supposedly immunized its proponents against racial prejudice. Yet in the same article, Romero assures his readers that, in spite of the repugnance they surely feel toward the Chinese race, he cannot imagine that any employer, if presented with inexpensive laborers, would refuse them on racial grounds.[7] Thus from the very beginning of the public debate of the merits of Chinese immigration, the positivist-influenced, *científico* elites understood Chinese immigration in terms of latent racial or cultural prejudice, a position merely mediated, not obliterated, by economic pragmatism. Romero, who was "a prominent member of the new generation of Liberals who rose to power after 1856," served as the Mexican ambassador to the United States from 1863 to 1867, then as finance minister, and again as ambassador to the United States from 1882 until his death.[8] His comments may therefore be read as more than the opinions of a private citizen; he was a well-established representative of the Porfirian government.

The Porfiriato responded to an anti-immigration opposition present in various sectors of society. Before the Treaty of Amity and Commerce between China and Mexico was signed in 1899, most critics of Chinese immigration concentrated on the threat the Chinese posed to national identity as defined by cultural capital. Before 1899 the Chinese were not seen as competitors, as they were entirely distinct from any group of Mexicans. Their sole claim to membership in Mexican society was as contracted laborers, a social position other Mexicans disdained. Imported Chinese laborers were to be isolated through geographic, linguistic, and ultimately "cultural" means. Several of these means Romero described in a letter of 1886, where he responded to charges that the presence of Chinese in Mexican society might incite social violence:

> We do not have the same reasons as our northern neighbor to fear that the Chinese will arrive in great numbers. In America they work for a lesser wage than the natives . . . the government has been forced to accede to the demands of its citizens. The same things will not occur here. The Chinese arriving on the Pacific coast will be in completely undeveloped regions, whose unhealthfulness has made them heretofore uninhabitable, even to Indians. If they should penetrate the districts cultivated by the Indians, they cannot seriously compete, since [the Indians'] wages are even lower than the immigrants'; as for the inconveniences resulting from race mixture, they should not exist here, since it is not the custom of the Chinese to mix with peoples different from themselves, and after having amassed a modest fortune, they dream of nothing but returning to their homeland.[9]

This letter reveals a view of the Chinese as unassailable, culturally primitive, and morally corrupt.[10] Newspapers read by businessmen and workers, such as *El tráfico* and *Siglo XIX*, ran a series of articles criticizing the government's stand, claiming that the Mexican homeless and vagrant population should all be employed before any laborers were imported.[11] However, this incipient vision of the "Mexican," defined as including the indigenous peoples, had yet to gain popularity at the time.

U.S. anti-Chinese propaganda also influenced proponents of this position, although they remained opposed to the Porfiriato's perceived dependence on foreign investors. After the passage of the Exclusion Act of 1882, Mexico faced heavy pressure from the United States to avoid increasing Chinese immigration. A resolution introduced into the U.S. Senate called on the Porfirian government and Canada to pass similar laws.[12] The Mexican elites prevailed, however, and Romero, who was now the Mexican ambassador to the United States, began negotiations in 1882 to establish diplomatic relations with the Chinese. The result was the Treaty of Amity and Commerce, signed in 1899.[13] Regardless of U.S. heavy-handed diplomacy or the existence of the treaty, Chinese had begun immigrating long before 1899.

CHINESE IMMIGRATION AND SETTLEMENT IN NORTHERN MEXICO

Promises of land, opportunity, and short labor contracts, generally lasting only two years, enticed Chinese immigrants to Mexico. One circular posted in Hong Kong read: "Chinese colony in Mexico. All will receive a lot of money there. You will have land. In the first year you will earn $500, and in the next year $1000. You will soon have more money than the

Mandarins. Lots of good rice and cheap vegetables. Good ship; without sickness, and lots of space."[14]

This advertisement directly addressed any potential immigrant's concerns. Many Chinese died on the voyage.[15] Those immigrants fortunate enough to disembark faced a two-year labor contract, earning only one peso per month. Even if employed by a large mining company, such as the Cananea Consolidated Copper Company, Chinese were still at the bottom of the pay scale.[16] Those Chinese who were hired to work on large haciendas in the South and in the Yucatan remained laborers.[17] And some arrived only to discover that there was no work to be had. They then faced the dilemma of procuring passage home. In this record from July 13, 1906, Mr. Ah Sing, forty-nine years old, is interrogated by a U.S. judge:

> "I was born in China and I left 13 months ago. I lived in Mexico for eight months. I don't have an immigration certificate and I never had one. I walked from Imuris to Nogales, and I arrived at four in the morning. I was looking for work."
>
> The judge asked: "Did you come to the United States with the goal of returning to China for free?"
>
> Mr. Ah Sing answered: "I want very much to return to China. I don't have money for the expenses. The wages are not sufficient to live. I came to Mexico expecting work and money and I haven't found them."[18]

Mr. Ah Sing was deported within a week. Cases such as Mr. Ah Sing's were common, and the threat of U.S. intervention in Mexico's frontier control was imminent. U.S. border patrols frequently crossed into Mexican territory in their pursuit of undocumented Chinese immigrants, who were known to prefer this route into the United States after passage of the 1882 Exclusion Act. One editorial in Stockton, California, a hotbed of reactionary politics, went so far as to call for an invasion of Mexico. After the fire that followed the San Francisco earthquake, many Chinese found crossing the border, or near enough to it to merit harassment, claimed that their documentation had been destroyed. It is interesting to note that this strategy must have been communicated to immigrants before they entered the United States, strongly suggesting that there existed a highly developed system of communication stretching from the western coast of the United States down into the northwestern provinces of Mexico. The Chinese settlers in these areas were all members of this large economic and social nexus.[19] The situation for the majority of immigrants in the northwestern provinces, however, differed from that in southern Mexico.

Several provocative models have been proposed to explain the social mobility afforded the Chinese in the northern provinces. All emphasize the sparse population, the lack of an established social hierarchy, a rapidly developing economy, and the absence of the highly structured contract labor system that predominated in the south. Census records from 1890 to the 1930s show that the highest concentration of Chinese immigrants settled in the northern states. Statistics on the numbers of Chinese show that from 1885 to 1910 their

numbers increased from 900 to 13,000 in the entire country.[20] The 1895 census shows a total 1,026 Chinese in Mexico, 310 of whom were included in Sonora's total population of 192,721.[21] In 1910 there were 4,486 Chinese living in Sonora,[22] and by 1930 the number had risen to 17,865.[23] The large numbers of Chinese in the northern states reflects their ability not merely to immigrate, but to settle and to build communities. As Kennett Cott observes:

> With astonishing frequency workers managed to accumulate small amounts of capital. They then moved into the ambulatory sale of fruits and vegetables, or opened laundries, hotels, restaurants, or shops. In Sonora and Baja California, they quickly came to dominate shoe and clothing manufacturing. By 1910, they dominated small trade in much of Northern Mexico. Some had gone further. They owned some of the largest mercantile establishments in Sonora. They were reported to own a financial house in Mexico City capitalized at one million pesos, which had branches in New York and Hong Kong. Their most notable success was in Torreón, where they owned a major bank and one of the city's streetcar lines.[24]

Census polls also document the upward social mobility of the Chinese, from laborer to merchant, in the northwestern states. In 1890, 70 percent of the Chinese listed their profession as employees; by 1910 they were predominately merchants.[25] Furthermore, in spite of charges by the Porfirian elites and anti-Chinese agitators that the Chinese were unassimilable, as the Chinese established sustainable communities, from 1893 to 1910, the Chinese became the largest group of naturalized Mexican citizens.[26] While statistics from different areas vary greatly, taken as a group, they clearly support the contention that the Chinese communities in northern Mexico were attaining some semblance of permanence. Chinese were marrying Mexican women, becoming naturalized citizens, and speaking and writing Spanish.

KANG YOUWEI, THE BAOHUANG HUI, AND CHINESE COMMUNITY BUILDING IN TORREÓN

From the signing of the 1899 Treaty of Amity and Commerce until the beginning of the Revolutionary period in 1910, the Chinese community in Torreón flourished.[27] The first Chinese immigrants were involved in the city's early development even before the treaty was signed. They arrived shortly after 1893, when the town of Torreón was just large enough to separate from the municipality of Matamoros and had become its own municipality.[28] One of the first seven doctors to move to the town in 1895 was Walter Sam Lin, a Cantonese who converted to Protestantism while still living in the United States.[29] Another prominent early Chinese in Torreón was Wong Foon Chuck, who arrived in 1887 and established the Banco Wah Yic (Wah Yic Bank) in 1898.[30] By 1911 there were around six hundred Chinese living in the city of Torreón, with no recorded case of unemployment among them.[31] The town's hosting of Kang Youwei highlights the preeminent position Torreón held in relation to the other largely successful Chinese communities of Mexico's northwest.

Kang went to Mexico after first traveling in 1899 to British Columbia, where he attempted to raise money for the numerous branches of his reform-oriented organization. While in Canada he organized Chinese merchants and businessmen to found the Protect the Emperor Society, the *Baohuang Hui*. The merchants originally proposed to name the organization the "Merchant Protection Society," which indicates that the Chinese Americans' goals were somewhat disparate from Kang's. Between its founding in 1899 and 1903, the Baohuang Hui spread to every Chinese community in the United States.[32] In 1903 the Chinese of Torreón formed a charter of the Baohuang Hui, and in 1906 Kang Youwei traveled to Torreón to investigate investment opportunities there. Kang's interest in Torreón and Mexico was, however, not limited to funding alone.[33] Kang thought that Chinese settlement in Mexico or Brazil might alleviate problems of overpopulation in China's Pearl River Delta.[34] Seen in this light, Kang's trip to Torreón and other parts of Mexico, and his meeting with Porfirio Díaz in 1905 suggest that Torreón was something of a test case for future Chinese immigration.

The changes effected by the arrival of the Baohuang Hui and Kang Youwei himself at Torreón brought the activities of the Chinese community into a much more prominent position in the daily life of all inhabitants of Torreón. Juan Puig has noted the flurry of activity surrounding these new developments:

> On the corner of the Avenida Júarez and the Calle de Valdés Carrillo, the successful Foon Chuck and his Chinese associates—they accepted no other—raised a sumptuous building, of the Compañía Bancaria y de Transvías Wah-Yic and of a new institution which did not cease to surprise its neighbors: the Asociación Reformista del Imperio Chino [Baohuang Hui], a liberal political club in which the rich Cantonese of Torreón and others who were not quite so [rich] discussed the manner in which to support the initiative of Kang Youwei and, later, the rebellions of Sun Yatsen.[35]

In addition, Kang's arrival brought about the construction of one of the most luxurious buildings in town, the Sino-Mexican Bank (Huamo yinghang). In 1906 Dr. Huang Jih-ch'u and Kang devised a plan to bid on a Mexican grant to build a tram line in Torreón.[36] Then, in 1907 Kang returned to Torreón with a financial advisor brought from Canada, Lee Fook Kee, the director of Kang's Commercial Corporation. They reorganized the bank and invested heavily in city real estate.[37] The profits from these Torreón-centered businesses were so high that they directly supported the Commercial Corporation's other business ventures.[38] In short, Chinese-Mexican business prospects in Torreón appeared, from 1906 to 1908, so promising that Chinese American businessmen invested heavily in the bank, purchasing a rumored total of 937,268 pesos worth of stock.[39]

Changes in the international and Mexican economies, combined with inept management and corruption, however, brought the Commercial Corporation in Mexico to its knees. Kang Youwei wrote: "I am at a loss as to what to do. Our great enterprise is now almost ruined by a few men. The bank in the U.S. may fall, the business in Mexico is not going well, land there is falling in value so that a po-lo (city block) is now worth only 5,000 pesos . . . It has been eight or nine years since I have been in a position as bad as this."[40] Although Wong and Huang's personal power struggle did retard the progress of several projects, Kang overestimated the culpability of these two men in the Mexican fiasco. An international recession as well as several years of drought brought financial ruin to many in Torreón. And those Chinese who survived the recession better than their neighbors unintentionally generated strong prejudice.

From the end of 1907 onwards, a new, reinvigorated phase of anti-Chinese sentiment began in Torreón. This resurgence closely followed the rise of Chinese institutional success and was a manifestation of the perceived economic challenge presented by Chinese merchants, who originally weathered the recession better than their neighbors. Thus, in Torreón and other northern communities, the threat was now explicitly acknowledged as one of economic and not merely social pollution, as the case had previously been perceived. The resurgence of this sentiment, however, continued to be articulated in terms of racial and ethnic prejudice, ultimately effecting a new definition of "el Mexicano."

THE RESURGENCE AND MODIFICATION OF ANTI-CHINESE SENTIMENT

Common charges against the Chinese claimed that they were ruled by Chinese tongs, that all of their money was sent outside of Mexico, and that they sought to stay in Mexico only until they had accumulated enough money to return home. Although the Chinese frequently lived in their place of business to save money, compared to the majority of the laborers of northern Mexico, they had attained relative wealth. One Mexican miner interviewed by his company in relation to anti-Chinese violence described his frustration with the Chinese in terms of economic competition: "In the beginning the Chinese were not merchants. They worked in the mines and some of them were able to get out of the company jobs. They worked as laundry men and as vegetable sellers. But they were entering commerce and displacing the "Mexican." The Chinese don't like mexcalito or tequila, and they dedicate themselves entirely to work . . . And they licked us! Later they monopolized commerce in the entire state."[41] The miner used the precise concept of "*el Mexicano*," a term which was defined in popular culture, as opposed to the Chinese. He and others like him used an all-encompassing Mexican identity, uniting those previously excluded from the Porfirian ideal of the Mexican: working classes, indigenous people, and regional elites. Economic competition played a major role in fueling anti-Chinese sentiment and, in the process, helped solidify a new national identity.

In 1907 the Mexican economy reacted to a U.S. recession, which, combined with several bad harvests, brought about a state of crisis. Many Mexican workers could not find work in the United States and returned to towns such as Torreón, where prospects for their employment were rarely better.[42] As the markets were predominantly run by the Chinese, they were blamed for inflated prices and real shortages of food. Simpish, a U.S. consul in Torreón, wrote: ". . . the feeling against all foreigners and against the Chinese in particular is very strong; the continued depreciation of money, and the subsequent rise in the cost of food . . . and the mistaken idea of the ignorant miners that American capitalists and Chinese merchants are in some way very responsible for this condition, is driving the people to increasing unrest."[43] Further exacerbating the situation, local strong-men and bandits frequently forced Chinese merchants to sell goods below cost, causing the Chinese merchants to order less food.[44] Here, the historian Hu-Dehart cites a common explanation of why the Chinese, rather than some other group, were targeted: "Moreover, in the north, Mexicans began to focus a widespread, general hatred of foreigners more narrowly on the Chinese, who were numerous and visible in their capacity as small local merchants, yet totally vulnerable because of China's own internal chaos and weak international position."[45] This explanation contends that because the Chinese were the only foreign settlers who had no strong international defense, they were targeted. The Japanese, in contrast, had consular representatives in Mexico. Thus, the Chinese could be attacked without fear of retribution. This argument, however, cannot completely account for the specific targeting of the Chinese when violence erupted. Mexicans were presented with an entire pantheon of marginalized groups, many of whom lacked international advocates. As the case of Torreón demonstrates, the causes of Chinese persecution were domestic.

Just as there was no definitive break in the earlier expression of anti-Chinese sentiment, there was also no single event marking a distinct revival. By 1906, however, the movement had gained enormous support. Regional opposition to the centralizing forces of the Porfiriato combined with the harsh economic conditions in the northern states led to the formation of anti-Porfirian political parties. The political expression of anti-Chinese rhetoric came mostly from the Partido Nacional Revolucionario.[46] Their northwestern power base reflected the power of the new, regional bourgeoisie in the national field. They appealed to and led the middle classes, merchants, and public functionaries. These previously distinct social groups coalesced around their mutual prejudice against the Chinese, whose existence allowed the category of "Mexican" to be expanded to include social elements previously distasteful to members of their coalition. This new

"Mexican" identity also directly opposed the Porfirian emulation of and openness to the foreign.[47]

The educated elite were forced to realign themselves by forming regional allegiances or defending the central power of the dictatorship. In either case, the new idea of "the Mexican" and the anti-Chinese sentiment through which it was articulated had become so prevalent that one could no longer defend the Chinese immigration policy. One document demonstrating the Porfiriato's retreat was the suppression of a study written by José María Romero, engineer and senator. The study was first commissioned in 1903 by Porfirio Díaz as a means of appeasing anti-Chinese agitators. The study's findings were never published, nor were its recommendations enacted.

After the Revolution and several months after the March 1911 massacre at Torreón, the new government contacted José María Romero and requested a revised version of the report to be prepared for publication. Even though Romero was revising his study for the new government, he structured his argument in the pseudoscientific language of the positivist-influenced *científicos* associated with the Porfirian elite. Aside from the usual anti-Chinese rhetoric alleging that the Chinese were incompatible with Western cultures, that they were morally corrupt, that they were filthy and brought plague, Romero's 1911 report expressed several new themes of prejudice:

> Consequently, the Chinese do not emigrate to the United States, nor to any other country, as individuals responsible for their own actions, following the example of the European immigrants, but rather they work in offices and positions as they are designated, under a regime so strict and in such absolute obedience that not one of them can enter negotiations of his own accord, move to other locales, nor even purchase a ticket to return to his country, without the consent of the company or association with which he is affiliated.[48]

Any activity on the part of secret societies, in the United States or Mexico, provided effective ammunition for the anti-Chinese movement. Romero's characterization of the Chinese also served to dehumanize them. Being portrayed in the popular press as void of any individual volition could also have contributed to the later persecution of the Chinese. In the same publication Romero bolsters his argument by assessing the potential Chinese impact on the indigenous communities, a group who were being claimed as "Mexicans" as part of the new articulation of Mexican identity.

> Rigorous methods and multiple precautions ought to be adopted in order to defend our body of workers from this disastrous competition and from contagion of depraved customs; now with the state of ignorance and misery in which groups of indigenous live, contact with the Chinese could produce grave degeneration, supposing that they cannot avert (this threat), as they do not possess the moral force that a good economic state and the intellectual culture of the masses [would instill].[49]

As the indigenous were incorporated into the new Mexican identity, they assumed a very traditional role: they were to be protected. What is revolutionary about Romero's defamatory statement is the explicit invocation of a dangerous Chinese population while simultaneously applauding a new formulation of the Mexican, which was broadened to include the indigenous. The Chinese thus became an "other" in relation to the new Mexican. One marginalized group replaced another, pushing the Chinese beyond the limits of acceptable society. As people completely excluded from the new conceptions of Mexico and Mexicans, they were stripped of the minimal protection previously afforded by social codes of behavior just as the violence began.

THE REVOLUTION REACHES TORREÓN

After the national elections of 1910, the situation in Torreón was unusually tense. The town expected the Maderista attack as early as April of 1910.[50] It came on March 13, 1911. During the intervening months, the leading business people of the town, Chinese and Mexican alike, convened a meeting in the impressive building of the Baohuang Hui. Wong Foon Chuck and another Chinese named Woo Lam Po were recorded as being present, although they did not speak during the meeting. Someone suggested that the merchants hire a small band to protect the city from the imminent attack, although no second was obtained. However, rumors later circulated that the Chinese merchants had hired bandits under the direction of Lojero to protect them.[51] There is no evidence suggesting that the Chinese took any such action; rather, Wong Foon Chuck circulated a statement to the Chinese of Torreón and the surrounding farms. This was later translated by Woo Lam Po from the original Spanish to English, his second language.

> Brother, attention! Attention! This is serious. Many unjust acts have happened during the revolution. Notice have been received that before ten o'clock today the revolutionists will unite their forces and attack the city. It is very probable that during the battle a mob will spring up and sack the stores. For this reason we advise all our people, when the crowds assemble, to close your door and hide yourselves and under no circumstances open your places for business or go outside to see the fighting. And, if any of your stores are broken into, offer no resistance but allow them to take what they please, since otherwise you might endanger your lives. THIS IS IMPORTANT. After the trouble is over, we will try to arrange a settlement./ Signed T. [Torreón] Merchants and Laborers Society.[52]

This circular illuminates the infrastructure of the Chinese community of Torreón. They expected to be the targets of looting and as a community were able to ensure the financial support necessary to recuperate. It is also clear, however, that by allowing their property to be looted, the Chinese hoped to avoid physical violence.

On March 13 and 14, the Maderistas engaged in skirmishes around the outlying farms. The only serious casualties were Chinese, some eighty-four of whom died before the day of the greatest casualties, March 15. Around three in the morning on March 15, the federal troops garrisoned at Torreón deserted the town. Another cause of the unbridled brutality of the massacre may have been that the Maderista leaders spent the evening in surrounding towns, totally unaware of the federal troops' flight.[53] Thus, it was the rank and file, unrestrained by their leadership and fearful of heavy opposition, who first entered Torreón and began killing. Another explanation for the targeting of the Chinese was that a drunkard named José María Grajeda, part-time herbalist and doctor, ran about yelling, "¡A matar chînos, muchachos!" (Let's kill Chinese, boys!). He was the only Mexican ever tried for the massacre.[54] One U.S. observer of the massacre and the following days wrote a letter to his father in Ottawa:

> The mob entered the Chinese Bank Building and on the third floor found a number of newly arrived Chinamen whom they threw out of the windows to the street and their friends below finished them. Little children were stood up against the wall and shot down, crying "No me matten" [Don't kill me]. Chinese women were served the same way. Mounted troopers rode to the outskirts of the town and dragged Chinamen in to the plaza by the hair to execution. . . . For three hours the slaughter of Chinese and the sacking of buildings went on, until the arrival of Castro and Emilio Madero . . . put an end to the most savage display even seen or heard of in a supposedly civilized country. . . . Last Thursday or Friday the lower classes gave a "baile" [dance] in the Chinese laundry, where the previous Monday they had slaughtered all the inmates. . . . Then began the burial of the dead. They were loaded into carts and taken to the cemetery, where the Mexicans were buried in trenches inside and the Chinese outside.[55]

Mrs. Lindquist, the wife of the Swedish consul and town tailor, sheltered the employees of a neighborhood Chinese restaurant in her home. The Maderistas called at her door three times for the Chinese hidden within; each time Mrs. Lindquist told them they would have to wait until her husband returned and could be consulted.[56] Although the Chinese were victims of revolutionary violence, it was not random. The interregnum freedom of revolution allowed latent anti-Chinese sentiment to be expressed.

The results of the massacre were both few and many. On the international level, there was little change in Mexican-Chinese relations. Negotiations for indemnities were conducted, with the unofficial help of U.S. investigators, for several months; seven months after the fact the Mexican government agreed to pay more than three million pesos. Still, by 1931 no money had ever been paid to survivors or to the Chinese government.[57] In terms of domestic Mexican-Chinese relations, the events in Torreón provoked the formation of anti-Chinese committees, and they have subsequently been seen as the major watershed in the anti-Chinese movements of northern Mexico. From 1911 through the 1930s, the northern states waged anti-Chinese campaigns that attained varied levels of effect. From 1910 to 1914 violence was prevalent in Pilares de Nacozari, Sonora; Mazatlán and Orozco, Coahuila; Piedra Negra; Chihuahua; and Nueva Leon.[58] The most virulent of these campaigns occurred in Sonora, where many of the 180 Chinese survivors of Torreón had relocated.[59] One Chinese held for deportation on Angel Island despairingly addressed the resulting situation:

> Stay at home and lose opportunities;
> A hundred considerations lead me to sojourn in Mexico.
> Political parties are like wolves and tigers eliminating each other;
> Hatred and prejudice against foreigners take away our property and many lives.
> Unable to stay on—
> I sneak across the border to the American side,
> But bump into an immigration officer who sternly throws the book at me
> And orders my expulsion back to China.[60]

THE CASE OF TORREÓN AND THE REVOLUTIONARY MEXICAN IDENTITY

This study of the history of Torreón from the early 1870s to 1911 suggests a radically different picture of the beginnings of the Mexican revolutionary era than we have seen before. Previous scholarship has examined the rise of Mexican nationalism and the emerging idea of "*el Mexicano.*" Scholars investigating ethnic relations in Mexico have likewise written on the role of the Chinese in the northern Mexican states, but no investigation of their relationship has yet been published. By linking these events, this essay suggests that the formation of a Mexican national identity at the regional, popular level was accomplished by toppling the Porfirian definition of "*el mexicano.*" The presence of so many successful Chinese in precisely the northern areas where the Maderista revolution gained strength, the numerous anti-Chinese editorials in labor and commercial newspapers, the explicit targeting of Chinese when violence did occur, and the legacy of Torreón as seen through the anti-Chinese laws of Sonora all suggest interrelated phenomena. They occurred over a period of forty years, from the first Chinese arrivals in the 1870s to the anti-Chinese campaigns beginning in 1911. Through this process, a regional, northern identity took shape in popular culture, constructed and reified by excluding a group more foreign than the indigenous people, the lower classes, or even the creole elite of the Porfiriato. Thus, the Chinese provided the vocabulary through which a new definition of nationalism could be structured by the northern Maderistas.

NOTES

I would like to thank the following individuals for their helpful critiques: Raymond B. Craib III, Valerie Hansen, Madeline Hsu, Elisa Milkes, and Jonathan Spence.

1. Francisco Madero, "a northern landowner and industrialist, led a broad coalition of nationalistic, middle-class entrepreneurs, *petit bourgeois* elements, peons, workers and peasants"
to launch a revolution. Evelyn Hu-DeHart, "Immigrant to a Developing Society: The Chinese in Northern Mexico, 1875–1932," *The Journal of Arizona History,* Autumn 1980, 283.

2. Raymond B. Craib III, "Ethnicity and Economy: The Legitimation of Anti-Chinese Sentiment in Porfirian México, 1870–1910" (master's thesis in Latin American Studies, University of New Mexico, 1994); and Kennett Cott, "Mexican Diplomacy and the Chinese Issue, 1876–1910," *Hispanic American Historical Review* 67, no.1 (Feb. 1987): 63–85.

3. My thoughts on the emergence of Mexican nationalism and the formation of a national identity have been greatly influenced by Joseph and Nugent, eds., *Everyday Forms of State Formation: Revolution and the Negotiation of Rule in Modern Mexico* (Durham and London: Duke University Press, 1994). See especially the editors' introduction, "Popular Culture and State Formation in Revolutionary Mexico"; and Alan Knight's "Weapons and Arches in the Mexican Revolutionary Landscape." I am also indebted to Professor Holquist for providing me with his notes from his lecture "Some Theses on the Relation of Secularism to Nationalism," Panel on Nationalism/National Identity, Whitney Humanities Center, 20, Feb. 1995.

4. Chang-tai Hung, "Paper Bullets: Fan Changjiang and New Journalism in Wartime China," *Modern China* 17, no. 4 (Oct. 1991): 427–69.

5. José Jorge Gómez Izquierdo, *El Movimiento Antichino en México (1871–1934): Problemas del racismo y del nacionalismo durante la Revolución Mexicana,* Colección Divulgación. (Mexico: Instituto Nacional de Antropología e Historia, 1991), 41.

6. Cott, "Mexican Diplomacy and the Chinese Issue, 1876–1910," 65.

7. Juan Puig, *Entre el Río Perla y el Nazas: La China decimonónica y sus Braceros Emigrantes, la Colonia China de Torreón y la Matanza de 1911,* Regiones (Mexico: Consejo Nacional para la Cultura y las Artes, 1992), 134.

8. Cott, "Mexican Diplomacy and the Chinese Issue, 1876–1910," 64–65.

9. As quoted in Ibid., 73.

10. Craib, "Ethnicity and Economy: The Legitimation of Anti-Chinese Sentiment in Porfirian México, 1870–1910," 58.

11. Izquierdo, *El Movimiento Antichino en México (1871–1934),* 47.

12. Cott, "Mexican Diplomacy and the Chinese Issue, 1876–1910," 73.

13. Ibid., 69.

14. James R. Thomas, "Los Chinos en Arizona y el Norte de México, 1880–1937," in *Sonora: Textos de su Historia,* ed. Mario Cuevas Arámburu, 1st ed. (San Juan, Mexico: Gobierno del Estado de Sonora, Instituto de Investigaciones, 1989), 35; my trans. from Spanish.

15. Thomas, "Los Chinos en Arizona y el Norte de México, 1880–1937," 34. On one of the earliest voyages to the Americas, 28 percent of the immigrants died in transit.

16. In 1907 a Chinese earned 2.50 pesos to a Mexican's 5.50 and an American's 12.50; wages rose and fell, but the Chinese continued to earn less than one-third of an American's wages and always less than a Mexican's. José Luis Trueba Lara, "La xenofobia en la legislación Sonorense: El Caso de los Chinos," in *Los Chinos en Sonora: Una historia olvidada* (Hermosillo, Sonora, Mexico: Instituto de Investigaciones Históricas, Universidad de Sonora, 1990), 49.

17. Izquierdo, *El Movimiento Antichino en México (1871–1934),* 59.

18. Thomas, "Los Chinos en Arizona y el Norte de México, 1880–1937," 38; my trans. from Spanish.

19. Cott, "Mexican Diplomacy and the Chinese Issue, 1876–1910," 73. See also Raymond B. Craib III, "Re-'Covering'

the Chinese in Mexico: The Uses of Philately in Historical Inquiry," *The American Philatelist*, 1998, forthcoming. Using envelope addresses, Craib reconstructs the trilingual commercial network of the Mexican and Californian Chinese.

20. Leo M. Jacques, "Have Quick More Money Than Mandarins: The Chinese in Sonora," *The Journal of Arizona History* 17 (summer 1976): 203.

21. Izquierdo, *El Movimiento Antichino en México (1871–1934)*, 64; and Dr. Antonio Peñafiel, ed. *Censo general de la Republica Mexicana, Sonora*, Direccion General de Estadistica, Ministerio de Fomento, 1987, 72.

22. Izquierdo, *El Movimiento Antichino en México (1871–1934)*, 75; and Craib, "Ethnicity and Economy," 76–78.

23. Trueba Lara, "La xenofobia en la legislación Sonorense," 49.

24. Cott, "Mexican Diplomacy and the Chinese Issue, 1876–1910," 79.

25. Jacques, "Have Quick More Money than Mandarins," 203.

26. Cott, "Mexican Diplomacy and the Chinese Issue, 1876–1910," 79. The first records show that in 1893 two Chinese became naturalized. In 1898 there were thirty-four naturalized Chinese, and by 1910 over half of all naturalized Mexicans were of Chinese descent.

27. Kang Youwei was by this time a famous Chinese reformer. In contrast to Dr. Sun Yatsen, who advocated revolution, Kang devoted his life to reforming the dynastic system of the Manchu, Qing dynasty. For a biography of Kang Youwei, see Kung-Chuan Hsiao, *A Modern China and a New World: K'ang Yu-wei, Reformer and Utopian, 1858–1927*, Publications on Asia of the Institute for Comparative and Foreign Area Studies, 25 (Seattle and London: University of Washington Press, 1975).

28. Puig, *Entre el Río Perla y el Nazas*, 153.

29. Ibid., 156. During the Massacre of 1911, Dr. Lin treated Chinese and Mexican victims at one of three Red Cross stations set up in the town. Later that night, he searched the streets for survivors. I have found no study of Chinese conversion to Christian religions in Mexico, but the question deserves further investigation.

30. Puig, *Entre el Río Perla y el Nazas*, 157. This is the same Wong Foon Chuck who later became involved in the Torreón chapter of the Baohuang Hui.

31. Ibid., 165.

32. Hsiao, *A Modern China and a New World*, 235.

33. Although Armentrout-Ma asserts that Latin America was a "political backwater," her dissertation was published before a flood of English-language articles arguing that Latin America played an important role in the Chinese American sphere. See L. Eve McIver Ballard Armentrout-Ma, "Chinese Politics in the Western Hemisphere, 1893–1911: Rivalry between Reformers and Revolutionaries in the Americas" (Ph.D. dissertation, University of California at Davis, 1977), 23.

34. Jung-Pang Lo, ed., *K'ang Yu-wei: A Biography and a Symposium*, Association for Asian Studies: Monographs and Papers, No. 23 (Tucson: University of Arizona Press, 1967), 200. I am indebted to Jonathan Spence for this citation.

35. Puig, *Entre el Río Perla y el Nazas*, 161–162. my trans. from Spanish.

36. Lo, *K'ang Yu-wei*, 203.

37. Puig, *Entre el Río Perla y el Nazas*, 164.

38. Lo, *K'ang Yu-wei*, 203.

39. Lo, *K'ang Yu-wei*, 208, note 49. This figure of 937,268 should be viewed cautiously, as Puig cites it not as the total of Chinese American bond purchases, but as the total profit cleared by the bank from 1906 to 1908. See Puig, *Entre el Río Perla y el Nazas*, 105–6.

40. Lo, *K'ang Yu-wei*, 211.

41. Trueba Lara, "La xenofobia en la legislación Sonorense," 55; my trans. from Spanish.

42. Craib, "Ethnicity and Economy," 26.

43. Hu-DeHart, "Immigrant to a Developing Society," 286.

44. Ibid., 288.

45. Ibid., 283. Cumberland calls the Chinese "vicarious victims." Charles C. Cumberland, "The Sonora Chinese and the Mexican Revolution," *Hispanic American Historical Review* 40 (1960): 210.

46. Izquierdo, *El Movimiento Antichino en México (1871–1934)*, 12.

47. Ibid., 25.

48. José María Romero, Ingeniero, *Comisión de Inmigración*, Dictamen del Vocal. Encargado de Estudiar la Influencia Social y Económica de la Inmigración Asiática en México (México: Imprenta de A. Garranza e Hijos, 1911), 84; my trans. from Spanish.

49. Ibid., 105; my trans. from Spanish.

50. Puig, *Entre el Río Perla y el Nazas*, 174.

51. Ibid., 176.

52. Ibid., 176–7.

53. Ibid., 184.

54. Ibid., 186.

55. Letter dated May 24, 1911, from William Jamieson to his father in Canada, who published it in an Ottawa newspaper, cited in Tulitas Jamieson, *Tulitas of Torreón: Reminiscences of Life in Mexico, As Told to Evelyn Payne* (Texas Western Press: University of Texas at El Paso, 1969), 119–21. The veracity of the account is bolstered by the knowledge that the author was later dismayed to be called upon to escort and protect the surviving Chinese across town to a safer building. As was the case with other U.S. national of the time, Billee Jamieson revealed his own prejudice against the Chinese even as he condemned the brutality of the Mexican massacre.

56. Jamieson, *Tulitas of Torreón*, 121–22.

57. Puig, *Entre el Río Perla y el Nazas*, 204.

58. Cumberland, "The Sonora Chinese and the Mexican Revolution," 193.

59. The events in Sonora from 1921–1931 merit a separate study. Anti-Chinese legislation includes the March 1919 passage of the Sonoran Organic Law of Internal Administration, Article 60 of which stated that municipal councils, for reasons of hygiene and health, would relegate all Chinese houses and stores to special barrios; and Article 106 of the labor law in the National Constitution of April 1919, requiring all businesses to employ 80 percent Mexican labor, and excluding Chinese. Other provinces passed laws prohibiting landlords from renting to Chinese, invalidating contracts with Chinese, and prohibiting Chinese from selling comestibles. Further, discriminatory taxes were leveled only on Chinese merchants, and in Agua Prieta, Chinese were forced to take public baths before municipal officers. In December 1923 the Sonoran state congress passed a law prohibiting Chinese-Mexican marriages, marriages between naturalized Chinese and Mexicans, and retroactively dissolving all Chinese-Mexican marriages. Finally, on August 25, 1931, the governor of Sonora, Elías, ordered all Chinese out of the state. They were to liquidate their stocks and leave the state by September 5. This was a major flight: by 1919 there were already fifteen thousand Chinese living in Sonora. See Cumberland, "The Sonora Chinese and the Mexican Revolution"; Jacques, "Have Quick More Money than Mandarins"; and Trueba Lara, *Los Chinos en Sonora: Una historia olvidada*, vol. 2 of *El tejabán* (Hermosillo, Sonora, Mexico: Instituto de Investigaciones Históricas, Universidad de Sonora, 1990).

60. Marlon K. Hom, *Songs of Gold Mountain: Cantonese Rhymes from San Francisco Chinatown* (Berkeley, Los Angeles, Oxford: University of California Press, 1987), 89.

BIBLIOGRAPHY

XV Simposio de Historia y Antropología de Sonora. Ed. Marco Antonio Valencia Arvizu. Hermosillo, Sonora, México: Instituto de Investigaciones Históricas, Universidad de Sonora, January 1991.

Armentrout-Ma, L. Eve McIver Ballard. "Chinese Politics in the Western Hemisphere, 1893–1911: Rivalry Between Reformers and Revolutionaries in the Americas." Ph.D. dissertation. University of California at Davis, 1977.

Auyon Gerardo, Eduardo. *El Dragón en el Desierto: Los Pioneros Chinos en Mexicali*. Mexicali: Instituto de Cultura de Baja California, 1991.

Cott, Kennett. "Mexican Diplomacy and the Chinese Issue, 1876–1910." *Hispanic American Historical Review* 67:1. February (1987): 63–86.

Craib, Raymond B. III. "Ethnicity and the Economy: The Legitimation of Anti-Chinese Sentiment in Porfirian México, 1870–1910." Master's Thesis in Latin American Studies. University of New Mexico, 1994.

Cumberland, Charles C. "The Sonora Chinese and the Mexican Revolution." *Hispanic American Historical Review* XL (1960): 191–211.

Gómez Izquierdo, José Jorge. *El Movimiento Antichino en México (1871–1934): Problemas del racismo y del nacionalism durante la Revolución Mexicana. Colección Divulgación*. México: Instituto Nacional de Antropología e Historia, 1991.

González Félix, Maricela. *El Proceso de Aculturación de la Población de Origen Chino en la Cuidad de Mexicale*. Vol. 7.4 of *Cuadernos de Ciencias Sociales*. Baja California, Mexico: Universidad Autónoma de Baja California, Instituto de Investigaciones Sociales, 1990.

Holquist, Michael. "Some Theses on the Relation of Secularism to Nationalism," Panel on Nationalism/National Identity. Whitney Humanities Center. Yale University. February 20, 1995.

Hom, Marlon K. *Songs of Gold Mountain: Cantonese Rhymes from San Francisco Chinatown*. Berkeley, Los Angeles, Oxford: University of California Press, 1987, 109.

Hsiao, Kung-Chuan. *A Modern China and a New World: K'ang Yu-wei, Reformer and Utopian, 1858–1927. Publications on Asia of the Institute for Comparative and Foreign Area Studies, 25*. Seattle and London: University of Washington Press, 1975.

Hu-DeHart, Evelyn. "Immigrants to Developing Society: The Chinese in Northern Mexico, 1875–1932." *The Journal of Arizona History*. Autumn (1980): 275–312.

Jacques, Leo M. "Have Quick More Money than Mandarins: The Chinese in Sonora." *The Journal of Arizona History* 17. Summer (1976): 201–218.

Jamieson, Tulitas. *Tulitas of Torreón: Reminiscences of Life in Mexico*. As told to Evelyn Payne. Texas Western Press: University of Texas at El Paso, 1969.

Joseph and Nugent, eds. *Everyday Forms of State Formation: Revolution and the Negotiation of Rule in Modern Mexico*. Durham and London: Duke University Press, 1994.

Lo, Jung-Pang, ed. *K'ang Yu-wei: A Biography and a Symposium*. The Association for Asian Studies: Monographs and Papers, No. XXIII. Tucson: University of Arizona Press, 1967.

Ota Mishima, María Elena. *Seite Migraciones Japonesas en México 1890–1978. Centro de Estudios de Asia y Africa*. México: El Colegio de México, 1982.

Puig, Juan. *Entre el Río Perla y el Nazas: La China decimonónica y sus Braceros Emigrantes, la Colonia China de Torreón y la Matanza de 1911. Regiones*. México: Consejo Nacional para la Cultura y las Artes, 1992.

Roméro, José María. *Comisión de Inmigración;* Dictamen del Vocal Ingeniero José María Roméro, Encargado de Estudiar la Influencia social y económica de la Inmigración Asiática en México. Microform. México: Impresa de A. Carranza e Hijos, 1911.

Thomas, James R. "Los Chinos en Arizona y el Norte de México, 1880–1937." *Sonora: Textos de su Historia*. Ed. Mario Cuevas Arámburu. Primera ed. San Juan, México: Gobierno del Estado de Sonora, Instituto de Investigaciones, 1989. 3: 31–40.

Trueba Lara, José Luis. "La Xenofobia en la Legislación Sonorense: el Caso de los Chinos." *Los Chinos en Sonora: una historia olvidada*. Vol. 2 of *El tejabán*. Hermosillo, Sonora, México: Instituto de Investigaciones Históricas, Universidad de Sonora, 1990. 47–65.

Trueba Lara, José Luis. "El Tráfico: un periódico guaymense ante la inmigración china." *Los Chinos en Sonora: una historia olvidada*. Vol. 2 of *El tejabán*. Hermosillo, Sonora, México: Instituto de Investigaciones Históricas, Universidad de Sonora, 1990. 33–44.

Valdés Lakowski, Vera. *Vinculaciones Sino-Mexicanas: Albores y Testimonios (1874–1899). Seminarios: Investigación*. Ciudad Universitaria, México: Universidad Nacional Autónoma de México, 1981.

Development of the San Diego Chinese American Community

A Preliminary Investigation

by Zeng Ying

In January 1996 the Chinese Historical Museum was opened to the public in the Asian/Pacific Thematic Historic District of downtown San Diego, California. As the leader of Chinese Historical Society of San Diego said, the purpose of this museum is "to preserve Chinese American history and heritage for all to enjoy." The museum is but one symbol that the Chinese American community in San Diego has been growing, maturing. It is also a reflection of the need of Chinese Americans in San Diego to sort out a united Chinese American identity.

The estimated population of Chinese Americans in San Diego County is approximately 50,000[1], only about 4 percent of the total population of San Diego. But considering the Chinese American population of one century before (70 in 1870, 229 in 1880, 909 in 1890, and 414 in 1900), the community in San Diego has grown significantly. How is the San Diego Chinese American community organized? With the growing population, what kinds of changes have been taking place in this community? Based on two months of fieldwork conducted during the summer of 1996, I will draw a general picture of the contemporary Chinese American community in San Diego. In doing so I hope to highlight many of the changes, areas of solidarity, and areas of difference within the community. But these are only preliminary findings, further research with finer detail will become available in the near future.

HISTORICAL BACKGROUND

The first Chinese to appear in southern California drifted down from the Sierra Nevada goldfields, where Chinese were excluded from the best-paying diggings. Many of them had been fishermen back in their homes in the Pearl River Delta area of Guangdong Province. "Given a chance to pursue their former livelihoods without the harassment they had experienced in the mining counties, they did so."[2]

The early Chinese immigrants established San Diego's fishing industry, which would later become one of San Diego's most important industries. In the 1870s and 1880s the Chinese supplied all the fresh fish requirements of San Diego and also exported dried fish products to other Chinese communities worldwide. During the peak there were eighteen Chinese junks based in San Diego. Since the local market was not lucrative enough to attract fishermen of other nationalities, the Chinese were left alone until the middle of 1880s in command of the rich resources.[3]

However, good times did not last long. As had already happened in the goldfields, Chinese once again became the target of exclusion. In 1888 Congress passed the Scott Act. Under the Chinese Exclusion Act of 1882, Chinese laborers already living in the United States had been allowed to return after leaving the country by presenting certificates of residence to the Collector of Customs at their port of entry. However, the Scott Act invalidated these certificates and denied reentry to any noncitizen laborer who went past the three-mile territorial limit of the United States. In 1892 the McGreary Amendment to the Geary Act classified fishermen as laborers, which threatened the fishermen who went south to fish in Mexican territorial waters. By 1893 there was only one Chinese junk left fishing in San Diego County.[4]

Besides being fishermen, the Chinese were employed as laborers on the railroad, and worked in the service industry as launderers, cooks, servants, and gardeners. In the 1880s many Chinese were involved in building the Hotel Del Coronado. Between 1881 and 1884 some 1,500 Chinese laborers in San Diego were employed to build the California Southern Railroad. In 1887 seventeen of the twenty-three laundries in San Diego were operated by Chinese. Later, as their capital accumulated, they became merchants, restaurateurs, and grocers. When the Scott Act brought about the end of the Chinese fishing industry in San Diego, many of the Chinese went into market gardening. By 1900 there were twenty-seven market gardens in San Diego. Chinese farmers introduced varieties of Chinese fruits and vegetables to San Diego.[5]

The early Chinese fisherman established a fishing village at the foot of San Diego's New Town, which later became Chinatown. The community grew with the arrival of the railroad laborers, but many of them had left by the end of the century. Since the Chinese community of San Diego never had a chance to grow large enough before the anti-Chinese immigration laws in the late 1800s, it was never able to solidify into a large centralized Chinatown area.

After the Chinese exclusion laws were repealed in 1943, especially after the passage of the Immigration Act of 1965, Chinese immigration increased sharply. Many of the newer immigrants had relocated to Hong Kong after the People's Republic of China was established in 1949. In 1947 the restrictive covenant on real estate was lifted and Chinese were able to purchase real estate in San Diego for the first time. It became much easier for Chinese to establish families and businesses outside of Chinatown. At the end of the 1960s, most of the people in the community had moved out of Chinatown, and San Diego became another city in America without a Chinatown.[6]

Since the latter half of 1970s, there has been a surge of immigrants from Southeast Asian countries owing to the turbulent political situation and unfavorable economic conditions for the ethnic Chinese there. After the Vietnam War, thousands and thousands of refugees escaped from Vietnam, Cambodia, and Laos in old and fragile boats. Most of these "boat people" were ethnic Chinese. A great number of them settled in San Diego, since Camp Pendleton was the biggest of the four receiving centers in the United States. The normalization of relations between China and the United States in 1979 opened the door for people from mainland China to immigrate to the United States. In 1981 Congress granted a separate immigration quota of twenty thousand to people from Taiwan.[7] A large number of students, professionals, and professors from Taiwan have immigrated to San Diego since then.

Today, the Chinese community in San Diego consists of old-timers; American-born Chinese; new immigrants from Hong Kong, Taiwan, mainland China, and other countries; and refugees from Vietnam, Cambodia, and Laos. Although they all may share the same ancestral roots, they were raised in different cultural environments. The Chinese Americans in San Diego now have to deal with different languages and traditions within the Chinese community.

THE SOCIAL ORGANIZATION OF THE CHINESE AMERICAN COMMUNITY

In an attempt to escape anti-Chinese hostility, which started almost from the moment Chinese immigrants arrived in the United States, Chinese immigrants created their own distinctive society in Chinatowns. The main community organizations in Chinatowns are district associations (*huiguan*), family or clan associations (*gongsuo*), secret societies or tongs (*tang*), and business guilds (*hanghui*). The fundamental conception of these associations came from traditional Chinese society, but the forms they took were unique to the overseas Chinese community.

District associations united all those who spoke a common subdialect or were from the same district. These associations primarily represented the Chinese from seven counties of heaviest Chinese emigration to America, the Sze Yap (Xin-

hui, Xinning, Kaiping, and Enping) and Sam Yap (Nanhai, Panyu, and Shunde) of Guangdong. The clan associations, originated from the lineage and clan organizations of South China, included all members bearing the same surname. Both district and clan associations played an important role in early Chinese American history as immigrant receiving stations. They provided employment, housing, and welfare, and protected members from the harmful action of other associations.[8]

Business guilds, based on mutual interests, originated from the craft and labor guilds in China. They upheld standards of workmanship, set prices, enforced territorial rights, collected funds, and hired lawyers to fight against anti-Chinese ordinances.[9]

Tongs were fraternal organizations that bound members together through secret initiation rites and sworn brotherhood. The best-known tong was Chee Kung Tong, an outgrowth of secret societies in China formed originally to espouse the overthrow of the Qing dynasty and the restoration of the Ming dynasty.[10] Tongs provided mutual aid for their members and a host of social and economic activities.

In the early San Diego Chinese community, unlike those communities in cities with big Chinatowns, district associations, clan associations, and business guilds were lacking. Many of the early bachelor immigrants were involved in tongs. As early as 1885, a Chee Kung Tong branch was established in San Diego. However, members of Chee Kung Tong were known for their protection of illegal activities such as gambling, opium, and smuggling immigrants across the Mexican border. In 1922 Bing Kung Tong and in 1945 Ying On Tong, both of which were headquartered in San Francisco, established branches in San Diego.[11]

It is difficult to say why the district, clan, or guild associations, which played central roles in other Chinatowns, were lacking in the San Diego Chinese community. It is probably related to the small size of the community. Or, perhaps, because many of the early immigrants moved to San Diego from other cities, where they already belonged to such associations, they did not feel the need to form new ones. But "perhaps the most significant factor was the role of the Chinese Congregational Mission in facilitating the adjustment of Chinese immigrants in San Diego and providing the necessary organization and functions normally provided by voluntary associations elsewhere."[12]

In 1870 the first Chinese mission was organized by the First Presbyterian Church as a branch of their Sunday school program. In 1885 the Chinese Mission School of the Congregational Church was founded. This early mission school served several important functions for the Chinese community. For example, English classes were provided free of charge six evenings a week. Since the small size of the Chinese community precluded its isolation from the larger society, knowledge of English was vital to anyone who hoped to work for or conduct business with the non-Chinese community. The mission school helped the Chinese to solve many problems involving housing, employment, and so forth. In 1907 the mission moved into a new building that included a long dormitory containing tiny rooms, which were rented to unmarried Chinese males. These rooms were always filled to capacity with recent arrivals to San Diego, providing an opportunity to meet other Chinese and to find employment. Besides providing religious instruction, the Chinese Mission in its new location became a center where Chinese immigrants (mostly bachelors) could learn English in order to adapt better to their new environment and to find employment. The Mission also served as living quarters and a social center, functions that in communities with big Chinatowns were usually served by voluntary associations like district, clan, or guild associations.[13]

In 1907 the Chinese Consolidated Benevolent Association (CCBA) was established in San Diego to represent the interests of the Chinese community in the larger society. The antipathy held by the CCBA toward the Chinese churches in other Chinatown communities appears to have been relatively absent in San Diego. This is most likely because the leaders of the local CCBA were usually members of the Chinese Congregational Mission as well. The association worked hand in hand with the Chinese Mission School for the social welfare of the Chinese community. In 1937 the first Chinese school (Chung Wah School) was opened in the Chinese Congregational Mission, and it was supported financially by the CCBA.[14] Even today, both organizations serve as cosponsors for many of the community activities in San Diego.

In 1935 the House of China was opened as one of the cultural programs of the California Pacific International Exposition (1935–36). On October 13 the House organized a China Day, which was chronicled as one of the biggest days in the history of the San Diego Chinese community. About 15,000 people were reported to have enjoyed the almost continuous program from afternoon to late at night.[15] After that, the House of China provided cultural displays and festival performances to the public every Sunday afternoon. It became one of the windows connecting the Chinese community with the larger society.

In 1946 the Chinese Congregational Mission became an independent and self-supporting church. It was later renamed the Chinese Community Church to express its community involvement.[16] In 1970 the Chinese Social Service Center was organized, and it was funded by the County of San Diego until 1980, when funding for social service programs was cut across the board.[17] The center provided resources and support for job assistance, information and referral, assistance in filling out forms, counseling, and other basic social services. It was later renamed the San Diego Chinese Center. In 1971 the Chung Wah Women's Club and the Chinese Senior Citizens Club were organized to meet the social needs of older women who did not speak English and to provide a social life for senior citizens.

With the recent growth in population, the Chinese community has many new active organizations in San Diego today. They include the Chinese Community Action Committee, a first-of-its-kind political action group; the Chinese Friendship Association, a "home" for many Chinese from Vietnam; the Indo-Chinese Association; the San Diego Chinese Cultural Association; the San Diego Chinese Association; and the San Diego Chinese American Scientists and Engineers Association. There are now nearly two dozen organizations serving the Chinese community in San Diego, which reflect the broad and diverse nature of the community.

CHANGES IN THE SAN DIEGO CHINESE COMMUNITY

The number of Chinese living in the San Diego has increased dramatically from 414 in 1900, to 3,259 in 1970, to an estimated 50,000 today. With the growing population, what kinds of changes have been taking place in this community?

First, their professions have changed from labor and small business to varied domains. Most of the early Chinese residents of San Diego, like those in other parts of the United States, were male laborers who worked in fishing, railroad building, agriculture, and other types of physical labor. A few merchants and their families had small mom-and-pop businesses, such as grocery stores, laundries, and restaurants. The Chinese Exclusion Act in 1882 barred wives of Chinese laborers in America from coming to this country, admitting only wives of Chinese merchants. In 1924 an immigrant act stated that not even the wives of Chinese merchants and the wives of American-born Chinese were allowed to enter this country. The Chinese community remained a bachelor society in the early years.

The easing of immigration restrictions following the war and the 1945 War Brides Act helped to increase the number of Chinese American women. The influx of war brides, wives, and other women immigrants in the late 1940s resulted in a Chinese American baby boom.[18] Because of the Chinese tradition of attaching importance to education, a great number of the American-born Chinese were sent for higher education. Together with the well-educated new immigrants from mainland China,[19] Hong Kong, and Taiwan, increased numbers of Chinese Americans entered the technical and professional fields.

Today there are many prominent Chinese Americans in San Diego with accomplishments in the fields of science, engineering, education, law, medicine, art, media, and business. Among these are Dr. Lily Cheng, professor at San Diego State University and the only Chinese member of the American Speech, Language, and Hearing Associate Academy; Dr. Catherine Yi-yu Cho Woo, professor and director of the Chinese Studies Institute, San Diego State University, the first Asian American woman to serve on the National Council of the Arts; Cindy Hom, news anchor of a national TV network; Joseph Wong, architect and the owner of Joseph Wong Design Associates; Susan Lew, Chairman of S. Lew and Associates, Inc., and commissioner of San Diego County international trade; David Chang, real estate developer; and Tom Hom, the first member of a minority in San Diego to be elected to the city council and the first Chinese American in town to serve in the State Assembly.

Second, Chinese Americans in San Diego have a new consciousness of political power. When Tom Hom started to run for city council in San Diego in the early sixties, he did not get much support from the Chinese community. The reaction from the Chinese community, as he recalled it, was "I don't want the embarrassment. He's losing. "But," he noted, "as I campaigned further and further, there came a point where the poll showed that I could win, then many of them started coming out. They supported me financially, but they did not support me openly. When obviously the poll showed that I would win, many of them put my sign on their business, passed out pencils and all such kind of things, because they were proud to see a person of Chinese background win."[20]

He was elected in 1963 with 87 percent of the vote, at a time when the Chinese population in San Diego accounted for less than one percent of the total population. In 1967 Tom Hom won again, with the second highest vote of any winner in a contested general election in San Diego. He served five years on the San Diego City Council, until he was elected to the State Assembly in 1969. During his tenure Hom helped pass a resolution in the State Assembly to cancel remaining anti-Chinese laws, including the Sunset Law from the 1800s, which prohibited Chinese from leaving Chinatown after sunset. He was also part of a group in San Diego that put the first minority-owned TV station (channel 69) in town on the air.[21]

Thirty-five years have passed since Tom Hom first ran for public office and became the first elected Chinese American politician in San Diego. Today more and more Chinese American names are showing up on lists of politicians and government office holders, because they "want to be the leader, want to make decisions."[22] There are still political lines and ethnic boundaries that Chinese Americans need to cross, but there is no doubt that the growing Chinese American political power will make a difference not only for the Chinese community but for the whole society.

Finally, today's San Diego Chinese community is made up of a more diverse and heterogeneous population than ever before. "I had never heard Mandarin in San Diego until the late fifties or early sixties," said Tom Hom, a native-born Chinese American whose parents were from Kaiping, one of the Sze Yap areas of Guangdong Province. Almost all of the first-generation immigrants in San Diego were from two areas of Guangdong Province: Kaiping and Taishan. Many of them were even from the same village. Until the early 1960s there were only a few Chinese families, most of them named Hom

or Tom.[23] As Susan Lew recalled, "Thirty years ago, in San Diego almost every Chinese you run into, if you call him Mr. Hom (Tom), most likely you're right."

Now the Chinese community in San Diego is made up of a diverse population: older Cantonese-speaking foreign-born, first-generation early immigrants; their English-speaking native-born descendants; Mandarin-speaking and Cantonese-speaking foreign-born immigrants from mainland China, Taiwan, and Hong Kong, consisting mostly of scholars, students, and professionals; Hokkien-speaking immigrants from Taiwan, most of whom are students or white-collar workers; and ethnic Chinese who have moved to the United States from Southeast Asian countries, primarily from Vietnam. These different social groups make the community socially and culturally heterogeneous. The owner of a Chinese video rental shop, who is from mainland China, has noted that his customers have differences in video appreciation, depending on where they are originally from and how many years they have been in the United States.[24] This is but one piece of collateral evidence of the cultural differences among these different groups.

Differences in language and cultural background often led to tension among the groups. The Sunday attendance of the Chinese Community Church grew from an average of fewer than 50 in 1946 to 155 in 1977, owing to a large increase of students, professors, and professionals from Hong Kong and Taiwan. Besides theological differences among the old-timers, the American-born Chinese (ABC), and the overseas-born Chinese (OBC),[25] cultural differences and language barriers became sources of tension among these groups. Many OBC had advanced academic degrees and had good reading and writing ability in English, but it was difficult for them to express themselves in spoken English. Their cultural pride often inhibited them from trying. As a result, they tended to be socially withdrawn from the English-speaking society. On many occasions, the OBC would use Cantonese or Mandarin to converse in spite of the presence of ABC, who often could not understand the dialect. This made the ABC feel offended. For their part, the ABC failed to be sensitive to the language needs and cultural pride of the OBC. This tension resulted in a church schism, which started as a controversy over the rental and use of the community center for a social dance. In 1978 a group made up mainly of OBC formed a new church, the Chinese Evangelical Church. This schism caused bitterness, pain, and frustration, resulting in the separation of friends and families.[26]

A similar schism occurred in the first Mandarin church in San Diego, which was established in 1973. In 1979 the church split into three separate groups. One formed another Mandarin-speaking church, and the second group, consisting of Hokkien-speaking immigrants, formed a new Taiwanese Lutheran church. In this case, besides differences of language and cultural background, socioeconomic differences among the groups also played an important role in causing the schism.[27] By 1985, out of eight Chinese churches in San Diego, four of them were results of schism.

Sometimes, different political views also resulted in tension in the community. In 1948 Rev. Peter Ahwah Lee, who was instrumental in leading the Chinese Congregational Mission to be an independent church (now the Chinese Community Church), had to leave the church because of his liberal political views. Most of the Chinese in those days supported Chiang Kai-shek and his Nationalist government. Lee, who believed that the Communists would have a moderating effect on the Nationalist government, lost the support of many church members by suggesting his opposing view. In 1973 the House of China also had a difficult time. As a result of an increase in supporters from varied backgrounds, the issue of political loyalty to either the government of mainland China or that of Taiwan was debated. The result of the debate was that the House of China should represent the San Diego Chinese community only and not offer political loyalty to either Chinese government.[28]

SEARCHING FOR A UNITED CHINESE AMERICAN IDENTITY

The growth of the Chinese community in San Diego made it a diverse and heterogeneous entity. However, the existence of differences does not necessarily mean that the Chinese community is not an integrated one. There are times when the differences between groups can split the community into diverse segments, but at other times members of the community find it advantageous to act as a cohesive unit.

In a common effort of the pastors of the Chinese Community Church, the Chinese Baptist Church, the Southern California Mandarin Church, and the Chinese Evangelical Church, a prayer meeting was organized for all the pastors of Chinese churches in San Diego. At the end of the 1980s, a joint Good Friday service was established. The tension of schism among the Chinese churches was slowly reduced.[29]

In the beginning of the nineties, there was an attempt to establish one umbrella Chinese organization in San Diego in order to organize a San Diego Greater Chinese Community.[30] This attempt did not work out for many reasons, but it showed the common aspiration of different groups to be united. In fact, when there is a cultural event or a community activity, the leaders of different groups and organizations usually get together and serve as cosponsors.

There are forces that act to integrate Chinese Americans—forces that crosscut diverse subcultural groups, emphasize what is common to all groups, and maintain a united community. Chinese Americans share the same ancestral roots. In spite of the differences in the cultural environments in which they were raised, they have been influenced, more or less, by Chinese cultural tradition, which separates them from other Americans. Familism, one of the most important characteris-

tics of Chinese culture, has been emphasized by Chinese Americans. A Chinese communication network, attaching importance to ties of kinship and friendship, is consciously maintained in the Chinese American community. This informal yet efficient information exchange system unites the community by cutting across generational and cultural boundaries.[31]

Although the status of Chinese Americans in San Diego has dramatically improved, racial and cultural barriers (external as well as internal) still prevent the Chinese and other minorities from full membership in mainstream society. A *San Diego Tribune* survey has shown that, although the population of minorities is about a quarter of San Diego County's total population, there were only two minority representatives in the boardrooms of San Diego's top twenty-five publicly held corporations. The San Diego Police Department, with 448 members of minorities among its 1,894 officers and support staff, counted only three among its top-ranked officials, including one assistant chief. The San Diego County Sheriff's Department had 423 minority members among its 1,506 employees, none in high ranks. Out of ninety-nine elected officials on eighteen city councils and county boards of supervisors, only five were minorities. Of 240 school and community college board members, only twenty-six were minorities.[32] As long as this "glass ceiling" exists to distinguish the Chinese from other Americans, it will push Chinese Americans back to their still diverse community.

In the late eighties, a group of concerned native-born Chinese Americans in San Diego started a movement to establish a Chinese/Asian Thematic Historic District.[33] Although this was a large commercial development project,[34] one of the main aims was to save the remaining buildings in the old Chinatown that had a significant Chinese or Asian history but were being torn down because of the San Diego downtown redevelopment program. Organizers had to fight an uphill battle against city hall to prove the value of the plan. In 1988 plans to save the building of the old Chinese Mission were approved by the Center City Development Corporation, an advisory group to the city council. One board member voted against the plan, saying, "$325,000 is a lot of money to move a building that most San Diegans don't even know exist."[35] When they began the effort to restore the old Chinese Mission and convert it into a Chinese historical museum, the plan's backers did not receive much support from other Chinese American groups either. But as a result of speeches and slide shows showing the importance of retaining their cultural background, other groups became very involved. As a result, a large part of the money raised for the museum fund came from Mandarin-speaking new immigrants. The newly formed Museum Operations Committee includes members from varied subculture groups: native-born English-speaking Chinese Americans, Cantonese-speaking and Mandarin-speaking new immigrants, and so on. The successful opening of the museum on January 13, 1996, became a real symbol of a united Chinese American identity.

CONCLUSION

This preliminary look into the San Diego Chinese American community reveals a vibrant, living community of a different sort than is most often brought to academic light. For lack of strong voluntary associations like district and clan associations found in communities in cities with big Chinatowns, the Chinese Community Church and other Chinese churches played a central role in the social organization of the San Diego Chinese American community. In addition to the political and historical reasons seen in other communities, the San Diego Chinese community has grown dramatically and become a diverse and heterogeneous entity for geographic reasons. Many new organizations that reflect the broader and more diverse nature of the new community, working together with the old organizations, provide aid and comfort for those in need as well as represent the community's interests to the larger society. At times there is tension among different social groups of the community, which sometime lead to schism. But at other times the community acts as a cohesive unit. This enables the members of the community to maintain their ethnic identity as well as to participate in mainstream society.

The San Diego Chinese American community has, with the exception of a smattering of articles, been largely ignored to date. A valuable window into Chinese American history has thus been left shut. In San Diego layers of history and culture, from the early immigrants with their important contributions to San Diego history and their struggles against oppressive laws to the recent immigrants and the variety they have brought to the community, can be viewed superimposed upon one another. San Diego further offers a look into a community never able to establish a lasting Chinatown. Thus today's Chinese community in San Diego offers many avenues for further research into Chinese American identity.

The older established community and the various immigrant groups all bring their own histories and cultures. I have shown here that there has not always been harmony and that, despite these differences, there are certain ties that still link these diverse groups, bringing them together in efforts to support, at least on some level, a unified community without a center. Although the main thrust of this article has been to explore the basic internal workings of the community, as seen in the battle with city hall over the construction of the Chinese Historical Museum, external influences on the community's development must also be investigated. Therefore, my next step will be to explore in finer detail, the unique history of this community and its environment.

NOTES

1. This figure is from the *San Diego Union*, Sept. 18, 1990, D-1. According to the 1990 census, Chinese in San Diego County number 19,686. However, a large part of the Vietnamese population and some of those from Cambodia, Laos, and other Southeast Asian countries are also of Chinese descent.

2 Arthur F. McEvoy, "In Places Men Reject: Chinese Fishermen at San Diego, 1870–1893," *The Journal of San Diego History* 23, no. 4 (1977): 14.

3 Murray K Lee, "A Short History of the Chinese in San Diego, California," unpublished paper (1996); McEvoy, "In Places Men Reject," 15.

4. McEvoy, "In Places Men Reject," 18–19; Karl Fung, *The Dragon Pilgrims: A Historical Study of a Chinese-American Church* (San Diego, Calif.: Providence Press, 1989), 14.

5. Lee, "A Short History of the Chinese in San Diego"; Suber Joyce, Lanell Alston, and David Vigilante, *San Diego People: The Chinese Pioneers* (San Diego: San Diego City Schools, 1982), 23; Fung, *The Dragon Pilgrims*, 15–16.

6. Fung, *The Dragon Pilgrims*, 75.

7. Betty Lee Sung, *The Adjustment Experience of Chinese Immigrant Children in New York City* (New York: Center for Migration Studies, 1987), 22.

8. Him Mark Lai, *From Huaqiao to Huaren* (Hong Kong: Joint Publishing Co., Ltd., 1992), 2932; Sucheng Chan, *Asian Americans: An Interpretive History* (Boston: Twayne Publishers, 1991), 63–65; Melford S. Weiss, *Valley City: A Chinese Community in America* (Cambridge, Mass.: Schenkman Publishing Company, 1974), 35–37.

9. Chan, *Asian Americans: An Interpretive History*, 67.

10. Ibid.

11. Fung, *The Dragon Pilgrims*, 48–49.

12. Lawrence A. Palinkas, *Rhetoric and Religious Experience: The Discourse of Immigrant Chinese Churches* (Fairfax, Va.: George Mason University Press, 1989), 21.

13. Elizabeth C. MacPhail, "San Diego's Chinese Mission," *Journal of San Diego History* 23, no. 2 (1977), 11–14; Fung, *The Dragon Pilgrims*, 23–26; Palinkas, *Rhetoric and Religious Experience*, 21–22.

14. Fung, *The Dragon Pilgrims*, 49; Palinkas, *Rhetoric and Religious Experience*, 24.

15. Fung, *The Dragon Pilgrims*, 107.

16. Centennial Book Committee, *Centennial Celebration: One Hundred Years of Leadership and Service* (San Diego, Calif.: Chinese Community Church, 1985), 20.

17. Fung, *The Dragon Pilgrims*, 108.

18. Judy Yung, *Chinese Women of America: A Pictorial History* (Seattle and London: University of Washington Press, 1986), 80–88.

19. When the People's Republic of China was founded in 1949, about five thousand Chinese college and graduate students then studying in the United States remained in the United States. A large number of highly educated and well-trained Chinese, primarily from central and northern China, came to America under the refugee acts.

20. Tom Hom, interview, July 25, 1996.

21. Tom Hom, interview; Fung, *The Dragon Pilgrims*, 98–99; *San Diego Tribune*, Nov. 5, 1986, B-9, Aug. 14, 1990, D-1.

22. Susan Lew, interview, Aug. 11, 1996.

23. Hom and Tom are different romanizations of the same Chinese surname, which arose simply because different immigration officials wrote down their own interpretations of the name.

24. Huang Kunning, interview, Aug. 15, 1996.

25. According to Karl Fung, most of the OBC were more conservative in their theological orientation for several reasons: (1) Since the mainline missionary movement in China had been phased out after the Communists took over China in 1949, small conservative denominations took over many missionary works in Hong Kong or Taiwan, so many OBC were brought up in conservative churches; (2) OBC who experienced traumatic social change and wars looked for absolute authority and clear direction, and conservatism provided that feeling of security; (3) OBC Christians from Hong Kong and Taiwan were raised in a society where political involvement and civil liberties were discouraged, so they were satisfied with what conservative theology could offer. Fung, *The Dragon Pilgrims*, 111.
26. Fung, *The Dragon Pilgrims*, 111–17; Robert Fung, interview, Aug. 11, 1996.
27. Palinkas, *Rhetoric and Religious Experience*, 29–36.
28. Fung, *The Dragon Pilgrims*, 71, 107.
29. Ibid., 126.
30. Susan Lew, interview.
31. Weiss, *Valley City*, 253–56.
32. *San Diego Tribune*, Nov. 21, 1991, A-19.
33. This district is now called the Asian Pacific Thematic Historic District. The new name demonstrates the interests of the larger Asian community, whereas the earlier name reflects the leading role played by the Chinese community in its creation.
34. The plan called for the creation of a Chinese/Asian thematic district downtown. The overall aim is now to redevelop the downtown area while emphasizing the history and importance of Asians and Asia to San Diego. The Chinese Historical Museum is but one part of this and represents the efforts of the combined Chinese American community. Recently ground was broken in the Asian Pacific Thematic Historic District for the construction of a senior citizen apartment building, the first such project by the Chinese American community of San Diego. *San Diego Union*, May 10, 1997.
35. Mark T. Sullivan, "Chinese Mission, Hotel May Be Rescued by Plans," *San Diego Tribune*, Feb. 27, 1988, B-2.

CHINESE GLOSSARY

Bing Kung Tong	秉公堂	Guangdong	广东	**Panyu**	番禺	Xinhui	新会
Chee Kung Tong	致公堂	hanghui	行会	Sam Yap	三邑	Xinning	新宁
Chung Wah	中华	huiguan	会馆	Shunde	顺德	Zhongshan	中山
Enping	恩平	Kaiping	开平	Sze Yap	四邑		
gongsuo	公所	Nanhai	南海	tang	堂		

"He's a Chinaman"

by Edmund D. Jung, M.D.

May 1986

Editors' Note: *During the half century that has elapsed since WW II, the status of the Chinese in America has undergone vast changes and in general has improved. However, as illustrated in the following essay, the path has not always been smooth and tranquil. Dr. Edmund Jung's account of his courageous and tenacious fight against bigotry and racial prejudice at the workplace is but one of thousands of similar personal experiences during this era, often poignant and at times harrowing and heartbreaking, of Chinese Americans as they have sought to play the role of equal partners in America's multicultural society.*

Racial discrimination against the Chinese in America reached its culmination in the series of so-called Chinese Exclusion Acts between 1882 and 1904. Not until six decades later was a major step taken to correct this injustice, when President Franklin D. Roosevelt, on December 13, 1943, signed the Act to Repeal the Chinese Exclusion Acts, to Establish Quotas, and for Other Purposes.[1] It was in the 1970s and the 1980s that I became a target and suffered from the effects of such discrimination. However, legislation alone can do little to diminish racial discrimination even in federal agencies. What follows is a recount of my personal ordeal and the anguish it caused in my life.

BACKGROUND

I graduated from the University of California at San Francisco (UCSF) School of Medicine in 1944, completed an internship at Kaiser-Permanente Hospital in Oakland, and then served in the U.S. Army as a medical officer in the United States Army, with overseas duty in the South Pacific at the end of World War II. After returning home I began a residency training program in internal medicine. I did the first year of my residency at the UCSF Hospital, followed by three years at the San Francisco Veterans Administration Hospital. Although a total of only three years of residency were required for the specialty, I stayed an extra year when I was chosen by the chief of medicine to be the chief medical resident. Afterwards I passed the rigorous examination of the

American Board of Internal Medicine, certifying me as a specialist in that field.

My next step was to decide what to do in my chosen specialty. Private practice was eliminated from consideration because of my limited finances, recent marriage, and a distaste for the business aspects of private practice. The alternative was a salaried position. From my training I was already familiar with the excellent medical care provided at the San Francisco Veterans Administration Hospital, where we were able to offer patients the best care possible without worrying about how much to charge them.

It was 1951 when I decided to begin my professional career as an internist on the full-time staff at the Veterans Administration Hospital in Oakland. This decision led initially to my most productive and satisfying years in medical practice. My main duty was the primary care of acutely ill patients who had been screened in the admitting office and were found to require hospitalization. These were truly sick patients, with diagnostic and therapeutic problems, who needed the skills of trained internists. Because I also had training in allergy, I was additionally appointed chief of the Allergy Section. Our working environment was ideal. The Medical Service consisted of eight other board-certified internists, each one with a different subspecialty interest so that we could consult with each other. Our chief of medicine, Dr. Eli Movitt, and the assistant chief of medicine, Dr. Mervin Goldman, were excellent clinicians, teachers, and administrators. They and several of the staff held clinical faculty appointments at the UCSF Medical School, where they did volunteer teaching.

The staff of the Medical Service was remarkably stable and worked harmoniously during the two decades that we were together. We each made morning ward rounds on our patients with either Dr. Movitt or Dr. Goldman. The interchange of knowledge and experience was invaluable not only in the care that the patients received but in our own development. Medical conferences several times a week conducted by professors from UCSF, Stanford, or other medical schools added to the creation of an atmosphere of the highest professional caliber. It provided me the opportunity for continued advancement in my medical skills and knowledge. In the late 1950s the medical staff assumed the added responsibility of training interns and residents, who were added to our staff. A bonus of this program was the release of senior physicians from the rotation of nighttime and weekend duty at the hospital.

The V.A. Hospital moves to Martinez in 1963

In World War II, the conversion of the old Hotel Oakland into an Army Hospital (which was later transferred to the Veterans Administration) was originally intended as a temporary measure during wartime. A new hospital for the Veterans Administration had been planned for several years, but political and other problems in finding a location delayed its construction. Finally the new Veterans Administration Hospital was completed in Martinez, and we moved there in 1963. Although my commuting distance from San Francisco was trebled, I decided to stay with the new location because of the time I had already put in and also because of the congenial working conditions.

The new Martinez V.A. Hospital was located forty-five miles from the University of California at Davis (UCD) Medical School. At the time that the Veterans Administration Hospital moved to Martinez, UCD Medical School needed more hospital beds and patients for its teaching program. For many years the Veterans Administration policy nationwide was to affiliate with local medical schools in order to improve patient care and to provide for medical research. The merger of the Martinez V.A. Hospital with the UCD Medical School finally took place ten years later, in 1973. Unfortunately, in that year our chief of medicine, Dr. Eli Movitt, retired. He had been my one and only chief for twenty-two years, a man for whom I had the highest regard and respect. I was very sorry to see him leave; it marked the end of an era not only for him but, as it turned out, also for me.

THE NEW CHIEF OF MEDICINE 1974

Dr. Michael Geokas arrived at the Martinez V.A. Hospital on March 14, 1974, as the new chief of medicine.[2] He was concurrently appointed professor and vice chairman of the Department of Medicine at the UCD Medical School. A native of Greece, he received his M.D. degree there. He subsequently earned a Ph.D. degree in Biochemistry in Canada, and then trained in gastroenterology at UCSF. He was not a diplomate (i.e., certified as a specialist) of the American Board of Internal Medicine. Before coming to Martinez, he was the chief of medicine at the Sepulveda V.A. Hospital and professor of medicine at the University of California at Los Angeles (UCLA) Medical School. We later learned that he had to resign from both places.

Dr. Geokas made a strong initial impression on us with his dynamic and forceful personality. Realizing that some

changes would be inevitable, I was willing to make adjustments under the new regime. But I did not expect my whole professional career to be affected. Shortly after his arrival, one of the first things Dr. Geokas did, without any obvious reason, was to fire Mrs. Caroline Lowe, a capable and experienced Chinese American secretary at the Medical Service who had worked for Dr. Movitt for many years. Her departure was a portent of things to come.

Dr. Geokas's aim to replace the original staff physicians then became more overt. Gradually a few of the old staff left and were replaced by new men he recruited. Perhaps a minor incident will illustrate the tactics he used. Dr. Geokas gave a "get acquainted" dinner party at his home, ostensibly for the old and the new staff members and their spouses to meet each other and to meet him and his wife. The disparity in treatment became obvious when the old staff and their spouses were shunted down to the basement playroom almost immediately after their arrival at the house, while the new members and the hosts remained upstairs. There was little or no attempt by the hosts to see to the mingling of the two groups and no chance for the two groups to become acquainted with each other. We actually saw little of the host and hostess during the entire evening.

In time many of the old staff left the hospital, either by transfer elsewhere, by resignation, or by retirement. They could not tolerate Dr. Geokas's abrasive and abusive ways any longer. Only three of the original staff remained, Dr. Robert Livingston, Dr. Selig Weinstein, and myself. But our prestige and self-esteem were eroded by a progressive decline in our professional responsibilities. One of the first changes made was to eliminate us from the primary care of the hospitalized patients. This had been our principal function during all the previous years. At first I mistakenly attributed this move to the anticipation of gaining a full house staff (medical interns and residents) who would be assigned to the patients while the senior staff, myself included, would supervise them. But Dr. Geokas assigned the teaching duties only to his new staff members.

Allergy Section

In 1959 I had been appointed chief of the Allergy Section by Dr. Movitt,[3] but soon after Dr. Geokas arrived in 1974, he abolished the Allergy Section by incorporating it into the Chest Section, thus eliminating my position. Dr. Geokas's excuse was that this was what had been done at the Sepulveda V.A. Hospital, where he had come from. I realized later that this was one of many ploys he would use to disempower me.

In this connection, during the early recruitment of his new staff, Dr. Geokas interviewed Dr. Ian Smith from the University of Iowa School of Medicine for the position of chief of infectious disease. His wife, Dr. Jeanne Smith, an allergist at the same institution, was also offered a position as chief of Allergy to induce both of them to accept positions. Dr. Geokas asked me to show her around the hospital and my allergy clinic. He confided to me that, with the addition of Dr. Jeanne Smith, the Allergy Section would be expanded (ignoring the fact that he had abolished it) and that the Martinez V.A. Hospital would be one up on U.C. Davis, since the Medical School did not have an Allergy Section at that time. The Smiths, however, declined Dr. Geokas's offers to join his staff.

Through the years that I was at the V.A. Hospital, I had built up a considerable allergy practice, so I continued to take care of these veterans despite the abolition of the Allergy Section. I also continued to consult on allergy problems in our hospital as well as on referrals from V.A. Hospitals in San Francisco, Palo Alto, and Livermore. During this time I also served as the allergy consultant once a week at the V.A. Regional Office in San Francisco. Because of this added responsibility during the years before Dr. Geokas arrived, I did not seek a faculty appointment at the UCSF Medical School as several of my colleagues had done.

Acupuncture

As part of my cultural heritage, I had long been interested in and had studied Chinese medicine, herbology, and acupuncture. My interest in acupuncture was accelerated and intensified following President Nixon's trip to China in 1972, when interest in and scientific reports on acupuncture started appearing in medical literature. Between 1972 and 1973, Dr. Alan Shifman, a resident in neurology, carried out acupuncture treatments at the Martinez V.A. Hospital with the approval of his chief of neurology and the chief of staff, Dr. Robert Nolan. Dr. Shifman had received training in acupuncture before coming to Martinez. I had learned the technique from reading and from international experts at workshops given at the Second World Symposium on Acupuncture in San Francisco. I also gained practical experience with Dr. Shifman at his office after he went into private practice.

During the one-year interim between Dr. Movitt's retirement and the arrival of Dr. Geokas, I followed Dr. Shifman's example and obtained permission from the acting chief of medicine, Dr. Joseph Belber, to use acupuncture in the treatment of selected patients—with their written consent—who were suffering from various pain syndromes and who had not responded to conventional methods of therapy. I was gaining valuable experience and getting good results in this modality by the time Dr. Geokas took over. I thought it best to let him know what I was doing but sensed an immediate negative reaction when he asked if I had been cleared by the Research Committee to do acupuncture. Such a directive had been issued long after I had started my program. He ignored my initial inquiry as to whether I could submit a research proposal until I pressed the question again. After working a week preparing what I thought was a well-constructed pro-

posal,[4] I submitted it to his office on May 16, 1974. That was the last I heard or saw of the proposal; it never went beyond Dr. Geoka's desk. Thus ended my short-lived practice of acupuncture.

Faculty appointment

Soon after he arrived, Dr. Geokas began referring to the old staff physicians as his "faculty" because of the new affiliation with U.C. Davis Medical School. He asked us to submit curricula vitae and applications for faculty appointments. We did this, but I heard no more about my application. When the new men he had recruited came in, they were immediately appointed assistant clinical professors of medicine. Eventually the other two old-timers (both Caucasians) also received their appointments, but I did not. In a subsequent Equal Employment Opportunity (EEO) investigation,[5] Dr. Geokas's explanation for withholding recommendation for my appointment was that he was still "observing" me. I then went to the UCSF Medical School, my alma mater, and was quickly appointed to the faculty as assistant clinical professor of medicine based on my qualifications, experience, and references. But I still was "not good enough" to be on Dr. Geokas's "faculty".

However, I encountered difficulty getting time off from the V.A. Hospital to teach one-half day a week in San Francisco. The only way I could do it was to be charged with annual leave. Other staff physicians, who also had UCSF appointments, did not have this problem; they were granted excused absence for teaching, in accordance with V.A. regulations.[6]

On-call roster

During my years of service at the V.A. Hospital, an on-call roster of physicians was posted each month. This was a list of senior physicians who were available nights and weekends for the house staff on duty to call if they needed help. My name always appeared on the list until July 1975, when it did not appear. After three months, during which time I realized that only my name and no others was deleted, I asked Dr. Geokas's secretary why. She replied that it was an order from Dr. Geokas. My name continued to be missing from the roster for nine months. This deletion was noted by my few remaining colleagues, who jokingly asked how I was so lucky as to get off the list. Later, when my EEO complaint became known, the names of other physicians started to be dropped from the list temporarily and randomly until my name was eventually restored. I could only assume that this was Dr. Geokas's devious method of covering up. In this connection, it should be noted that my name was also omitted from the hospital telephone directory by order of Dr. Geokas; this was another way for him to demean me. This deletion lasted for six months until a memorandum on April 6, 1976, indicated that my name should be added to the telephone directory.

"Blond, blue-eyed, real American boys"

Prior to the affiliation with U.C. Davis, the house staff at the Martinez V.A. Hospital included Asian American graduates of American medical schools and also foreign medical graduates from India, the Philippines, and other Asian countries. The Veterans Administration later on issued a directive stating that at least 80 percent of the house staff must be graduates of American or Canadian medical schools. Soon after Dr. Geokas arrived, he announced widely throughout the hospital that he would bring in "blond, blue-eyed, real American boys."[7] Clearly there was nothing in the V.A. regulations designating the hair, skin, or eye color of the house staff that could have prompted his remarks. In view of his own dark complexion and thick foreign accent, I could only presume that he was attempting to overcompensate for his own foreignness. After Dr. Geokas was successful in recruiting a full complement of medical residents for his first house staff, he proudly announced throughout the hospital that "the Yanks are coming."[8]

"Chinaman" and slant-eye gesture

In the summer of 1974, Dr. Geokas was talking one day to Dr. Glenn Lubeck (of the original staff and my close friend) and Dr. Yurchak (the new chief medical resident chosen by Dr. Geokas) when my name was mentioned. Dr. Geokas referred to me as the "Chinaman" and mimicked the stereotype "slant eyes" of Asians by pulling the outer corners of his eyes up with his fingers. This was the first indication that Dr. Geokas's prejudice against me was blatantly racial. Other acts, albeit less outspoken, were to follow. Both Drs. Lubeck and Yurchak were astounded by the uncalled for racist remark and gesture. They reported the incident to me later, and I incorporated it in my subsequent EEO complaint.[9]

Asian Americans who have grown up in this country have all experienced the humiliation of these racist gestures and slurs, particularly during childhood. Such stereotyping of Asian racial features has been used as a source of ridicule for more than a century and is as old as it is offensive. It is especially unbecoming and uncalled for from a supposedly educated professor and chief of medicine.

A few weeks after his arrival, Dr. Geokas was discussing patient care with the staff at a weekly meeting of the Medical Service. At that time, I was the only Asian American on the staff and was present at the meeting. For no reason that I could discern, Dr. Geokas told a story concerning an elderly, confused patient and, without it having any relevance, stated that the patient said "He's a Chinaman." I could only assume that by attributing the remark to the hypothetical patient, the story afforded Dr. Geokas a chance to direct the racial slur toward me.[10]

I am a third-generation American and, although not blond and blue-eyed, I am as all-American as Mom, apple pie, and chop suey. I lived in a Eurocentric America in my early years in the small mining towns of Mason and Yerington, Nevada, and later in a more cosmopolitan San Francisco. At that time racial slurs and gestures were common. To this day, such ignorant and insensitive remarks and gestures have not disappeared. In fact, they are even considered by some to be acceptable when they are regarded as merely a "joke."

As a child I had been brought up in the Chinese tradition of respecting my elders and those in authority, so I overlooked the earlier acts of discrimination by Dr. Geokas; I attributed them to the faux pas of an immigrant who was unfamiliar with the social mores here. At the beginning I was also intimidated by Dr. Geokas's domineering persona.

Plotting against the whites

On a number of occasions during the year after Dr. Geokas came to Martinez, whenever he saw me chatting in the hallways with one or more of my colleagues, Dr. Geokas would pointedly exclaim within hearing of everyone in the vicinity, "Oh, plotting against the whites again, eh!"[11] Since I was the only nonwhite present in each and every instance, my only interpretation was that the remark was directed at me and my race.

Intermediate Care Program

After Dr. Geokas removed the three of us original staff men from primary care responsibilities for patients, we were left in limbo for a few months. We had no specific duties until Dr. Geokas came up with the idea of an "Intermediate Care Program" for us. This program consisted of taking care of patients who were no longer in need of acute medical attention and therefore were of "no teaching value" (his words, although he denied them later). These were patients who had recovered from their acute illnesses and were either waiting for placement in a nursing home or for other disposition; some were cancer patients referred to the Martinez V.A. Hospital, which at that time was a V.A. center for cobalt therapy. Their care did not require the experience of senior staff physicians and Board-certified internists. We felt that it was another scheme by Dr. Geokas to downgrade and insult us.

Transfer off the Medical Service

In October 1975 I was "loaned" to the Ambulatory Care Service "temporarily." The duties there consisted of screening applicants who were seeking hospitalization or were requesting ambulatory care. These duties were usually handled by physicians who had no specialty training. Thus, I was removed from what little, but more responsible, in-patient care I was still doing. The other two old-timers, Dr. Weinstein and Dr. Livingston, managed to remain on the wards. I probably would have been kept in the Admitting Office longer, but my EEO complaint became known in December 1975. At that time I was brought back to the Medical Service. This was at the time during which the Intermediate Care Program was instituted, so my functions were still negligible. Eventually, in September 1977, the final blow occurred; all three of us remaining old-timers were removed from the Medical Service and transferred to the Ambulatory Care Service. The transfer of the three of us together made it appear this time that there was no disparate treatment of me. The other two were willing to get out from under Dr. Geokas's control, but I was just starting my battle with him. When I protested the transfer, the hospital director, Mr. Nixon, assumed the responsibility for the transfer. He claimed that the move was due to the need to fill vacancies in the Ambulatory Care Service and to hire sub-specialists for the Medical Service. Thus Dr. Geokas finally accomplished what he had set out to do, but it took him over three years to get rid of the last of us.

THE EQUAL EMPLOYMENT OPPORTUNITY (EEO) COMPLAINT

While all these acts of discrimination and harassment were going on, I was disinclined to "rock the boat," since I was within a year or two of retirement; I thought I could endure the humiliation until then. I was also in awe of Dr. Geokas's domineering power, which contrasted with my low-key, mild-mannered demeanor. But as each demeaning incident accumulated, I became increasingly less sanguine. In the fall of 1975, about a year and a half after Dr. Geokas arrived, I had had enough, and I decided to take action at the urging of Dr. Robert L. Nolan (an M.D. and a lawyer). He was the previous chief of staff at the hospital and was familiar with Dr. Geokas. Dr. Nolan helped me prepare my first EEO complaint.[12] We filed it on December 17, 1975. This marked the beginning of what proved to be a long, drawn-out battle, which I had not anticipated would last five and a half years. The agony and distress involved in the subsequent countless hours of work filing complaints, making depositions, appearing at hearings, preparing and filing appeals, writing letters, and making telephone calls and personal contacts made my life a shambles. It occupied time and energy that I could have spent more meaningfully. The burden was shared by my family during all those troubled years.

The EEO Investigation

After a delay of three months, the EEO investigation took place between March 29 and April 7, 1976. It was conducted by Mr. Henry Gonzalez, an employee of the Wadsworth V.A. Hospital. In my complaint, I listed twenty-two charges of racial discrimination by Dr. Geokas. Depositions were obtained from Drs. Nolan, Geokas, William McFarland, Selig B. Weinstein, Sam Thal, and Mr. Steven Gulyas and Mr. Amando Rao. After concluding the investigation, Mr. Gonzalez decided that the "allegations" were "not determined" in two of the charges and "not sustained" in the rest. Bias was apparent in the Gonzalez report in the description of my testimony as "allegations," while the assertions of my opposing witnesses were called "evidence."[13] The decisions made by Mr. Gonzalez were a disappointment, but they were not entirely unexpected. The fallacy of the EEO investigative process lies in the assignment of a V.A. employee to probe complaints made against the agency in which he is employed. On July 16, 1976, an attempt at informal resolution was unsuccessful, so on July 21, 1976, the agency issued a proposed disposition reflecting a finding of "no discrimination."

Interference

About the same time that I was involved with my case, Dr. Matthew Baggett, an African American medical resident, filed an EEO complaint of racial discrimination against Dr. Geokas.[14] Dr. Geokas learned about this and warned Dr. Baggett that he would need recommendations for further training and for the examination of the American Board of Internal Medicine.

Later on, when my Civil Service Commission hearing was about to come up, Dr. Baggett prepared a deposition on my behalf. Dr. Geokas heard about this also and again threatened Dr. Baggett, using the same warning as before. As a result, Dr. Baggett did not sign or transmit his deposition.

When Dr. Baggett did not withdraw his own EEO complaint, he was summoned a third time by Dr. Geokas and warned of the adverse effects on his career if the complaint was not withdrawn. These were clearcut acts of interference with a witness and probable obstruction of justice, conspiracy against the rights of a citizen, and interference with the enjoyment of federal employment, which could involve violation of the Criminal Code.

Dr. Nolan and I referred this aspect of the problem to Congressman Philip Burton[15] who in turn asked the Department of Justice to investigate.[16] In his reply to Congressman Burton, the Assistant Attorney General stated that he had asked the FBI in San Francisco to conduct a preliminary investigation and that "upon receiving a report on the results of the investigation, appropriate action would then be determined."[17] However, that was as far as it went; nothing more was heard about the issue.

A Filipina medical resident

In the fall of 1976, a racial incident occurred that concerned a Filipina physician who had started as a medical resident during the last year that Dr. Movitt was chief of medicine. When

Dr. Geokas took over, she needed one more year to complete her training but was told by Dr. Geokas that she would not be kept on because of her sex and national origin. She related this to me one day when we were having lunch together. I included this incident in my charges against Dr. Geokas in a Civil Service Commission hearing. When Dr. Geokas learned of my move, he reversed his decision and allowed her to continue her residency. She then decided not to testify in my case for fear of reprisal.

THE CIVIL SERVICE COMMISSION HEARING

Dr. Nolan and I continued the fight by filing an appeal with the Civil Service Commission.[18] The hearing was not scheduled until October 27, 1976. Through further delays it finally took place on November 9, 10, and 17, 1976. Dr. Nolan served as my attorney while the V.A. was represented by David Firestone from the legal staff of the V.A. Regional Office. Five witnesses, including myself, Dr. Nolan, and Dr. Geokas, testified. Seventeen documents were entered into evidence. One of these documents revealed that Dr. Geokas had been effectively induced to resign under pressure from his position as chief of medicine at the Sepulveda V.A. Hospital in 1974 because of abusive practices against the personnel there. He was also required to resign from a concurrent post as vice-chairman of the UCLA Department of Medicine. Yet, in spite of this knowledge regarding his previous problems with personnel, he had been hired to come to the Martinez V.A. Hospital and the UCD Medical School. If more attention had been paid to the records about Dr. Geokas, both institutions, my colleagues, and I would have been spared all the trouble he was to cause.

During his testimony at the Civil Service Commission hearing, Dr. Geokas did not specifically deny many of the charges of discrimination made against him but stated repeatedly that he did not have any recollection of making a particular remark or, in some instances, that if he had made such a remark, it was meant as a joke. On some charges, he arrogantly claimed that it was his prerogative as chief of medicine to do what he did.

Findings by the Civil Service Commission hearing examiner

About five months later, on April 6, 1977, the Civil Service Commission complaints examiner, William C. Jenkins, issued a 254-page report of his findings.[19] The conclusion was that I had been discriminated against because of my race and national origin as evidenced by the derogatory comment and gesture directed at me were made by Dr. Geokas and when my name was removed from the on-call roster. The events surrounding Dr. Baggett's refusal to sign and return a deposition to the EEO investigator were also shown to have

interfered with the processing of my case. Thus, of the seventeen charges presented, only three were found in my favor; the others were rejected. Still, this was better than none found in my favor in the EEO investigation. Recommendations were made for corrective action with regard to the derogatory comment and gestures, and the actions and statements shown to have constituted interference with the complaint. Recommendation was also made for "consideration for inclusion" of my name on future on-call rosters and that the "eventual determination of this matter and the reasons therefore be communicated to the complainant."

These findings and recommendations of the Civil Service Commission Complaints examiner were adopted by the V.A. on May 11, 1977.[20] The Veterans Administration decided that "some allegations of discrimination and interference are substantiated by the evidence of record," a small gain in the fight.

CHINESE FOR AFFIRMATIVE ACTION (CAA) GETS INVOLVED

After we had launched into the battle, Dr. Nolan learned about and contacted Chinese for Affirmation Action (CAA), "a San Francisco community based organization dedicated to defend the civil rights of and to promote equal employment opportunity for Chinese Americans." Henry Der, the brilliant and capable executive director of the organization, made on-site visits to the hospital, spoke to the hospital director, and wrote forceful letters to congressmen, the administrator of the V.A.,[21] and others. What had been my private affair now became a concern of the Asian community; my fight had become theirs also. I had never expected such a heart-warming response, as the community rallied to my support. This must have been a collective expression of pentup emotions felt over the injustices caused by racial discrimination and suffered by so many for the past century.

Dr. Geokas and the Board of Medical Quality Assurance

Two months after the Civil Service Commission hearing results were released, a small and inconspicuous announcement appeared on a back page of the *San Francisco Chronicle* on June 10, 1977, stating that Governor Jerry Brown had appointed Dr. Geokas to the Board of Medical Quality Assurance. This board licenses and controls health professionals to practice in California. Chinese for Affirmative Action immediately sprang into action, and the next day the *San Francisco Chronicle* published Chinese for Affirmative Action's opposition to the nomination because of Dr. Geokas's proven record of racial discrimination. Bay Area Chinese Americans, both individuals and organizations such as Asian Americans for Community Involvement,[22] were outraged and joined in a concerted effort during the next two months to protest the Geokas appointment. However, the Brown administration took no action, stating only that it was investigating the case. Finally, Henry Der and a group from Chinese for Affirmative Action went to Sacramento on August 19, 1977, to hold a press conference at the Capitol. Brown's office exerted pressure on Chinese for Affirmative Action to call it off. About ten minutes before the scheduled news conference, Brown's staff notified Henry Der that Dr. Geokas had submitted a request at midnight that his name be withdrawn. This was an apparent move to undercut the need for the conference. But the conference was held anyway. Because the Brown staff had been unwilling to make a simple statement about the Geokas resignation, Chinese for Affirmative Action decided to notify the press themselves. Dr. Rolland Lowe stated that Chinese American physicians throughout the state were opposed to all forms of racial discrimination. Dr. George Wong added that the governor should appoint only qualified persons who are sensitive to the needs of all Californians. All of the San Francisco Bay Area, and neighboring city newspapers (including *East West* and *Asian Week*), reported on the progress of the case.[23]

ANOTHER EEO COMPLAINT AND THE CIVIL SERVICE COMMISSION APPEAL BOARD

Following the incomplete victory resulting from the Civil Service Commission examination, Dr. Nolan and I were far from finished. We filed an appeal with the Civil Service Commission Appeal and Review Board. Knowing there would be delays before this board made its decision, we also filed a second EEO complaint on October 27, 1977.[24] This was done because, after the first EEO investigation and the Civil Service Commission examination, Dr. Geokas continued his harassment and abuse with continued degrading assignments and by ignoring my very existence. He showed no sign that he had done anything wrong and repeatedly denied in public that he was guilty of any wrongdoing. In my second EEO complaint, I listed seventy-seven discrimination reprisal specifications against Dr. Geokas for the harassment and disparate treatment toward me since the time he was "reprimanded." The second EEO investigation was held on October 16, 1978, again by a V.A. employee. It resulted in the finding that there was no evidence of reprisal, race, national origin, and/or race discrimination to substantiate my allegations.

We were dissatisfied with these findings and sent an appeal to the Equal Employment Opportunity Commission in Washington, D.C. On November 8, 1979, a final decision was rendered in which the agency was found to have erred in rejecting for investigation seven of the allegations I had made.[25] This was an example of the many steps we had to take in our struggle.

A third EEO complaint was lodged on May 12, 1980, and partial findings of discrimination were returned on October 10, 1980. Unfortunately, the documents regarding these findings are missing from my files and I am unable to provide further details.

Meeting of ward secretaries with Dr. Geokas

One important charge we had made in the second EEO complaint that we thought was convincingly documented although it failed to impress the investigator, concerned a ward secretaries meeting called by Dr. Geokas in December 1975. Dr. Nolan and I had not heard about that meeting until after the Civil Service Commission hearing, when the secretaries told us about it. About twenty ward secretaries were present at the meeting when, according to a sworn deposition by Mary Jane Lenca, Dr. Geokas started by relating his qualifications and then his accomplishments in creating a "new image." He then stated that "when I first came here all the doctors spoke like this" [he then made a slant-eyed gesture]—'chee, chang, fewg, goo'—but I changed that right away."[26] Ms. Lenca, a Caucasian who was born in Japan and who had a high regard for Asian culture, was "extremely shocked and very embarrassed" by his remarks. Another deposition by Ernie Johnson,[27] an African American male secretary, stated that he was late to the meeting and had just walked in when Dr. Geokas said, "When I first got here all we had were foreigners, sing, sang, jung." Johnson was an EEO counselor at the time and felt it especially peculiar for Dr. Geokas, who spoke with a thick foreign accent, to imply that he didn't like foreigners. A deposition by Carol del Grande stated that Dr. Geokas "was talking about his plans and that in the past most of the interns and residents all had slanted eyes, and he made a motion, and spoke 'Chin, Chan, Yung.'"[28] Thus, there were three independent depositions testifying to the same incident, but in different words. In spite of this strong testimony, Dr. Geokas was found not guilty by the EEO investigator. This investigator was again a V.A. employee.

Decision of the Civil Service Appeals Board

It took two years before I received the decision of the Civil Service Commission Board of Appeals and Review in Washington, D.C., on May 16, 1979.[29] They reaffirmed the findings of discrimination previously made by the agency regarding the remark "Chinaman," the mimicking of facial appearance, and the removal of my name from the on-call roster. In addition, the board reversed the agency decision of no discrimination on four other charges, namely: the Geokas statement at a staff meeting regarding a patient saying "Chinaman," the Geokas statement concerning "plotting against the whites," the failure to answer my application for academic appointment, and the failure to respond to my research proposal on acupuncture. Thus, in addition to the three charges previously won, I had gained four more. Actually, with the charge of interference, the total was eight charges won. This marked another major step in winning the fight.

FEDERAL COURT

As a crowning step toward seeking justice, Dr. Nolan and I filed a "Complaint for Damages, Injunctive Relief, and Declaratory Relief (Civil Rights)" with the United States District Court of Northern California on July 31, 1978.[30] There ensued a chain of interrogations and depositions, followed by filing of motions for summary judgment, defendant's opposition, plaintiff's reply memorandum, plaintiff's objections to exhibits lodged and motions to strike, motions for leave to file post-hearing memoranda, and plaintiff's notice and opposition and objections to portions of proposed order received April 18, 1980, and so forth, for a total of thirteen procedures in three years. On June 4, 1981, United States District Judge Spencer Williams approved a compromise settlement.[31] By doing so, an expensive and drawn-out trial was avoided. Also by that time many of my former witnesses were no longer available and I would have been at a disadvantage if the case were tried de novo. The terms of the stipulation and order approving compromise settlement were as follows:

> (1) The defendant, Donald L. Curtis, in his capacity as Acting Administrator of Veterans Affairs, acknowledges, concedes, and admits those findings and conclusions that were made by the Civil Service Commission Complaints Examiner on April 6, 1977, the Veterans Administration Final Agency Decision letter of May 11, 1977, the Civil Service Commission Appeals and Review Board decision of May 16, 1979, and the partial findings of the Veterans Administration Report of Investigation of October 10, 1980, that the plaintiff was discriminated against while employed at the Veterans Administration Hospital in Martinez, California as specified in the aforementioned documents. (2) Defendant, Donald L. Curtis . . . , agrees that the plaintiff will not be subject to discrimination on the basis of race, national origin, or age, and will be free from any restraint, reprisal, or retaliation as a result of filing the administrative complaints and causes of action herein. (3) Defendant, Donald L. Curtis . . . , agrees that the Agency will sponsor a hospital program at the V.A. Hospital, Martinez, in Asian History, similar to its Black History Week, providing sufficient employee interest is manifested. Defendant Donald L. Curtis . . . , agrees to promptly pay to plaintiff the sum of Five Hundred Dollars ($500.00) in full settlement of plaintiff's claims for costs herein, following entry of this stipulation, order and dismissal of these actions.

(I never received the $500 nor did I pursue it.)

THE MALPRACTICE SUIT

Although on the surface it would appear that we had not won much of a victory, the whole affair has to be considered from the point of view that it is extremely rare for a federal agency to make any concessions. We were satisfied that we had done the best we could. Interestingly, it was during this time frame that the Martinez V.A. Hospital was being sued for malpractice by the widow of one of my former patients. Without going into a lengthy exposition of the suit, suffice it to say that there was no basis for the litigation. It was a nui-

sance case without merit. My deposition, taken on February 22, 1978,[32] as the principal witness, helped to win the suit for the V.A. Hospital. In working with and on the side of the V.A. legal staff this time, I probably impressed them that I was not as professionally inept as Dr. Geokas had painted me to be during the discrimination hearings. This malpractice suit took place prior to my civil rights complaints in federal court. I doubt, however, that it had any influence on the V.A. lawyers' agreement to the compromise settlement made in federal court.

THE AFTERMATH OF THE LEGAL BATTLE

After a long, drawn-out five and a half years, the legal battle had come to closure for me. What I had won was the admission that there was racial discrimination practiced against me by Dr. Geokas at the V.A. Hospital. What I had lost was prestige and self-esteem in having been knocked off the Medical Service, I was no longer practicing primary care of hospitalized patients, I was not teaching the house staff, I was no longer the chief of Allergy, I was denied the pursuit of acupuncture practice, and I was denied a faculty appointment at UCD Medical School. My medical career had started out gloriously and continued to be fulfilling during the first twenty-four years. Unfortunately, the last seven years brought it to a close with an unhappy ending. My only consolation was that I was still able to offer some medical attention and help to a few patients in the Outpatient Service during the periods of diminished responsibility. Also, at the end, I felt a tremendous relief from the burden that was lifted from me. And I was happy to see that at last my efforts had resulted in justice being served.

Corrective action

Dr. Geokas was apparently "admonished" as a result of the federal court orders, but whatever corrective actions were taken by the Veterans Administration were not disclosed, in order "to protect him." However, as a result of one of the hearings, it was revealed that Dr. Geokas was to be "afforded the opportunity of taking courses in equal opportunity employment, basic supervisory duties, or other courses deemed appropriate." Dr. Geokas enrolled in such a program at Harvard, an intensive course conducted jointly by the Harvard School of Public Health and the School of Business Administration. The course "places emphasis on leadership style and interpersonal effectiveness." No doubt the program was attended at government expense, including travel vouchers, tuition, per diem expenses, and official leave time for Dr. Geokas. As will be shown later, Dr. Geokas did not learn anything from the course to make him change his behavior. In spite of the findings of racial discrimination by the Civil Service Commission, the Civil Service Commission

Appeals Board, and the Federal Court, Dr. Geokas continued as the chief of medicine at the Martinez V.A. Hospital and as vice chairman and professor at the Department of Medicine at UCD Medical School. He also continued to deny repeatedly that he was guilty of discrimination; instead, he accused me of lying! He also continued the abusive treatment of his staff, as will be shown below.

Efforts to oust Dr. Geokas

Following the federal court settlement, renewed efforts were made by the Asian American community and its organizations to remove Dr. Geokas from his dual positions of responsibility at the V.A. Hospital and the UCD Medical School. Letters were sent to both institutions by Chinese for Affirmative Action and by Asian Americans for Community Involvement,[33] but no action was taken in response. Later on, help came from a source that was not entirely unexpected; it had just taken time to develop. On March 14, 1982, the *Sacramento Bee* reported: "More recent allegations of harassment, intimidation, and threats against Martinez employees made last year have become the subject of pending investigation and the main preoccupation of Martinez staffers. Five of eleven technicians in Geokas's enzymology research laboratory have quit and the other six are expected to either quit or file complaints against him when the investigation is completed."

On August 19, 1981, the *Contra Costa Times* reported that a group calling itself "Concerned V.A. Physicians" had written a letter to the newspaper "charging Geokas with harassment, intimidation, and obnoxious comments."[34] These were the same men that Dr. Geokas had hand-picked to replace the old staff when he arrived in 1974. They were my adversaries during the early years of my fight. They sided with Dr. Geokas then and, as they progressively took charge, made my presence on the Medical Service increasingly uncomfortable and unwanted. Now they were suffering abuses. Now they were turning against Dr. Geokas and wanted him ousted. Other newspapers from Martinez, Oakland, Sacramento, and San Francisco reported that Dr. Geokas had been charged with or was guilty of racism and was being investigated by a team from Washington.[35]

While I was on terminal (accumulated annual and sick) leave before official retirement from the hospital, I was surprised one evening to receive a phone call from Dr. Harry Adams, the assistant chief of medicine and one of my former foes, asking me for advice on fighting Dr. Geokas on behalf of their group.

The Proposed discharge of Dr. Geokas by the V.A.

On April 12, 1982, a letter from Dr. Earl Brown, V.A. associate deputy chief medical director, informed Dr. Geokas that his discharge from the V.A. was proposed because of his demonstrated ineptitude, inefficiency, and misconduct" and cited more than twenty charges against him.[36] The V.A. investigative team from Washington, D.C., began a one-week hearing on Dr. Geokas on July 12, 1982. More then three hundred witnesses were interviewed and two hundred affidavits filed. This investigation resulted in a recommendation on October 8, 1982, that Dr. Geokas be transferred to the Livermore V.A. Hospital.[37] He was to report there in sixty days, or he could appeal the decision in fifteen days. Livermore V.A. Hospital is a small 190-bed facility without medical school affiliation. Dr. Geokas was to be chief of medicine there, replacing Dr. Glenn Lubeck, my old friend, who was retiring. Because of the transfer, Dr. Geokas, who was still professor of medicine at U.C. Davis Medical School, would lose that faculty position. He had already been deposed as vice chairman of the Medical Department when that appointment was not renewed.[38]

Dr. Geokas's transfer overruled

But the proposed transfer of Dr. Geokas to Livermore did not come to pass. The outgoing V.A. administrator, Mr. Robert Nimmo, in a stunning decision dated October 26, 1982, ruled that Dr. Geokas would remain as chief of medicine at Martinez V.A. Hospital. Mr. Nimmo officially admonished Dr. Geokas but overruled the recommendation for his transfer to Livermore, which had been made by his own top medical director. Mr. Nimmo cited Dr. Geokas's "record of distinguished accomplishments in the field of medicine and contributions to the V.A., as well as conflicting testimony, support from a variety of medical groups, and the effects of reassignment on Dr. Geokas's career as reasons against tougher punishment."[39]

The V.A. medical staff, the Asian American community, Chinese for Affirmative Action, and others were angered and surprised by Mr. Nimmo's decision. The contention was that Congressman George Miller, D-Martinez (to whose campaign fund Dr. Geokas reportedly gave a $300 contribution earlier in the week), intervened with top V.A. officials on Dr. Geokas's behalf. Some V.A. sources suggested that Mr. Nimmo went ahead with the unusual decision because he himself had given notice of resignation from his post under duress. Mr. Nimmo had been under fire because of a costly redecoration of his Washington office, his personal use of chauffeurs, the running up of other big expenses, and for his rocky relations with veterans groups.[40]

The V.A. medical staff petitions President Reagan

In November 1982, nine of the ten permanent full-time staff physicians under Dr. Geokas signed a letter petitioning President Reagan asking for the ouster of Dr. Geokas.[41] A White House spokesman said that the letter would be sent through channels. However, existing law prevented the president from intervening in such cases and authorized the V.A.

administrator to make the final decisions. President Reagan never replied to the physicians' appeal. The aftermath to all this was that eventually nearly all of the medical staff departed and were replaced by still another group.

CONCLUSION

After delaying my retirement until I had seen this matter through to the end, I retired in June 1982, after thirty-one years of service at the hospital and a total of thirty-seven years of federal service (including time in the Army in World War II). This was several years beyond the time I was eligible to retire but I felt that I could not leave until I had finished what I had started. Since retirement, I have continued teaching part-time at UCSF Medical School as an associate clinical professor of medicine. I have greatly enjoyed this time spent with bright, young medical students as well as the time spent pursuing other activities in the company of my wife, time we did not have when we were both still in medical practice. At the time of this writing in May 1986, Dr. Geokas was still the chief of medicine at Martinez V.A. Hospital, with his second personally selected medical staff, and professor of medicine on the U.C. Davis Medical School faculty.

Prejudice is a horrible thing. My own experience as its target is only one example of a never-ending onslaught practiced by one individual or many against an individual or a group designated as "different." The results are as devastating as the denial of employment or promotion—a livelihood essentially—and as subtle as devaluating a person's worth and contribution to a career for which that individual is well trained and eminently qualified. That person is robbed ultimately of the satisfaction one is entitled to feel from a lifetime dedicated to work. And yet, we seem unable to check the growth of such prejudice to this day. Indeed, it would appear that attempts to deal with the problems brought on by prejudice may even now be escalating to an increasingly controversial level, however hard we may try to correct for the resulting injustices.

ADDENDUM (1997)

The denouement to the Geokas affair took place in 1990, when I heard that Dr. Geokas had finally retired (or had been fired) from Martinez V.A. Hospital. He had applied for a faculty position at the University of California at San Francisco (UCSF), School of Medicine, Department of Medicine. I wrote a letter to the department, of which I was a member, giving them a detailed exposition of Dr. Geokas's past record earlier in Sepulveda and Los Angeles and later in Martinez and Davis.[42]

Whether my letter had any influence or not, I was satisfied with the outcome that Dr. Geokas was not accepted for the faculty appointment at UCSF Medical School.[43] This out-

come gave me a feeling of relief, knowing that he would not do any harm at my school. It was also a partial pay back for all the grief he had caused me by making my last years of medical practice such disturbed and unhappy ones.

NOTES

Acknowledgment: I am deeply indebted to Dr. Robert L. Nolan for his guidance, legal skills, and tireless effort in pursuing this battle from the beginning through to the end. Without him, victory would not have been possible.

1. Thomas W. Chinn, Him Mark Lai, and Philip P. Choy, *A History of the Chinese in America: A Syllabus* (San Francisco: Chinese Historical Society of America, 1969), 26–28.
2. *Daily Bulletin* (VAH Martinez) Mar. 19, 1974.
3. Memorandum 13–59, V.A. Hospital, Oakland, California, Apr. 24, 1959.
4. Edmund D. Jung, M.D., "Acupuncture: Clinical Investigation" (research proposal), Apr. 24, 1974.
5. Equal Employment Opportunity complaint held Mar. 29 through Apr. 7, 1976, at the V.A. Hospital Martinez, Calif. "Report of Investigation" by Henry Gonzalez, June 17, 1976. Hereafter cited as EEO complaint.
6. DM&S Supplement, MP-5, part II, chapter 7, change 1, paragraph 7.08, Mar. 26, 1976: "Full time physicians . . . may accept teaching responsibilities in private and public colleges and universities, providing the teaching obligations do not conflict with the performance of their duties in DM&S. Absences resulting from such teaching assignments, if no remuneration is involved, may be excused without charge to leave."
7. EEO complaint.
8. Ibid.
9. Ibid.
10. Ibid.
11. Ibid.
12. Ibid.
13. Ibid.
14. Equal Employment Opportunity complaint, "Affidavit of Matthew Alvin Baggett, M.D.," June 4, 1976.
15. Letter from Dr. Edmund D. Jung to Honorable Philip Burton, House of Representatives, Washington, D.C., Feb. 2, 1977.
16. Letter from Honorable Philip Burton to Hugh M. Durham, Legislative Counsel, Office of Legislative Affairs, Department of Justice, Washington, D.C., Feb. 8, 1977; letter from Honorable Philip Burton to Drew Saunders Day III, Assistant Attorney General, Civil Rights Division, Department of Justice, Washington, D.C., Aug. 12, 1977; letter from Honorable Philip Burton to Benjamin R. Civiletti, Assistant Attorney General, Criminal Section, Department of Justice, Washington, D.C., Mar. 25, 1977.
17. Letter from Drew S. Days III by Maceo W. Hubbard, Supervisory Trial Attorney, Criminal Section, to Honorable Philip Burton, Apr. 8, 1977.
18. Civil Service Commission, "Findings and Recommended Decision in the Discrimination Complaint of Dr. Edmund D. Jung," investigated at the V.A. Hospital, Martinez, Calif., report by examiner William Jenkins on Apr. 6, 1977.
19. Ibid.
20. Letter from Veterans Administration, Office of General Counsel, Washington, D.C., May 11, 1977, to Edmund D. Jung, M.D.

21. Letter from Henry Der, Executive Director, Chinese for Affirmative Action, San Francisco, Calif., to Max Clelland, Administrator of Veterans Affairs, Washington, D.C., Apr. 15, 1977.

22. Letter from Theodore T. Fong, Chairperson, Asian Americans for Community Involvement, Palo Alto, Calif., to Congressman Philip Burton, Sept. 20, 1978; letter from Theodore T. Fong, Chairperson, Asian Americans for Community Involvement, Palo Alto, Calif., to Senator Alan Cranston, Sept. 20, 1978.

23. "Medical Board Pick—Is He a Racist?" *San Francisco Examiner,* June 23, 1977; "CAA Fights Medical Board Nomination of Dr. Geokas," *East West,* June 22, 1977; "Bay Area Chinese Outraged Over Medical Board Choice," *Sacramento Bee,* June 24, 1977; "Race Row Doctor Resigns," *San Francisco Examiner,* Aug. 19, 1977; "Brown Pick Withdraws Under Fire," *Oakland Tribune,* Aug.19, 1977; "Brown Nominee Quits in Doctor Bias Dispute," *San Francisco Chronicle,* Aug. 19, 1977; "Martinez Doctor Pulls Name," *Contra Costa Times,* Aug. 19, 1977; "Gov. Brown Withdraws Dr. Geokas Nomination," *East West,* Aug. 24, 1977.

24. Second Equal Employment Opportunity complaint of discrimination in the Federal Government, filed Oct. 27, 1977.

25. Final Decision of Equal Employment Opportunity Commission, Philadelphia, Pa.—*Edmund D. Jung Appellant vs. Veterans Administration.* Appeal No. B01780284, Nov. 8, 1979.

26. Deposition of Mary Jane Lenca, May 15, 1980.

27. Deposition of Ernest Johnson, May 15, 1980.

28. Deposition of Carol del Grande, May 15, 1980.

29. U.S. Civil Service Commission, Appeals Review Board, Washington, D.C., "Decision in the Matter of Edmund D. Jung, Veterans Administration, San Francisco," May 16, 1979.

30. United States District Court for the Northern District of California, Civil No. 78-1719 SW, *Edmund D. Jung, M.D., Plaintiff vs. Michael C. Geokas, M.D., Chief of Medical Service; Wallace R. Koseluk and Clarence H. Nixon, Hospital Directors, V.A. Hospital, Martinez, Calif.; John D. Chase, M.D., Chief Medical Director of the V.A.; and Joseph Maxwell Clelland, Administrator of Veterans Affairs, Defendants.* "Complaint for Damages, Injunctive Relief, and Declaratory Relief (Civil Rights)," filed on July 31, 1978.

31. United States District Court, Northern District of California, C-78-1719 and C-78-1866, *Edmund D. Jung, M.D., Plaintiff vs. Donald L. Custis, Acting Administrator of Veterans Affairs, Defendant,* "Stipulation and Order Approving Compromise Settlement," June 4, 1981; "Plaintiff's Motion for Dismissal," June 5, 1981.

32. Letter from John F. Barg, Assistant U.S. Attorney, Department of Justice, San Francisco, to Edmund D. Jung, M.D., V.A. Hospital, Martinez, Calif. re: *Janet Rowen vs.Unites States of America. Civil No. C-77-2503-AJZ.* Mar. 10, 1978.

33. Letter from Henry Der, Executive Director, Chinese for Affirmative Action, San Francisco, Calif. to Dr. Donald L. Custis, Chief Medical Director, Veterans Administration, Washington, D.C., Aug. 20, 1981; letter from Henry Der to David Saxon, President, University of California, Berkeley, Calif., Sept. 2, 1981; letter from Henry Der to David Saxon—second letter of inquiry about Geokas racial discrimination, Feb.12, 1982; letter from Ronald Lee, Asian Americans for Community Involvement, Dr. Donald L. Custis, Sept.16, 1981.

34. "VA Hospital Staff Attacks Medical Chief," *Contra Costa Times,* Aug. 19, 1981.

35. "VA Doctor Guilty of Racism," *Martinez News Gazette,* Aug. 19, 1981; "VA Doctor Is Probed by Washington Team," *Oakland Tribune,* Aug. 20, 1981; "UC Med School Doctor Charged with Racism," *Sacramento Union,* Sept. 4, 1981; "VA Hospital Chief in Bias Probe," *Sacramento Bee,* Sept. 5, 1981; "Jung Wants Geokas out after VA Suit Settled," *Asian Week,* Sept. 17, 1981.

36. "VA Acts to Remove Doctor from Staff," *Sacramento Union,* Apr. 15, 1982; "VA Wants to Fire Hospital Chief for Misconduct," *Sacramento Bee,* Apr. 16, 1982.

37. "Med Center Doctor Transferred Following Harassment Charges," *Sacramento Union,* Oct. 9, 1982; "VA Doctor Transferred Because of Misconduct," *Sacramento Union,* Oct. 11, 1982; "VA Doctor Transferred for Alleged Misconduct," *San Francisco Examiner,* Oct. 14, 1982; "Dr. Michael Geokas Removed from VA Hospital in Martinez," *East West,* Oct. 20, 1982.

38. "UCD Physician Loses Executive Position," *Sacramento Union,* Sept. 8, 1982; "Davis Med School Revokes MD's Title," *Sacramento Bee,* Sept. 9, 1982; "Controversial Doctor at VA Hospital Loses Davis Post," *San Francisco Examiner,* Sept. 14, 1982; "Dr. Geokas Removed from UC Davis Vice-Chair Post," *East West,* Sept. 15, 1982.

39. "Outgoing VA Chief Clears Geokas," *Contra Costa Times,* Oct. 30, 1982; "VA Doctor Cleared of Conduct, Racism Charges," *Sacramento Bee,* Oct. 30, 1982; "VA Head Halts Geokas Transfer," *East West,* Nov. 17, 1982.

40. Ibid.

41. "VA Doctors Protest Chief's Retention," *Oakland Tribune,* Nov. 12, 1982; "Decision to Keep Geokas Upheld," *Contra Costa Times,* Jan. 15, 1983.

42. Letter from Edmund D. Jung, M.D., to Floyd C. Rector, M.D., Chairman, Department of Medicine, UCSF School of Medicine, San Francisco, Dec. 12, 1990.

43. Letter from Floyd C. Rector, M.D., to Edmund D. Jung, M.D., Jan. 17, 1991.

About the Contributors

HIM MARK LAI

Him Mark Lai is an adjunct professor of Asian American Studies at San Francisco State University, past president of the Chinese Historical Society of America and Chinese Culture Foundation of San Francisco, and consultant for the Asian American Studies Library at the University of California at Berkeley. He has lectured in Asian American Studies at San Francisco State University and the University of California. He is the author of numerous books and articles on Chinese American history, and his most recent work is a history of the Chinese American community, *From Overseas Chinese to Chinese American* (in Chinese), published by Joint Publishing Company (Hong Kong).

JUDY YUNG

Judy Yung is a second-generation Chinese American born and raised in San Francisco Chinatown. She received her Ph.D. in ethnic studies from the University of California, Berkeley, in 1990 and is currently Associate Professor of American Studies at the University of California, Santa Cruz. Her publications include *Unbound Feet: A Social History of Chinese Women in San Francisco*, *Chinese Women of America: A Pictorial History*, and *Island: Poetry and History of Chinese Immigrants on Angel Island, 1910–1940*.

LARISSA N. SCHWARTZ

Larissa N. Schwartz is currently a graduate student at Yale University in premodern Chinese history. She has a B.A. from Middlebury College in Chinese Language and Literature, and an M.A. in East Asian Studies at Yale University. In the fall of 1989 she studied at the University of Salamanca as an exchange student.

ZENG YING

Zeng Ying is currently a Ph.D. candidate in Comparative Culture at International Christian University, Tokyo. Her research interests include Chinese American history and Asian American literature.

EDMUND D. JUNG

Edmund D. Jung received his B.A. from Stanford University and M.S. and M.D. from the University of California San Francisco Medical School. He is a Diplomate of the American Board of Internal Medicine and a Fellow of the American College of Physicians. He served during World War II with the U.S. Army Medical Corps in the South Pacific theater. Dr. Jung retired after thirty-two years of medical practice at the Veterans Administration Hospital in Oakland and Martinez, California, as well as from UCSF Medical School as associate clinical professor of medicine. He is a former member of the board of trustees of the Chinese Historical Society of America.

Guidelines for Manuscript Submission

Chinese America: History and Perspectives is published annually by the Chinese Historical Society of America (CHSA).

The journal invites original contributions on all aspects of Chinese American history and culture. Manuscripts should not exceed five thousand words in length (excluding footnotes) and should follow the format outlined in *The Chicago Manual of Style*. A style sheet will be sent upon request. When the article is accepted, authors are asked to send three copies of the manuscript and, if possible, a final version of the article input in a commercial word-processing program (Microsoft Word, WordPerfect, Wordstar) on an IBM PC– or Macintosh-compatible diskette. Upon publication contributors will receive two complimentary copies of the journal.

Send manuscript to:

CHSA Journal
c/o Marlon Hom
Asian American Studies
San Francisco State University
1600 Holloway
San Francisco CA 94132

Chinese Historical Society of America

Established January 5, 1963

650 Commercial St. • San Francisco, CA 94111 • (415) 391-1188

MEMBERSHIP FORM

Please print.

❏ Check here if you add extended address information on back.

NAME _____

ADDRESS _____ CITY _____

STATE _____ ZIP _____ COUNTRY_____

PHONE NUMBER (OPTIONAL) _____ - _____ - _____ HOME/WORK

❏ Renewal Membership   ❏ New Membership

Membership and donations are **tax-deductible** as provided by federal tax laws. Membership expires December 31. Persons who join after September 30 are automatically members until December 31 of the *following* year. Please make checks payable to CHSA and send with this form.

❏ Regular (*individual*) . . . . $45   ❏ Institution (*group*) $60

❏ Senior (*age 60+*) . . . . $25   ❏ Foreign (*outside USA*) $60

❏ Student (*now enrolled*) . . . . $25   ❏ Life $1500

❏ Donation . . . . $_____

❏ I want to help with (*please circle*): Docents • Programs • Field Trips • Publications • Inventory • Special Events • Office Help •

Other (*please specify*) _____

❏ I want to give (*please circle*): a gift membership to • a donation in memory of • a donation in honor of

NAME _____

ADDRESS _____ CITY _____

STATE _____ ZIP _____ COUNTRY_____

CHSA will send a card to the honored or remembered or his/her family informing them of your gift.